ELEPHANTS IN THE VOLKSWAGEN:
Facing the Tough Questions
About Our Overcrowded Country

ELEPHANTS IN THE VOLKSWAGEN:
Facing the Tough Questions
About Our Overcrowded Country

LINDSEY GRANT

with contributions by

Martin Binkin
Leon F. Bouvier
Vernon M. Briggs, Jr.
Dennis Brownridge
Robert Costanza
Paul R. and Anne H. Ehrlich
Robert W. Fox
David and Marcia Pimentel
David E. Simcox
Alden Speare, Jr., and Michael J. White
Stephen E. Tennenbaum
John R. Weeks
Paul J. Werbos

W. H. Freeman and Company
New York

Library of Congress Cataloging-in-Publication Data

Grant, Lindsey
  Elephants in the Volkswagen: Facing the tough questions about our overcrowded
  country. By Lindsey Grant; with contributions by Martin Binkin . . . [et al.].
  p. cm.
  Includes bibliographical references and index.
  ISBN 0-7167-2267-4—ISBN 0-7167-2268-2 (pbk.)
  1. United States—Population. 2. Population—Economic aspects. 3. Population—
  Environmental aspects. I. Title.
  HB3505.G63 1992
  304.6'0973—dc20   91-37321
                                                                                CIP

Printed in the United States of America

2 3 4 5 6 7 8 9 0 VB 9 9 8 7 6 5 4 3 2

*This book is affectionately
dedicated to Donald Mann,
who has fought the good fight.*

CONTENTS

PREFACE

Elephant jokes were popular when my children were passing through adolescence. There was a riddle about how to get four elephants into a Volkswagen, and the answer was "two in front and two in back." The next question was "How do you put four giraffes in a Volkswagen?" and the answer was "Well, first you have to get the elephants out."

Fortunately for the quality of the humor, I was not there in the place where jokes are invented. If I had been, I would have started with another question: Do we *want* to put four elephants in a Volkswagen?

It is gratifying to see the resurgence of environmentalism on the national agenda but curious to find that very few people make the connection between environment and population—as if environmental issues could be addressed in isolation from the numbers of people who are generating them.

In a nation whose population has increased from 75 million to more than 250 million in this century, it is equally remarkable that few people have raised the question "When do we stop?" Only one organization—Negative Population Growth Inc.—has asked: "Have we already gone too far? Are we already overpopulated? Once we have passed through the brief fever of the fossil fuel era, will the optimum population for the country be smaller than it is now? If so, how do we get there?"

Such questions are not simply academic. They are real, immediate, and very important. The U.S. Geological Survey in 1989 warned that economically recoverable oil resources in the United States are about 86 billion barrels. We consume that much in sixteen years. Our dependence on the Persian Gulf states is increasing. The Kuwait crisis of 1991 demonstrated how vulnerable that makes us. In fact, four of the writers in the book, from very different backgrounds, have focused on energy as the principal factor in addressing population size. They all argue that scarcities and the protection of the environment will require that we learn again to live within our solar energy budget. They wrote their chapters before the Kuwait crisis, but they are not dealing with distant abstractions. Kuwait is only the most recent of a series of foreshocks that herald the end of the petroleum era.

Meanwhile, our population continues to increase. The fertility of American women appears to have risen about 20 percent from the 1976 low. Every major change in immigration laws in recent years has increased the rate of immigration. Congress in 1990 raised the rate by some 40 to 50 percent. We may be in for a crowded future.

Congress' behavior is perhaps understandable. Powerful interests are pressing for the immigration of specific groups, without concern about the effect of total immigration on population levels. The issue is volatile because ours is a generous nation, with deep ties to immigration, and our humane instincts call for us to welcome the distressed or persecuted. There are advocates of higher immigration levels and fertility rates. Julian Simon, in a recent Op-Ed piece in *The New York Times* suggested the doubling of immigration levels and a return to the 1957 fertility level as ways to meet the national budget deficit and to care for the elderly. No wonder that, for Congress, the line of least resistance is to raise the numbers.

Simon's proposed solution would lead to a U.S. population of about 2.5 billion in 2080 (assuming 1957 fertility levels and two million annual net immigration). That is equal to the entire population of the world two generations ago. Faced with a number like that, most Americans would probably agree that that is not the future they want. But a number alone—even 2.5 billion—is meaningless by itself. A particular population size or trend becomes good or bad only as it relates to the pursuit of national, social, or personal goals.

This book makes the connections between these goals through "foresight." Foresight is the process of examining the implications of current trends or proposed policies, to see how they may affect and be affected by the pursuit of other policies. As a systematic method of identifying problems and opportunities, foresight has frequently been advocated but seldom applied.

The best way to understand the connections between numbers and values is to ask experts in various fields to consider the impact different population levels would have on their fields of interest. In the chapters that make up the "Perspectives" section, the core of this book, the authors examine the labor force, the issues raised by an aging population, and national security. These areas underlie the principal arguments used by population expansionists in support of their position. But the authors go much farther. They connect population with the environment, with agricultural and energy futures, with the problems of the cities, the seacoast, the high country of the West, and the ecology of the Earth. They believe that the failure to consider such connections is a principal flaw in the thinking of those who advocate further population growth.

At a conceptual level, in the section "Rebuttals," I challenge the fundamental assumptions of those who believe that continuing growth is desirable or even possible. ("The Cornucopian Fallacies" was initially published in 1983, but I believe that the arguments stand the test of time. All other chapters in this book were drawn from *NPG Forum* essays for Negative Population Growth, Inc.; most were written for its "optimum population" project.)

Without a practical approach to influencing population change, speculating about optimum population would be little more than an interesting intellectual exercise. In the four chapters included in the section "Getting There," experts describe the scale of the problem and suggest ways that our society can consciously shape demographic change.

In the chapters on Europe and Central America, in "Alternatives," we contrast an example of a region that has come to grips with its population growth with one that has not. The Central American case is of interest not simply as an example; its demographic future is closely linked with our own.

When people address the population issue at all, they usually do so in terms of maximum populations: "How many people can this region support?" The authors in this book address a different question: "How many people would be **desirable**?" The object of population policy should not be to find out how many people we can cram in. Similarly, most commentators treat present population size as a minimum. The debate then is couched in terms of how to slow or eventually stop population growth. Yet, as we are presently learning from Europe, population can be rolled back, and society at present may profit from such a change.

There is another criterion for "optimum population" size, and it is legitimate even if it is necessarily a personal judgement. Some of us may feel, for example, that New York City is too crowded to enjoy and too big to escape, or that there is value in great open spaces, or that our overly successful species should refrain from taking over all the space that other species need, even when their contribution to our material well-being is not immediately apparent. These considerations have been slighted in this book because they do not lend themselves to systematic proof, but I hope that readers will consult their own feelings in coming to their conclusions about what population size is desirable and how it should be attained.

The nation needs to debate the idea of optimum population and, if possible, to come to some consensus. Right now, we are creating our demographic future by inadvertence, making decisions on other issues (such as energy or transportation) without ever considering their impact on population or recognizing that the connections are circular. Population growth may wipe out the progress we are trying to make in other areas of public policy.

This book is intended to be an opening salvo rather than the final word. It serves to dramatize that population is connected with many national issues. I hope it will remind governments and legislators that they may be shaping our demographic future when they make decisions about issues as disparate as tax policy, welfare policy, housing, transportation, and immigration. Governments are unlikely to change their ways unless they are confronted with informed pressures to address population issues and to develop processes to bring the population aspects into real world decisions. Without such processes, a population policy will remain a pious abstraction.

Before undertaking this exploration, I tried to interest several larger organizations in sponsoring a cross-disciplinary look at population. I had some nibbles, but no bites. The invitation is still open. A more ambitious effort would permit the ongoing interaction among experts that is central to refining the judgments reached.

Meanwhile, I am most appreciative to our authors for participating in the project. Donald Mann, President of Negative Population Growth, Inc., deserves particular credit for setting this project in motion. It was he who underwrote the series of papers on optimum population. He asked me to manage and edit the series. He has provided advice on the papers and seen to their distribution. The effort would not have been undertaken without him. I also thank the anonymous donor whose generosity made the project possible. And my nephew Keith Harwood for telling me the elephant joke.

Lindsey Grant
November 1991

RECONCILING TEXAS AND BERKELEY
The Concept of Optimum Population

Images float in the mind's eye. I recall (probably from some long-ago Western) a scene of horses in deep grasses, and I remember a passage in a history book describing the arrival of the Anglos in Arizona a century or so ago: "The grass was up to the horses' bellies."

More recently, I was in the Glorieta Pass in northern New Mexico, at a national monument surrounding the remains of the Pecos Pueblo. It sits on a low ridge partly enclosing a shallow swale. And that little flat valley was a miracle: a profusion of tall grasses and sedges and weeds, filled with birds. They owed their existence to their protection from the effects of domestic catttle grazing.

What have we lost? The ranch that surrounds that little valley is a rich man's ranch protected from the brutal overgrazing that one sees everywhere in the West. But it bears no comparision with that little protected area for beauty, for the diversity of life, or even for the amount of food that it could produce for human use if only we would live within our environment rather than savaging it.

To judge from the newspapers, people are discovering that the nation cannot go on running its affairs as it has. We are degrading the air, making the climate worse, poisoning our water supplies, wiping out the Chesapeake Bay fishery and the Everglades' wildlife, overgrazing the land, losing soil, and damaging our forest resources. We do not know what to do with radioactive wastes. Our bills for ordinary garbage disposal are quintupling, and our cities send garbage trucks to other states and garbage scows overseas seeking a place to unload. There are reports of beaches paved with human excrement.

These environmental problems are driven by three variables: population size, per capita consumption, and the technologies we use—the ways we produce and consume. To state the impact of population starkly: *At any given level of conservation and technology, the problems are roughly proportional to the size of the population involved.* (I say "roughly" because the experts will point to niceties such as thresholds and non-linearities; the experts are right, but those subtleties generally aggravate the problem rather than ameliorating it, and the statement remains a good rule of thumb.)

Having recognized its environmental problems, the nation seeks solutions in technological fixes and pleas for conservation. Population has been almost wholly ignored as a part of both the problem and the solutions. It is a bit like a Restoration bedroom farce, with the actors looking for the culprit in every direction but the right one, but this time it is not funny.

There are other problems linked intimately with population size and population change, in more complex ways. Consider, for example, the interconnected phenomena of urban housing costs, growing income disparities, drugs, violence, and alienation in the ghetto. These are not simply the results of Reaganite policies; they reflect underlying demographic trends. Yet they are seldom addressed in those terms.

Reconciling Texas and Berkeley

With injustice to some, I typify Texas as the spiritual home of the viewpoint typified by "I am entitled to a great big air-conditioned car, and

I have the right to drive it as fast as I want." (Our president, a Texan from Connecticut, relaxes by cruising about in a Cigarette speedboat, a vehicle distinguished principally for its high gas consumption.) I use Berkeley as the proxy for believers in alternative life-styles, bicycle transportation, and a vegetarian diet that lets us feed corn to hungry foreigners rather than to American beef cattle.

To disengage these opponents from each other's throat, I would like to suggest that their differences are driven by a force that neither of them addresses: population growth. To repeat my formula in another form: The big automobile becomes an environmental threat only when the number of automobiles exceeds the capacity of the atmosphere to buffer the exhaust. The steak is an immoral diversion of resources only when population outruns the capacity of the land to support a beef diet. Texas need not fear that it will lose its air-conditioned cars and thereby find summers once again intolerable *if* it will recognize that its views about cars are irreconcilable with the advocacy (among employers, at least) of population growth by way of an unfettered supply of cheap, illegal laborers from Mexico.

I believe that a nation that can land astronauts on the moon can learn the pentagonal relationship among (1) consumption levels, (2) population, and (3) environmental sustainability, as influenced by (4) foreseeable technologies and (5) the availability of capital to apply them. *The more we incline toward the "Texas" view of consumption, the smaller the population the environment can bear.*

Freedom, Social Constraints, and Population

Conspicuous consumption is only one aspect. The broader issue is the trade-off between freedom and social responsibility. The 13 million people of Los Angeles are already being told that they must give up their backyard barbeques to stop poisoning the air, and before long they will learn that they must trade in their beloved automobiles for public transportation, for their own good.

Throughout the country, industrialists and common folk alike chafe at being told by earnest environmentalists that they can no longer behave as they have been behaving. If the friction is intense, and probably increasing, it is perhaps because we are traversing the fault zone between powerful, antithetical world views.

The idea of personal freedom is very strong in this country, and it has deep roots. With a sparse population and seemingly limitless land and abundance, a person is worth a great deal, and a tree is not worth much. It is probably no accident that John Ball's ringing assertion of the rights of man came in the wake of the Black Plague, when labor in England was suddenly very scarce, and that it found an echo in the Declaration of Independence and the writings of Tom Paine four centuries later, when this embryonic nation stood on the edge of a wilderness.

Meanwhile, science has been revising Western civilization's image of humankind's place on Earth. That image has shrunk in less than four centuries from a central role, possessing and benefiting from a timeless Earth that is central to the universe, in personal communication with an anthropomorphic deity concerned about our fate, to a position among interdependent life forms, a recent species in the extraordinarily complex, evolving ecology of a small planet associated with a rather ordinary star partway toward the edge of one among countless galaxies. The Earth is no longer an infinite sheltering mother. It is, in Adlai Stevenson's indelible phrase, a fragile spaceship.

And many of us have become aware that we are managing the spaceship very badly—we may be appropriating as much as 41 percent of the Earth's primary terrestrial productivity for human uses.[1] We are suddenly learning the extent of the hazards we are creating: the greenhouse effect, for example, or acid precipitation. The 1983 report of the President's Acid Rain Review Panel warned that human activities may affect "the denitrifying microbes . . . upon which the entire biosphere depends."

Those of us who hear and understand these warnings respond (shrilly, perhaps) with demands that societies regulate human activities so as to bring such threats under control. Farewell to the heroic—the frontier—image of personal freedom. Enter the era of mutual coercion to save ourselves from the mess we are creating.

Again, there is the trade-off that "Texas" faces. If the problem is induced in part by population growth, the severity of mutual restraints will be harder if we choose not to address that source of environmental problems.

Maximum Population and "Sustainability"

The trade-off between population and consumption levels is almost universally ignored. When scientists have dealt with population limits at all, they have generally done so at a very crude stage, trying to estimate the maximum populations that can be fed. It seems to me that they have asked the wrong question. It would be better to investigate what numbers would be *desirable* for the good of all.

Maximum population studies have generally been flawed in two other ways:

1. They deal with one variable, food, as if the complexity of the Earth could be reduced to an equation of arable land, yields, and consumers. One Food and Agriculture Organization (FAO) study, for example, simply posited the conversion of forests into fields wherever the land was arable, without considering the likely effects: the loss of firewood to cook the food; the effects on rainfall, water supplies, and agriculture itself; the disruption of the ecosystem; the loss of plant and animal species; the economic impacts; the broader effects upon climate.

2. "Maximum population" is a one-shot concept. It does not examine whether it is sustainable over time.

Maximum population is a slippery number. It has moved up with the burst of agricultural technology. It can move down again as some of that technology proves environmentally unbearable, as climate changes, or as fields erode. It can also be driven down suddenly by a natural calamity, such as drought or a volcanic explosion like the one (Mt. Agung) that created the worldwide "year without a summer" in 1816, or by disruptions such as political disorder in oil-producing countries.

A maximum population is a vulnerable one, because it has no slack. It cannot drop back to lower consumption levels in the wake of a disaster, except through hunger and disease and rising death rates.

Given the weaknesses of the maximum population approach, the idea of sustainability has become a rallying point for environmentalists. It was a central theme of the report of the World Commission on Environment and Development (the "Brundtland Commission.")[2] Briefly, it denotes the goal of running the world's economies in a way that ensures that we pass along an undiminished environment to our heirs.

The proponents of sustainability have dealt only in passing with population, but they have added a new dimension to the idea of maximum population. Population should not be so large as to degrade the carrying capacity of the system, the ability to support future generations.

Environmental degradation—the failure of sustainability—is eroding carrying capacity in much of the third world and already reducing theoretical maximum populations. We should not assume that the United States is immune.[3] By the standard of sustainability, *the United States is overpopulated or mismanaged, or both, because we are depleting our per capita natural resources and impairing the environment.*

Environmental thinking must take the next step beyond sustainability. The issue is not just pollution control; we need to bring all human activities into better balance with the rest of the Earth's ecosystem. We need a way of reconciling the concern for humanity with the broader concern for the system that supports us.

It is no wonder that, with movements like Gaia and the Earth Firsters, the times are full of people trying to work their way toward some new philosophy that relates humankind to the totality of the Earth. Any such philosophy must incorporate a viewpoint on population. *Population, like sulfate emissions, must be treated as a variable subject to conscious human decisions.* In some instances, a technological fix alone may be enough, but I doubt there will be many. For an extreme case, take the Netherlands. The Dutch have an official goal of reducing sulfate and nitrogen oxide emissions by 70 to 80 percent. I think they will find that goal simply unattainable without a dramatic decline either in population or in living standards—especially as global warming drives the sea higher on their dikes. They do not have a population policy. They are going to need one—badly.

The next step is the idea of optimum population—not a calculation of the maximum human population that can be reached or sustained, but a determination of the population size that best satisfies our national and social goals within a functioning ecosystem of which we are only a part.

Population Policy by Default . . .

Here in the United States there is something of an intellectual vacuum at the heart of what is arguably the central issue of our time: Should governments attempt to influence demographic change? The vacuum is the lack of any systematic way of deciding what the optimum population might be.

I imagine that many people would agree that Africa or Central America would be better off with smaller populations, though the thought may be dismissed as visionary. The thought is hardly even raised with respect to the United States, however, although there is no reason for assuming that the only possible direction for U.S. population to go is up. The Rockefeller Commission in 1972 concluded that it saw no benefit from further population growth in the United States, and it proposed family planning and immigration policies to bring that growth gradually to a halt.[4] That was some forty million Americans ago, and the report seems to have been forgotten.

The failure to address the issue does not mean that we are avoiding it. *The United States has many population policies. We don't think we have any, however, and that is perhaps the most dangerous of situations.* Decisions about taxation, welfare, urban development and housing, transportation, day care, abortion or immigration, all influence population change, and population change in turn affects the pursuit of those policies. Perhaps it would be wise to have a conscious population policy rather than many inadvertent ones.

. . . *Or by Design: Optimum Population*

Sir Julian Huxley seems to have coined the term optimum population:

> The recognition of an optimum population size (of course relative to technological and social conditions) is an indispensable first step towards that planned control of population which is necessary if man's blind reproductive urges are not to wreck his ideals and his plans for material and spiritual betterment.[5]

There were, at about the time of the Rockefeller Commission study, at least two academic efforts to define optimum population.[6] Although much of what was said may seem dated, some of the arguments are appropriate two decades later: we must define optimum population, not as the largest number we can get away with, but as a target that would help us achieve the greatest human well-being. They did not try to agree on a definition or to propose numbers, but they suggested the direction for inquiry.

Obviously, optimum population must be small enough so that we do not endanger the environment that supports us, but it is not dictated by the capacity of the environment alone. It is, presumably, some magic point that best reconciles all the different goals related to demography: full employment and maximum productivity per person, livable housing accessible to employment, social equity and reasonable levels of consumption, national security, open spaces and the preservation of resources, clean air and water, leisure, education and cultural amenities, and indeed "liberty and the pursuit of happiness."

The Want of Tools

The process of groping toward optimum population will not be intellectually rigorous. That is the fault of the state of the art rather than of the researchers. The intellectual disciplines have not been developed to handle complex systems in which multiple causes lead to multiple results. And in the case of population, everything is connected.

Keynesian and post-Keynesian economics and the scientific method are the dominant disciplines of our era, and neither is satisfactory for our purposes. Macroeconomics hinders more than it guides the search for optimum population.

- It is a theory of equilibrium and does not contain the concepts for the study of growth, change, scale, or limits.

- It puts an economic value on the processes that destroy natural resources, as well as on the belated efforts to correct the damage, but it does not value the natural world until that world enters the economy.[7]

- It puts a value on the supply of amenities that once were free and thus overstates the well-being of a crowded society as compared to an uncrowded one. One can think of hundreds of economic goods and services that inflate the GNP, giving the illusion of prosperity while in fact they represent our efforts to deal with problems that exist only because of crowding. Start, perhaps, with parking meters and traffic jams.

The scientific method works best when one can study simple systems with simple causes, holding all other variables constant. In a world of bewilderingly complex interactions, it offers only limited help in defining "optimum population."

And there is the problem of value judgments. We still face the dilemma the British philosopher Jeremy Bentham encountered (but did not solve) two centuries ago, when he stated the goal of "the greatest good for the greatest number." One must make a value judgment in trying to decide which alternative is better—for example, one apple each for four people or two apples each for two? There is no objective way to judge the trade-offs among defending individual liberty, meeting social responsibilities, and protecting the Earth. Value judgments must be made.

There is also the complication brought about by technological change. Different technologies can support different numbers of people. In this study we will assume current U.S. technology as a starting point and attempt to identify technological changes that could change our assumptions about optimum population level. For example, labor-saving technology may come to seem much less important; the critical technologies may be those that offer benign ways of producing energy, increasing agricultural yields, and reducing pollution.

Finally, the pursuit of an optimum population would generate its own by-products. If, for instance, fertility and immigration were reduced in order to lead to an agreed-upon optimum, the age structure of the population would change, with fewer children, more old people, and fewer entrants annually into the labor force, particularly at the unskilled level. These changes would, in turn, affect capital formation, the labor market, education, Social Security, the problems of cities and minorities, military recruitment, and other national interests. I believe that the problems associated with such demographic change are usually overstated, and the benefits regularly ignored. We will return to these questions in several chapters in this book.

Despite all these conceptual problems in trying to describe optimum population, there are new approaches that may be of help. Foresight systems and alternative futures studies offer hope, precisely because they deal with multiple variables. The emerging methodology of systems analysis is an effort to bring mathematical discipline to the study of complex, interacting systems.[8]

There have been periodic journalistic exercises undertaken to measure the "livability" of cities using nine indexes:

- Climate and terrain
- Housing (stock, price, heating and cooling costs, mortgage rates and taxes)
- Health care and environment (air and water pollution, hay fever)
- Crime
- Transportation (the problem of getting to work)
- Education

- The arts

- Recreation and sports

- Personal economics (living costs, incomes, taxes and jobs)[9]

The high-scoring cities tend to be the smaller ones, with living space, stable neighborhoods, low housing prices and low taxes. A recent winner was Pittsburgh, despite its climate. Its population has declined by nearly one-half since 1950, to less than 400,000. The common wisdom holds that growth is needed for job opportunities. The steel industry has gone. Pittsburgh should be a basket case. However, in May 1989 the city had unemployment of only 4.3 percent. There must be a lesson in this. It would be interesting to run a population correlation with those "livability" studies.

Zero Population Growth, Inc. (ZPG), attempting a population correlation using somewhat different indexes, did indeed find that smaller cities tend to have better environmental and living conditions than larger ones.[10] We should not disdain the simple approach used in livability surveys. Identifying and weighting the elements of optimum population, we can come up with a composite number. No study is likely to result in a consensus, but it will have been useful if it suggests a range, or even

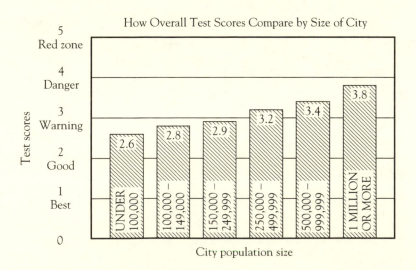

The urban stress test. This figure shows how overall test scores compare, by size of city. ©1988 Zero Population Growth, Inc., 1400 16th Street, NW, #320, Washington, D.C. 20036

a vector from the present level—and if it brings into focus connections that the nation has ignored in its population nonpolicy.

These suggestions are just a beginning. We need a systematic intellectual framework for studying optimum population, but we cannot wait indefinitely for a system to develop. Societies seldom have the luxury of knowing all about a problem before being obliged to deal with it. We do not have that much time.

The No-Cost Solution: *The Population Connection*

I have generalized about the connections among population and other issues. Other chapters will provide the details. Here I can only give a few brief examples.

AIR POLLUTION, ACID PRECIPITATION, AND THE GREENHOUSE   Nationally, we are beginning to recognize that we face serious environmental problems. We are trying to deal with them in a typically American way: bull our way through the problem by throwing money at it. President Bush's proposals on clean air were welcome after the drought of the Reagan years, but they still reflected the limited American mindset. The emphasis was upon technical fixes and alternative fuels. Later, in its energy proposals, the administration largely abandoned even this concession to environmental concerns, focusing instead on the illusory hope of finding more petroleum and calling for the removal of impediments to nuclear power.

Eventually we will have to face the issue of how many people there will be, using how many cars, and over what distances.

We can, and should, practice greater efficiency and seek cleaner technologies, but these are expensive remedies. By way of example, Los Angeles' problem is the worst in the nation. The annual cost of a recently proposed regional remedy was estimated at $4 billion for the first year, and at $12 billion by 2000.[11] However, because the scale of the environmental problem is generally proportional to the number of people, there may be cheaper solutions. If our present population were what it was in 1950, there would be about one-third as many people in Los Angeles, so its air pollution problems would be correspondingly smaller.

This observation can be made, *mutatis mutandis*, about many other national issues.

ENERGY   As the petroleum era begins to wind down, the United States is crossing the line of 50 percent dependence on foreign sources of petroleum. This dependence adds to our foreign exchange deficit and places the nation at risk in relying on unstable foreign sources for a vital share of its energy budget.

If our population were still at the 1950 level of 150 million, with current consumption patterns we would not need imported oil (see Chapter 10).

UNEMPLOYMENT AND THE GHETTO   If there has been one clear effect of current technology upon the labor market, it is to increase the demand for certain skills and to reduce the demand for mass labor. Our demographic nonpolicy and our immigration policies have been precisely the wrong ones for this situation. The baby boom and high fertility among the poor have created a large pool of unskilled labor. Immigration law has favored the immigration of the unskilled rather than the skilled. Moreover, the failure to enforce the immigration law has permitted an additional influx of workers competing for the bottom-level jobs. The results are visible in the impoverishment of the poor in the past decade[12] and in unemployment in the ghetto. According to current Census and Bureau of Labor Standards statistics, only 64 percent of blacks in their twenties have jobs, compared with 78 percent of other Americans in their twenties (Chapter 12).

If one seeks causes for social breakdown and drug problems in the ghetto or looks for potential sources of unrest, that is a good starting point.

It is tempting to proceed to agriculture and other issues, but I will leave them to the specialists—elsewhere in this book.

THE DEMOGRAPHIC ROLE IN THE SOLUTIONS   Fertility (the number of children borne by the average woman) fluctuates constantly. As I have said, it is currently at about replacement level. If immigration and emigration were in balance, the fertility level would lead eventually to population stabilization at a figure not much above the current 250 million; however, fertility is rising. With present fertility, net immigration of one million annually (which is a conservative guess at the level likely under the Immigration Law of 1990) would lead to a population in 2080 of more than 400 million, and rising.[13] There are ways of controlling immigration and influencing fertility, but they are not easy.

The capital costs of achieving a lower population would be negligible. It would require only a national resolve to limit immigration to refugees most in need of asylum and to potential immigrants who would bring needed skills to our economy. If we add to that a national goal of the two-child maximum and shape social policies (taxes, welfare, housing) to help realize the goal, we could achieve a lower population. (If women generally "stopped at two," the total fertility rate would decline, since many women have no children, or only one.)

The two-child family would have other advantages. It is already becoming the norm for more prosperous Americans, if only because of the cost of higher education. It would provide a rationale for encouraging the poor—and particularly the proliferating unwed teenage mothers—to exercise restraint. It would be easier for society to help educate smaller cohorts of poor children, enabling them to participate in the economy and to exploit new technologies. According to the Census Bureau's *Fertility of American Women* (June 1988), women with family incomes over $50,000 average 1.36 children; those with incomes under $10,000 average

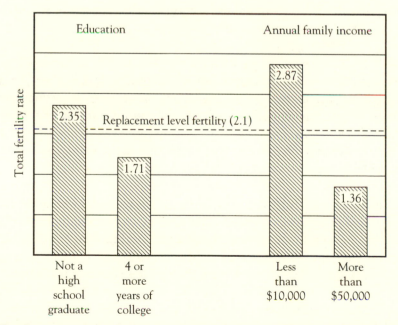

Fertility, income, and education of U.S. women, eighteen to forty-four, as of June 1988. Source: Derived from U.S. Bureau of the Census, "Fertility of American Women: June 1988" (Washington, D.C., 1989).

2.87. At that rate, the poorest will have 24 great grandchildren, the most prosperous will average 2.5.

Moreover, that policy would help to forestall an eventuality that most demographic projections ignore: fertility may rise if the poor continue to get poorer and as immigrants from high-fertility societies produce a rising proportion of the total population. If we could forestall or deal with the problems through population policy, and if there are very few visible economic costs in moving toward a smaller population, why not consider such a policy?

When these proposals are aired, the usual reaction is "You can't do it." The answer is "We haven't tried."

The Resistances

There is deep resistance, some of it with good reasons, to the idea of a government policy on population.

"BIGGER IS BETTER"   This slogan expresses deeply held feelings in our nation, which has been expanding for most of its existence and sees itself as a nation of immigrants.

SELF-INTEREST   As Garrett Hardin showed in *The Tragedy of the Commons*, self-interest can conflict with the common good. Realtors, land speculators, business people looking for a larger market, and educators worried about shrinking school-age populations may believe that their immediate interest is served by growing numbers, even if they recognize that it would harm the community. Private interest usually wins against the public interest when people take positions.

"BE FRUITFUL AND MULTIPLY"   To people who like children and who were raised on the injunction to "be fruitful and multiply," there is something viscerally disturbing about a proposal to limit the number of births. Perhaps this will change as we come to a shared understanding of humankind's place in the system, but the resistance is enormous.

THE FEAR OF COERCION   We have had a tradition of governmental noninterference in personal affairs, and it is a good one. The problem here is a conflict of objectives. What does society do if people's choices about fertility are leading to an unsustainable population? Crowded societies do not leave room for the kinds of freedom that uncrowded ones do.

This issue is inflamed by the abortion debate, and its sensitivity is well illustrated by the furor that practices in China have generated in the United States. Lower fertility can theoretically be achieved without abortions, but in practice it has yet to happen in any country.

We would do well to recognize at the outset that a country embarks upon a delicate course when it consciously brings fertility into social policy decisions. The line between incentives and disincentives, on the one hand, and coercion, on the other, will need to be honestly and publicly debated.

There is a related problem. How does one avoid penalizing the child—who is guiltless even if it is the eighth child—in the process of trying to dissuade the mother from having more children I think part of the answer would be feeding programs directed at the children rather than welfare provided to mothers, who might, in any case, be diverting it to drugs.

Finally, there is a question as to how much a government can do in a free-enterprise society. The historical evidence is mixed. Both recent and pre-World War II efforts in Europe to encourage higher fertility have had very limited success. On the other hand, through some alchemy of incentives and disincentives and public consensus, the so-called chopstick cultures of East Asia have done remarkably well at bringing fertility down; only in China have there been charges of coercion.

It will take patience and good government to thread a way through these issues. Even if all the problems are successfully handled, population change takes a long, long time.

Responsibility for a Small Planet

The argument is regularly heard that, because natural increase is now largely a third world phenomenon, population control is important for them but not for us. That argument founders on the facts of resource use and pollution. A first world person has a greater environmental impact than a third world counterpart. With 5 percent of the world's population, for example, the United States generates about one-quarter of the air pollution.

It is not a question of altruism. We share the Earth and its climate, and we cannot expect that others will reduce their pollution coefficients sufficiently to permit the United States to continue its present ways.

If a Peruvian migrates to the United States, he will pollute more than he did in Peru. We may be sure that one of the first things he will buy, to get to work, is a big old cheap automobile, belching smoke.

Optimize or Maximize

If we do not optimize, we will probably maximize at an unsustainable level, and that is not a very attractive option.

Human tribes have from time to time discovered new technologies or new lands and have prospered for a while until population growth brought them to the edge once again. In this century we have had, with the explosion of technology, the greatest opportunity of all to create a world in which all could live decently. But we are blowing that chance because we have been willing to control mortality but not fertility. We think of that imbalance as a third world phenomenon, but migration brings it home.

The United States courts the same fate as the third world because of our population growth. There is no assurance when we will stop growing. Fertility is rising as the population composition changes. Congress has been immune to the demographic implications of immigration and responsive to pressure groups. As a result, every "reform" of the past decade has increased the numbers of legal immigrants.

We in the United States still have an advantage that has been lost to Africa and India and China and Bangla Desh. Our range of options is much greater. We have more room for conservation, more money for technical fixes, and we can yield a bit on per capita consumption. We have not driven population up—and consumption down—to the point that the immediate issue is survival. In India despite the journalistic reports of the "green revolution," all the production gains have not been sufficient to maintain per capita grain consumption at the level of 1900.[14] As anybody familiar with Africa or Asia can attest, "maximum" population under their circumstances is grim indeed. We have been warned.

We think of our country as a breadbasket, but in 1988, for the first time in modern history, the United States consumed more grain than it produced.[15] With more bad years, perhaps connected with climate change, the first result is more expensive meat, and less of it for the poor.

What will be the next step? Gradual irreversible erosion? A sudden crisis? Or a conscious population policy to get us out of the mess?

The choice is ours, but the timing is not. If we do not foresee problems, we will have to try to live with them. If we did *all* the right things tomorrow, we could only slow down the global greenhouse effect; we could not avoid it. Even if we came to a consensus tomorrow that the population of the United States should be smaller, it might take a century or more to reach the level we seek. The momentum of change demands a long perspective.

On that note, we invite our readers into the joint exploration of a landscape still only dimly seen.

2

LAND, ENERGY AND WATER:
The Constraints Governing Ideal U.S. Population Size
DAVID AND MARCIA PIMENTEL

One frequently hears that U.S. agriculture is the most efficient in the world. It is so, indeed, if measured on the scale of output per hours of labor input. It is, however, very inefficient if measured in terms of output per unit of energy input. Like most agriculture, it is diminishing its own base through loss of topsoil, and the intensive use of fertilizer and pesticide poses a threat to groundwater sources, wetlands, and fisheries.

Along with air and water, agriculture supplies the first tier of human wants, and U.S. agriculture is of particular importance, because it has helped to fill the gap in food production in much of the world. Given the constraints on future energy availability that have been dramatized (again) by the Kuwait crisis, an examination of the connections between energy, food production, and sustainable agriculture provides a particularly appropriate starting point for the effort to define optimum U.S. population size.

For most of this century, leading scientists, public officials, and various organizations have been calling attention to the rapidly growing human population and the deteriorating environment throughout the world.[1] Based on these assessments, genuine concerns arise about maintaining prosperity and the quality of human life in the future.

In the United States, humankind is already managing and using more than half of all the solar energy captured by photosynthesis. Yet even this is insufficient for our needs, and we are actually using nearly three times that much energy, or about 40 percent more energy than is captured by all plants in the United States. This rate is made possible only because we are temporarily drawing upon stored fossil energy. We are approaching the end of the petroleum era, however, and other fossil fuels are not inexhaustible. Moreover, the very use of these fossil fuels, along with erosion and other misuse of our natural resources, is reducing the carrying capacity of our ecosystem.

These are not sustainable conditions, and our natural resources cannot be expected indefinitely to maintain a population as large as the present one, without a remarkable decline in our living standards.

Thus far, our society appears unable to deal successfully with problems of the environment, resources, and population. It has a poor record of effectively managing and protecting essential environmental and natural resources from overexploitation due to ignorance, mismanagement, and the impact of growing human numbers. Recent history suggests that these problems have been escalating, moreover, because the United States has not clearly acknowledged that the attainment of an unspecified but high general standard of living depends on the interaction of the environment, resources, and population density.

Decisions concerning the environment and natural resources that are made in the United States, and indeed throughout the world, are ad hoc in nature and designed to protect or to promote a particular or immediate aspect of human well-being or the environment, or both. All too often, solutions are sought only after a problem reaches a crisis status. As Benjamin Franklin wrote long ago in *Poor Richard's Almanac*, "it is not until the well runs dry, that we know the worth of water." Based on experience, it will not be until the pressure of human population on the environment and resources becomes intolerable that some corrective action will be taken by individuals and governments. But then it may be too late to avert hunger and poverty.

In this chapter, we examine the degradation of the environment, the consumption of nonrenewable resources, population growth, and the possible decline in U.S. prosperity. We also suggest that dramatically reduced U.S. population densities would ensure individual prosperity and quality environment for future generations. With sufficient information and understanding of our problems, we may be able to create sound policies.

Resources and Population Density

Each country in the world is unique in its resources of fertile land, forests, water, and energy, as well as its topography, temperature, and rainfall patterns. These and other factors influence the productivity of the people, their food supply, their economic and social welfare, and even to some degree their political security. Innate human behavior exhibits a strong will to survive and achieve some level of prosperity and quality of life. The specific characteristcs of the desired standard of living vary from person to person. Nonetheless, compared with those who have a relative wealth of resources, people inhabitating regions with fewer natural endowments must struggle harder to achieve the living standard they desire. Yet for both, large population size and rapid population growth lessen the availability of the vital resources and stresses the sustained functioning of all components of the environment.

A comparision of some aspects of life in the United States and China reveals startling extremes and suggests what Americans can expect if our population continues to grow at its current rate. Despite the government's policy of one child per couple, with a population of 1.1 billion, China is growing at a rate of 1.4 percent or 15 million per year.[2] The population of the United States currently stands at 252 million and is growing at a rate of about 0.8 percent per year (depending on one's estimates of emigration and illegal immigration); however, if the number of immigrants coming into the United States is allowed to increase, the rate of U.S. population growth will escalate.

China, with a land area similar to ours, is already experiencing diminished per capita supplies of food and other essential resources, as well as a deteriorating natural environment, as evidenced by the great deforestation and intense soil erosion. The relative affluence presently enjoyed by Americans has been made possible by our abundant supplies of arable land, water, and fossil energy relative to our present population numbers. As our population escalates, our resources will inevitably experience pressures similar to those now experienced by China.

Statistics suggest that we in the United States produce and consume about forty-seven times more goods and services per capita than do the Chinese.[3] Currently, approximately 3,300 pounds of agricultural products are produced annually to feed each American, while the Chinese make do with only 1,300 pounds per year. To produce food for each person in the United States, a total of 4.7 acres of cropland and

Foods and Feed Grains Consumed per Capita (in Pounds) per Year in the United States and China.

Food/feed	USA[a]	China
Food grain	152	592[b]
Vegetables	246	450[c]
Fruit	139	24[d]
Meat and fish	227	55[d]
Dairy products	583	7[d]
Eggs	33	13[d]
Fats and oils	62	13[d]
Sugar	145	13[d]
Total	1,587	1,128
Feed grains	1,762	141[b]
Grand Total	3,349	1,269
Kilocalories/person/day	3,500	2,484[e]

[a]USDA, 1985. Converted from kilograms (1 Kg = 2.2 lb.).

[b]Total grain production per capita in 1985 was 364 kg (802 lb.) (CDAAHF, 1986). It is estimated on the basis of some unpublished data that 8.5 percent of the total grain production was used for seeds and industrial materials, 17.5 percent for feed, and 74 percent for food (Wen, personal communication, 1987).

[c]Estimated on the basis of total vegetable planting area (Wen, personal communication, 1987).

[d]CDAAHF, 1986.

[e]CAA, 1986.

Source: D. Pimentel, L.M. Frederickson, D.B. Johnson, J.H. McShane, and H.-W. Yuan, "Environment and Population: Crises and Policies," in *Food and Natural Resources*, D. Pimentel and C.W. Hall, eds. (San Diego: Academic Press, 1989).

pastureland is used, whereas in China only 0.9 acres per person is used. Each person in China eats essentially a vegetarian diet, one that is low in animal protein. The Chinese have nearly reached the carrying capacity of their agricultural system. In contrast, the average U.S. diet is varied and high (66 percent) in animal protein foods.

Since colonial times and especially after 1850, Americans have relied increasingly on energy sources other than human power for their food and forestry production. Relatively cheap and abundant supplies of fossil fuel have been substituted for human energy. Fossil-based fertilizers and pesticides, as well as machinery, have made our farmers more productive while diminishing the level of personal energy they must expend to farm. The Chinese have not been as fortunate; they still depend on

Resources Used per Capita per Year in the United States and China to Supply Basic Needs

Resources	United States	China
Land (acres)		
Cropland	1.5[a]	0.2[b,c]
Pasture	3.2[a]	0.7[b]
Forests	3.2[a]	0.2[b,d]
Total	7.9	1.1
Water (gallons x 10^3/yr)	661	122
Fossil fuel		
Oil equivalents (gallons)	2,114[f]	109[g]
Forest products (tons)	15[a]	0.03[c,d]

[a]USDA, 1985.   [e]USWRC, 1979.

[b]Wu, 1981.   [f]DOE, 1983.

[c]Smil, 1984.   [g]State Statistical Bureau PROC, 1985.

[d]Vermeer, 1984.

Note: Figures converted from metric in sources. 1 hectare = 2.471 acres. 1 liter = 0.2642 gallons. 1 metric ton = 1.1023 tons.

Source: D. Pimentel, L.M. Frederickson, D.B. Johnson, J.H. McShane, and H.-W. Yuan, "Environment and Population: Crises and Policies," in *Food and Natural Resources*, D. Pimentel and C.W. Hall, eds. (San Diego: Academic Press, 1989).

about 500 hours per acre (h/a) of manual farm labor; compared with only 4 h/a in the United States.[4]

Industry, transportation, heating homes, and producing food account for most of the fossil energy consumed in the United States.[5] Most fossil energy in China is used by industry, a lesser amount for food production.[6] Per capita use of fossil energy in the United States amounts to about 2,100 gallons of oil equivalents per year, or twenty times the level in China.

Status of U.S. Environmental Resources

Basic to making decisions about our future is the need to assess both the quality and quantity of land, water, and energy, and the biological resources we will have at our disposal in coming decades. At our present population level of 252 million we are affluent consumers of our vital resources; however, in the face of increasing demands due in part to a growing population, many of these resources are being depleted, with no hope of renewal after the next one hundred years. Although these components function interdependently, they can be manipulated to make up for a partial shortfall in one or more. For example, to bring desert land into production, water can be applied to the land, but only if groundwater or river water is available and if sufficient fossil energy is available to pump the water. This is the current practice in California and many other western states, enabling some of our western agricultural regions to be highly productive.

Land, that vital natural resource, is all too often taken for granted, yet it is essential for food production and the supply of other basic human needs, such as fiber, fuel, and shelter. Currently, Americans use about 1.5 acres per capita of arable land per capita to produce our food. Nearly all the arable land is in production and in fact some marginal land is also in production.[7] Thus, Americans do not have new arable land to open up to take care of a growing U.S. population.

At present the soil on U.S. cropland is eroding at rates that average 8 tons per acre per year.[8] This is of particular concern because soil reformation is extremely slow; specifically, we are losing topsoil sixteen times faster than replacement.[9] Even now, in what used to be some of our most productive agricultural regions, soil productivity has been reduced 50 percent, and in some areas it has been so severely degraded that it has been abandoned.[10]

All arable land that is currently in production, and especially marginal land, continues to be highly susceptible to degradation.[11] Although some marginal land has been withdrawn under the Conservation Reserve Program, some marginal land cannot be removed from production, because it is essential to feed Americans. Certainly, more effort should be made to implement soil and water conservation practices on both arable and marginal land.[12]

Despite serious soil erosion, U.S. crop yields have been maintained or increased because of the availability of cheap fossil energy for inputs like fertilizers, pesticides, and irrigation.[13] Currently on U.S. farms, about 3 kilocalories (kcal) of fossil energy are being spent to produce just 1 kcal of food. Our policy of supporting this 3:1 energy ratio has serious implications for the future. One cannot help but wonder how long such intensive agriculture can be maintained on U.S. croplands while our nonrenewable fossil energy resources are being rapidly depleted.

In addition to use in agricultural production and throughout our entire food system for processing, packaging, and transportation, fossil energy is used to fuel diverse human activities. Overall fossil energy inputs in different economic sectors have increased twenty to one thousand-fold in the past three decades, attesting to our heavy reliance on this energy.[14]

Projections of the availability of these energy resources are not encouraging. In fact, a 1989 Department of the Interior study reports that, based on the most current oil-drilling data, the estimated amount of oil resources has plummeted. This means that instead of having about a thirty-five-year supply of oil, we are limited to a sixteen-year supply if use remains at about the current rate. Concurrently, natural gas, another important energy resource, is being rapidly depleted[15] and nuclear energy is also limited because uranium resources face eventual depletion.[16] Reliable estimates indicate that coal reserves are sufficient to last for more than a century.[17] However, larger populations can be expected to put additional stress on use of all energy resources. Thus, considering population growth and the forecasts about our nonrenewable energy supplies, all efforts need to be focused on conserving current supplies while intensifying research on developing new energy sources.

Along with land and energy supplies, we take water supplies for granted and often forget that all vegetation requires and transpires massive amounts of water. For example, a corn crop that produces about 112 bu per acre of grain will take up and transpire about 450,000 gallons per acre of water during just one growing season.[18] To supply this much water to the crop, not only must 1 million gallons (40 inches) of rain fall per acre, but it must be evenly distributed during the year and especially during the growing season.

Of the total water currently used in the United States, 85 percent is used in agriculture, while the remainder is needed for industry and for public use.[19] In the future, the rate of U.S. water consumption is projected to rise both because of population growth and because of greater per capita use.[20] The rapid increase in water use is already stressing both our surface and our groundwater resources. Currently, groundwater overdraft is 25 percent greater than its replenishment rate,[21] with the result that our mammoth groundwater aquifers are being mined at an alarming rate. In addition, both surface and groundwater pollution have become a serious problem in the United States, and concern about the future availability of pure water is justified.[22]

Threats to those Resources

Pollution is pervasive throughout our environment and degrades the quality and availability of resources like water, land, air, and biota (life forms). For example, when salts are leached from the land during irrigation (up to 8 tons of salts per acre during the growing season) and deposited in rivers, the effectiveness of this river water for further irrigation is reduced.[23]

Air pollution has a more pervasive impact than water pollution. In the United States, the estimated 23 million tons of sulfur dioxide from factories and cars that are released into the atmosphere annually cause serious environmental problems in both our natural and agricultural environments.[24] For example, acid rain, produced in part from sulfur dioxide, is having major environmental impacts on aquatic life in streams and life in U.S. forests.

Furthermore, a wide array of chemical pollutants is released to the air, water, and soil and is already adversely affecting the growth and survival of many of the 500,000 species of natural plants and animals that make up our natural environment. For example, each year about 550,000 million tons of toxic pesticides are applied to control pests, but all too often they kill beneficial species as well. Some of these pesticides leach into groundwater and streams, damaging the valuable plants and animals that inhabit surface waters.[25]

In addition to toxic chemicals, the conversion of forests and other natural habitats to croplands, pastures, roads, and urban spread in response to expanding population numbers is reducing the biological diversity of plants and animals. These natural biota are vital for the recycling of organic wastes, the degrading of chemical pollutants, and the purifying of water and soil.[26] They are also the essential reservoirs of genetic material for agriculture and forestry.

Transition from Fossil to Solar Energy

Instead of relying on the finite supplies of fossil energy, we must focus research on ways to convert solar energy into usable energy for society. Many solar energy technologies already exist, including solar thermal receivers, photovoltaics, solar ponds,* and hydropower, as well as the burning of biomass vegetation. Using some technologies, moreover, biomass can be converted into the liquid fuels ethanol and methanol.[27]

As recently as 1850, the United States was 91 percent dependent on biomass wood and solar power for energy.[28] Gradually that has changed, until today we are 92 percent dependent on fossil energy, while biomass energy makes up only 3 percent of the fuel we use.[29]

Looking to the future, reliance on biomass energy use undoubtedly will grow and again become one of our dominant forms of solar energy.[30] However, use of biomass has major limitations. The total amount of solar energy captured by vegetation each year in our country is about 13×10^{15} kcal.[31] This yield including all the solar energy captured by agricultural crops, forests, lawns, and natural plants, cannot, according to all estimates, be increased to any great extent.[32] Furthermore, the total solar energy captured by our agricultural crops and forest products is about 7×10^{15} kcal, or slightly more than half the total solar energy captured.[33] Because this portion of biomass energy provides us with food, fiber, pulp, and lumber, it cannot be burned or converted into biomass energy.

Biomass vegetation provides the food and shelter for a wide variety of important natural biota life forms that help keep our natural environment healthy. Some of these species recycle wastes and nutrients; others help clean our air, soil, and water of pollutants. Without sufficient biomass, these essential processes would stop.

---

* Solar ponds are water storage units that have a salt gradient where heat collects and is stored.

Another factor to consider is that only 0.1 percent to 0.2 percent of the total solar energy per acre can be harvested as biomass in the temperate region.[34] This is because solar energy is captured by plants only during their brief growing season, and for three-quarters of the year most plants are not growing.[35] The use of relatively large land areas and large capital equipment investments will be needed for the conversion of biomass energy into usable form.

Even at our present population level, to sustain our lives and activities we are burning 40 percent more fossil energy than the total amount of solar energy captured by all plant biomass.[36] Clearly, our consumption of resources, especially nonrenewable fossil fuels, is out of balance with our supplies. The plain fact is that we are depleting these resources at an alarming rate and need to find and develop other energy sources.

However great the investment we are prepared to make, the availability of land will be the major constraint to the expanded use of solar energy systems. Almost three-quarters of the land area in the United States is already devoted to agriculture and commercial forestry,[37] so only a relatively small percentage of our land area is available for

Land Resource Requirements for Construction of Energy Facilities That Produce 1 Billion Kilowatt-hours per Year of Electricity for a City of 100,000 People.

Electrical Energy Technology	Land in Acres
Solar thermal central receiver	1,976
Photovoltaics	1,482
Wind power	6,670
Hydropower	32,110
Forest biomass	815,100
Solar ponds	22,230
Nuclear	168
Coal	222

Source: D. Pimentel, L.M. Frederickson, D.B. Johnson, J.H. McShane, H.-W. Yuan, "Environment and Population: Crises and Policies," in *Food and Natural Resources*, D. Pimentel and C.W. Hall, eds. (Academic Press, San Diego, 1989).

harvesting biomass and other solar energy technologies to support a solar energy–based U.S. economy.

The amount of land required to provide solar-based electricity for a city of 100,000 people illustrates the land constraints. Providing the needed 1 billion kilowatt hours per year from wood biomass would require our maintaining 815,000 acres of permanent forest, as shown in the table. Even hydropower is, in part, land based, because on average it requires 32,000 acres of land for an adequate-size reservoir. Furthermore, the land used for the reservoir is often fertile, productive agricultural land.[38] Both solar energy and hydropower have serious land and environmental limitations. Compared to biomass and hydropower production, nuclear and coal-fired power plants, including mining, require relatively small areas of land.

The conversion of biomass into energy, such as, corn into liquid ethanol fuels, unfortunately requires enormous inputs of fossil energy. For example, about 1.5 gallons of oil equivalents are used to produce 1 gallon of ethanol equivalents.[39] Thus, under optimal conditions about 70 percent more energy is used to produce ethanol than there is energy in the ethanol produced.[40] Even if we quadrupled efficiency so that 1 kcal of fossil energy produced 2 kcal of ethanol, about 10 acres of corn land would be required to fuel one U.S. automobile per year.[41]

If we make the optimistic assumption that the amount of solar energy used today could be increased about three- to ten-fold without adversely affecting agriculture, forestry, or the environment, then from 3 to 10×10^{15} kcal of solar energy would be available.[42] This is at best only one-half the current level of energy consumption in the United States, which is about 20×10^{15} kcal and averages 2,100 gallons of oil equivalents per capita per year.[43] One possibility is that fusion energy will eventually be developed and make up the shortfall. However, odds for this happening in time are about 1 in 1,000[44]. Furthermore, the intense heat its production generates would have to be overcome.

Toward a Sustainable Agriculture

Analyzing the 120 gallons of oil we now use to produce food on one acre of land suggests ways we might decrease that fossil-based energy expenditure. Both fertilizers and pesticides are lost or wasted in agricultural production. For instance, about $18 billion per year of fertilizer nutrients are lost as they are eroded along with soils.[45] Further, livestock manures, which have five times the amount of fertilizer nitrogen used each year, are underutilized, wasted, or allowed to erode along with soil. Much fossil energy could be saved if effective soil conservation methods were to be implemented and manures were used more extensively.

Another waste occurring in agriculture that affects energy use can be attributed to pesticides. Since 1945 the use of synthetic pesticides in the United States has grown thirty-three-fold, yet our crop losses continue to increase.[46] More pesticides have been used because agricultural technology has drastically changed; for example, crop rotations have been abandoned for many major crops. About 40 percent of our corn acreage is now grown continuously as corn, and this has resulted in an increased number of corn pests. Despite a thousand-fold increase in use of pesticides on corn-on-corn (continuous corn), corn losses to insects have risen four-fold.

Improved agricultural technology and a return to crop rotations would stem soil erosion, conserve fertile land, reduce water requirements for irrigation, and decrease pesticide and fertilizer use, thereby saving both fossil fuels and water. With relatively small populations, more land is available for cultivation. *The use of more land to produce food reduces the total energy inputs needed in crop production and would make agriculture more solar energy dependent and sustainable.* For example, instead of raising a given crop on one acre with an energy input of about 120 gallons of oil, the use of two acres for the same crop would make possible a reduction in energy inputs from 50 percent to 66 percent.[47]

This, of course, assumes the availability of sufficient land, and a halving of yields per acre. Some estimates suggest that if losses, waste, and mismanagement were eliminated, we would be able to produce present yields of food on the same amounts of land with one-half the energy outputs and still have a more sustainable system.[48] This should probably be considered an upper limit. Since supplies of arable land cannot be much expanded, and since we have already hypothesized the diversion of some land to solar energy uses, prudence suggests that, in planning any such shift to sustainable practices, we anticipate lower yields and lower total production. This, in turn, forces a choice between a smaller population or one that is less well fed.

Prosperity and Population

If the United States were to move to a solar energy–based economy and become self-sustainable, what would be our options and levels of prosperity? With a self-sustaining solar energy system replacing our current dependence on fossil energy, the energy availability would be one-fifth to one-half the current level. If the U.S. population remained at its present level of 252 million, a significant reduction in our current standard of living would follow, even if all the energy conservation measures known today were adopted.

If the U.S. population wishes to continue to enjoy its current high level of energy use and standard of living and prosperity, its ideal population should be between forty and one hundred million people. With sound energy conservation practices and a drastic reduction of energy use per capita to less than one-half current usage, it might be possible to support the current population. One choice requires a significantly lower population level and the other results in a dramatic reduction in the standard of living because of the resource needs of the larger population. On the positive side, we do have sufficient fossil energy, especially coal, to help us make the needed transition in the use of energy resources and population numbers over the next century, provided we can manage to lessen the environmental impacts now damaging our ecosystem.

Conclusion

At present levels of fertility and migration, the U.S. population will rise by more than one-half by 2050. A modest increase in fertility could drive it past a half-billion, and we would be heading toward population densities like those in present-day China. Comparisons to China clearly show why the United States will be unable to maintain its current level of prosperity and high standard of living, which are based on its adequate fertile land, water, energy, and biological resources. Supplies of fossil energy, a nonrenewable resource, now are being rapidly depleted and in just a few years, most U.S. oil resources will be used up. Fortunately, natural gas reserves will last for nearly fifty years, while coal reserves will carry us beyond the next century.

Therefore, we must start now to make the slow transition from our dependence on fossil fuels to the development of solar energy power as our major energy resource. For the United States to be self-sustaining in solar energy, given our land, water, and biological resources, our population should be less than 100 million—significantly less than the current level of 252 million. If, however, the current population level is sustained, a drastic reduction in standards of living will follow.

The available supply of fossil fuels, especially coal, will provide the time we need to make the necessary adjustments involving new solar energy technologies and agriculture practices. Coupled with this, Americans will have time to improve their use and respect for natural resources and the environment.

With a population of forty to one hundred million, the United States could become self-sustaining on solar energy while maintaining a quality environment, provided that sound energy conservation and environmental policies were in effect to preserve soil, water, air, and biological resources that sustain life. With these far-reaching changes, we feel confident that future generations of Americans would be able to enjoy prosperity and have a high standard of living. Starting to deal with the future before it reaches crisis-level is the only way we will be able to avert real tragedy for our children's children. Through education, fair population control, sound resource policies, the support of scientific research, and the effort of all the people, we will be able to face the future with optimism and pride.

ENERGY AND POPULATION
Transitional Issues and Eventual Limits
PAUL J. WERBOS

The transition to sustainable energy sources, perhaps the most challenging task facing the nation over the next few decades, is complicated because we cannot predict the technologies that will help us to make that transistion. If we must rely on technologies presently in sight, the optimum population is dramatically lower than technological optimism might justify. In either event, however, we need to free the maximum possible resources to finance the transition, and population policy will be an essential element in determining whether funds and skills can be mobilized on the scale required.

The editor of this book has asked me to address what appears to be a straightforward set of questions: What U.S. population size is compatible with the environmental consequences of energy use? What levels of population would lead to maximum efficiency in the energy sector, as a guesstimate, in long-term equilibrium?

Many energy analysts tend to ignore the population question, or they treat population as a minor background variable in forecasting twenty years into the future. A few analysts, following the first report to the Club of Rome, decry all forms of economic and population growth. Both sides—the pessimists and the defenders of the status quo—have built elaborate models and theories to defend their viewpoints, often based on questionable hidden assumptions. After years of working through this maze of theories and building a few models myself, I would make the following personal judgments[1] about energy and population:

1. The present mix of fuels and energy technologies is not sustainable in the long term, even if population could be dramatically reduced. In the long term, fossil fuels will run out. Even now, our present ways of using energy have led to unhealthy levels of ozone in almost every American city and to toxic pollution leaking into groundwater and into natural bodies of water. In the next decade or two, oil imports may return to being a crisis-level problem as, almost inevitably, demand increases and domestic supply decreases. Sooner or later, we must also deal with the problem of greenhouse warming, which is associated with all realistic uses of fossil fuels.

To meet *all* our present energy demands, worldwide, and also achieve economic growth, with conventional nuclear power, would lead over time to a growth by orders of magnitude in key variables that are already growing due to simple accumulation over time: the volume of nuclear waste, the supply of nuclear material divertible to terrorists, the dangers of nuclear proliferation, and the probability of nuclear accident. Even at their present levels, one may argue that these variables present the greatest existing threat to national security.

2. Once a complete transition to sustainable technologies is achieved, we could probably sustain a wide range of possible populations at a reasonable level of efficiency. From an efficiency viewpoint, populations between 50 and 100 percent of the present population would probably be ideal, though environmental quality would probably be better at the lower end of the range. Populations as low as twenty-five million or so would probably be a problem, because it would be difficult to sustain a complex mix of technologies (even soft technologies) on such a small engineering base; however, we probably could not sustain a population much greater than that if we insisted on using only less expensive, less risky soft technologies. With a high degree of optimism about the soft technologies, and allowances for peak-load electricity supplied by solar power, we might hope to sustain a population as large as sixty million or so. For larger populations, we would probably have to rely mostly on direct solar technologies, including a certain mix of technologies as yet unproved. With much larger populations, solar energy would become more expensive due to higher land prices; furthermore, the concentration of water pollution tends to increase in proportion to population. With a per capita income as low as that of China, we could sustain a population of that size as well; however, an economy as rich as ours would surely face more difficult problems with water pollution and land supply.

3. Regardless of long-term sustainability, the growth of population and the composition of this growth in the next two to three decades is possibly the most serious problem reducing our chance of a successful transition to sustainable technology. At first glance, the connection may not be obvious, but it is really quite strong. Sustainable technologies will take a long time to bring onto the mass market, and the transition will cost billions upon billions of dollars. An important part of the cost will involve research and development which is highly profitable in the long term, but expensive in the short term. Finding the money in the next five years will clearly be a problem—and the next twenty years may not be radically different from the next five.

In these circumstances, the nation will be well advised to do whatever it can to slow the present rate of population growth and the concomitant increased energy demand created by a larger population. Perhaps more important, it needs to change its investment habits, accumulating capital to make the transition away from petroleum. The biggest obstacle to finding the money—in both the public and the private sectors—is the general shortage of capital associated with a low national savings rate and the federal budget deficit. The financial challenges aside, we are socially unprepared for current as well as future economic and environmental demands. Although we need a skilled and productive labor force, neither our immigration policies nor our national social policies are focused on this goal; we admit immigrants based on kinship rather than skills. Teenage pregnancy continues to rise, and increasingly it is the poorest, who can least afford to raise them, who are having the most children.

We wrestle with the costs and results of these problems, rather than trying to avoid them. The costs are very high, and they divert resources from the challenges ahead. A national policy preparing us to cope with those challenges would probably result in immigration and fertility levels corresponding roughly to the "hard path" described by Leon Bouvier in Chapter 13, with an immediate slowing of population growth.

In conclusion, it is not obvious that the United States will be able to make the transition to sustainable technologies in time to prevent severe, debilitating rises in energy prices and environmental problems worldwide. Rising energy prices and shifts in the composition of the labor force would slow down economic growth, making such a huge transition ever more difficult if we wait too long. The solutions and the problems will both take decades to develop, and no one knows which of the two will come first. If demographic problems over the next few decades result in too much delay, the consequences for our civilization might well be permanent.

In the following sections I will elaborate on some of these points. First, I will discuss the near-term problem of dependency on oil and the difficulty of achieving a transportation system that frees us from that dependency. Then I will discuss the longer-term issues of how we fuel this transportation sector and other sectors of the economy.

Oil: Its Importance, Its Future and How to Escape It

Oil and gas currently account for 66 percent of the primary energy consumed in the United States.[2] They are both in highly finite supply, and there will be major difficulties in replacing them. Oil in particular tends to be used in applications where it is difficult to substitute other fuels. Unless there is gross mismanagement of the electric utility sector, shortages and high prices for oil are likely to create the next major crisis in the energy sector, just as they did in the 1970s.

The last great oil crises came in 1974 and 1979, when oil prices rose 119 percent and 42 percent, respectively.[3] These oil crises led immediately to slowdowns in economic activity. From 1973 to 1975, GNP was reduced by 10.6 percent compared to the previous growth path (1961–1973); this works out to a loss of $285 billion in 1982 dollars, in 1975 alone. From 1978 to 1980, the loss was more like 6 percent. Those who remember living during those days of gas lines and uncertainty may appreciate how greatly this understates the actual pain involved. For example, time lost in gas lines does not show up in the GNP. Nor do these reductions account for the loss to our balance of payments, which has reduced our degree of ownership of our own economy. If we produce a lot of goods but do not own what we produce, our own well-being may suffer.

Was this loss of GNP in 1974 and 1979 really due to the oil price rises? Some economic models predict that price rises of this sort should have little short-term impact; however, most of those models have a "potential GNP" equation that does not depend on energy or assumes that it is easy to replace energy with capital or labor. In effect, they *assume* that we can easily produce goods without using energy (even in cases where energy is represented in great detail in *other* equations of the model). Naturally, they do not predict big impacts in the future either. One famous modeler, whose model could not explain the full impact of the 1974 price rises, came up with a very ingenious excuse he used in selling his model during the Reagan administration: He argued that it was the *government's* fault that the GNP fell so much due to mismanagement by the Nixon–Ford administration; however, the errors of his model can be explained more easily as the result of his assuming a very high price elasticity (that is, easy replacement of energy). In contrast, the Wharton Annual Energy Model of the 1970s, which contained a detailed account of the short-term influence of energy on the economy, using a detailed representation of production, *was* able to explain the economic downturn in 1973–75[4] and would also predict larger short-term effects in case of future price rises.

Does the loss of $285 billion in 1975 represent the full cost of the price rise of 1974? Many analysts simply calculate this kind of short-term loss and assume that the economy bounced back thereafter to its previous growth path. However, if the previous growth path depended on tangibles like investment, this becomes a questionable assumption. The well-known economist Dale Jorgenson has shown very convincingly that one would expect a *long-term* effect, shifting both the level and the rate of growth of GNP. In fact, the year 1974 marks a sudden and very disturbing shift in the U.S. economy, from a sustained growth in the 4 percent range—based on large growth in productivity—to sustained growth in the zero to one percent range. The growing percentage of women working for wages, along with tax cuts, has helped to keep up the growth in average monetary income over the past fifteen years, but real wages *per person working* have not grown in this period. Real wages are probably a better measure of economic well-being than is income per capita.

Although the evidence cited here suggests that the drop in productivity growth after 1974 might be due to higher energy prices, other explanations are possible. For example, one might argue that short-term efforts to keep up high standards of consumption despite the rise of energy prices led to shortsighted actions, such as cuts in research and development, that lowered productivity growth. Some economists have argued that changes in the labor force, related to the population issues alluded to in the overview, were the major culprit. If *any* of these arguments is correct, then the problems cited in the overview would be the main culprit for this chronic loss in economic growth since 1974. Our hopes of returning to sustainable economic growth, and restoring that high spirit and morale that led us to the moon, may depend on solving our energy and population problems. Those who believe that lower oil prices have already begun to bring back some of the old high spirits in the past few years should be concerned about the danger of going back into malaise if oil prices go back up again.*

What are the dangers of new oil crises, leading to effects as large as or larger than those of the 1970s? The basic situation that allowed an oil crisis in 1974 was the growth in U.S. dependency on imported oil. By 1974, U.S. oil imports had grown to 35 percent of our oil consumption, and 20 percent of the total came from OPEC.[5] *Those* are the numbers that made us vulnerable to unexpected events in the Middle East. By 1979, the situation was worse, with a 43 percent import dependency and a 30 percent OPEC dependency. In fact, the *steady* rise in oil prices from 1973 to 1981 was undoubtedly a factor in the lower economic growth in that period.

By the late 1970s, it seemed clear to many people that low or stable oil prices were a thing of the past. As a result, there were massive changes in energy use, including one-time improvements in efficiency and conversion from oil to other fuels in markets where conversion was relatively easy. This, in turn, led to reduced oil demand and downward pressure on prices. By 1986, there was talk of an oil glut. However, even

*As this book went to press, oil prices had begun to rise somewhat, as the result of yet another crisis in the Mideast, and the U.S. economy experienced its first real recession in almost ten years.

before prices bottomed out in 1986, oil imports began to rise again as certain inexorable forces began to reassert themselves. From 1986 to January 1990, oil prices rose back to $20 per barrel, about half again as large as the 1986 price.[6] However, from 1986 to 1989, our dependency on oil imports rose from 33 to 41 percent (and is still rising), and our dependency on OPEC rose from 17 to 24 percent, despite the rise in oil prices. We are now more vulnerable than we were in 1974, and we are moving rapidly back to the 1979 level. Based on a relatively conservative analysis of these trends, the Energy Information Agency (EIA) forecasts that U.S. oil imports from 1988 to 2010 will double.[7] This implies a relatively serious, steadily growing threat to the U.S. economy—one with no end in sight.

Looking beneath the surface, the dangers are even greater than the import numbers suggest. For one thing, the situation in the Mideast appears more intractable than it did in 1974, particularly in the light of nuclear and chemical weapons proliferation. For another thing, there is less slack in our use of energy than there was in 1974. The easy things have already been done. From 1974 to 1989, the use of oil in the residential/commercial sector dropped by 30 percent, and the electric utility use of oil dropped by 50 percent. Most people who could convert easily to natural gas have done so.[8] (Many areas still lack sufficient gas pipeline capacity, however.) As a result, oil use by the transportation sector grew from 53 to 63 percent of the national total. The remaining oil use in the United States is overwhelmingly concentrated in vehicle use in industry, for example, tractors and bulldozers, and in petrochemical feedstock use.[9] In brief, further reductions in oil use, either in a crisis or before, will have to come chiefly from cutbacks in motor vehicles or cutbacks in our use of bulk plastics and petrochemicals.

How hard would it be to make such cutbacks in a crisis, if we did not have time to change our capital stock? In a future crisis, our main opportunity to cut back on oil use would be through reductions in driving. From historical data it is overwhelmingly clear[10] that a 1.0 percent increase in the real price of gasoline reduces driving by only 0.2 percent; in economists' jargon this is a price elasticity of -0.2/1.0, or -20 percent. To cut back driving by 10 percent without a direct reduction in personal income would thus require something like a 60 percent increase in prices. The loss of all U.S. oil imports from OPEC—which are far more than 10 percent—would therefore seem to imply a bigger impact than we observed in 1974 or 1979.

What would happen if we allowed for the possibility of conservation? What if we assume that cars will become more efficient but still use gasoline? In actuality, the EIA forecasts have *already assumed* a very high level of conservation, rising to 35 miles per gallon (mpg) for the *average* new car.[11] Higher mpg is possible, of course, in small or slower cars, but the research embedded in these assumptions was based on very extensive studies of what the public is willing to buy under different price regimes—something that the private sector has been very sincere about wanting to know.[12] Phil Patterson, of the Conservation Office of the Department of Energy (DOE), published a critical review of the EIA efficiency assumptions in a recent World Energy Conference in Paris. Patterson argued very persuasively that the EIA assumptions were on the optimistic side. His review was especially persuasive because it drew heavily on work by engineering research groups who had worked with people like Amory Lovins (who is arguably the world's most famous champion of conservation), and it came from an office that seriously tries to champion the cause of conservation. In summary, continued conservation is expected to have an important impact on oil use, but it will not be enough by itself to prevent a worsening situation on imports.

There are laws in thermodynamics, discovered by Sadi Carnot in the early nineteenth century, that limit the ultimate efficiency of internal combustion engines and other heat engines. Back when engines were highly inefficient, there was substantial waste and slack, which allowed a rapid improvement in mpg until 1982. Many econometric models show more potential for conservation because they are based in large part on data from that period and do not account for the diminishing returns that are obvious in the engineering. (Also, they usually focus on "new car" mpg, without accounting for the shift of many car buyers toward pickup trucks and vans.) Nowadays, engines are pushing the limits of what is physically possible with this class of engine; already the complexity of new systems has begun to create problems involving cost and maintenance. Serious improvements in aerodynamics and lighter materials are certainly possible, but they are already assumed in the forecasts. To do a whole lot *better* than the existing forecasts—and to avoid massive disruptions in the case of import cutbacks—one would have to go beyond the use of gasoline in heat engines.

Back in the administration of Jimmy Carter, synthetic fuels were supposed to solve these problems. However, early cost estimates for synthetic fuels—like estimates for nuclear power and many other complex new technologies—were off by a factor of two or three. Ed Merrow of the RAND Corporation performed a more in-depth analysis of cost escalation, and predicted costs more like $3 per gallon (in 1980 dollars) for gasoline based on synfuels technologies. This did not include the environmental costs, which would have been large. If the United States consumes one hundred billion gallons of gasoline per year, now priced at under $1 per gallon (in 1980 dollars), then the cost of switching entirely to synfuels would have been over $200 billion per year—not the kind of thing one likes to do a decade early for the sake of insurance.

The current President has chosen, for excellent reasons, to focus on methanol as the immediate way out of this dilemma. Economists from Ford Motor Company have argued that one gets more miles per ton of coal if one converts the coal to methanol, and uses it as methanol, rather than making synthetic gasoline.[13] Furthermore, the use of methanol opens the door to a whole variety of other fuel supplies (such as wood alcohol) and makes it far easier, as I will discuss, to change over to fuels like hydrogen in the more distant future.

If we assume 60 cents per gallon to produce methanol using established technologies,[14] and 30 cents per gallon for distribution, and account for the lower heat content of methanol, we arrive at a price of $1.80 per gallon equivalent, in 1989 dollars and in conventional automobiles. This is far less than what synfuels would cost. Unfortunately, it is still not as cheap as gasoline, and it still requires an expensive transition. Moreover, it only helps a little in reducing those emissions that cause ozone buildup, a major health hazard in most American cities (about 20 percent, in my judgment—less than the 50 percent claimed by some authoritative advocates but more than the 0 percent claimed by critics). Finally, dual-fueled methanol–gasoline vehicles would have only half the driving range using methanol that they would with gasoline. (Driving range would be a serious problem with other alternate fuels as well, except for ethanol.) At any rate, in 1989 Congress rejected an administration version of the Clean Air Bill that would have mandated an initial effort to begin deploying this technology.

There are ways to move vehicles that are *not* covered by the Carnot limitations. Los Alamos National Laboratories (LANL) has made substantial breakthroughs in the development of methanol-powered fuel cells for transportation, breakthroughs that solve a wide variety of earlier problems.[15] Such vehicles are expected to be twice as efficient as cars based on heat engines, *if* we use low-temperature technologies like the LANL technology (or others discussed by the National Hydrogen Association of Washington, D.C.). These technologies now require the use of methanol or hydrogen as fuels (natural gas *might* become possible someday, with further research); ozone-related emissions are reduced by a factor of ten or twenty, conservatively. In this technology, a fuel cell provides electricity to an electric motor; therefore, if breakthroughs in battery technology should occur, the widespread use of the fuel-cell technology would make a further transition much easier.

Money has gone into this technology from both DOE and the private sector, and the most recent (unpublished) results are extremely promising.* However, we are rapidly approaching a point where large investments will be required from the private sector, and it is uncertain whether the incentives now available are large enough. The House of Representatives added an amendment to the Clean Air Act of 1990 mandating an advanced vehicle program in Southern California, that might conceivably provide the required incentives; however, this new law is only a first step. There is room for much stronger incentives giving more positive (and profitable) encouragement to the automobile manufacturers. The most optimistic among us are hoping for thousands of fuel-cell vehicles per year by the year 2000, under a sustained push beyond what present circumstances point toward. Sober forecasters are expecting something more like 2010 to 2030—and many years more to achieve full penetration of the existing automotive fleet. Between the methanol suppliers and the auto manufacturers, the required investments will undoubtedly add up to hundreds of billions of dollars by the time we are through.

In summary, as stated at the beginning of this chapter, the solutions to oil dependency will take a long time and a lot of money, and may or may not actually happen, given our present political and budgetary climate. If we are lucky, they may come on-line before oil prices ratchet way up again, but no one knows which will happen first—the crisis or the cure. Anything that improves the budgetary climate could make a big difference here, and an early cessation of growth in the population dependent on federal income support would certainly help.

---

*As this book goes to press, DOE has announced a major new effort including LANL, Dow Chemical, and General Motors.

Transition to Sustainable Energy Supplies

Billions of dollars and decades of work will be required just to complete the transition away from oil as described above. This transition away from oil is justifiably our most immediate priority in the energy sector because of the need to minimize the threat of a big new oil crisis and to eliminate unhealthy levels of ozone in American cities. However, this still does not solve the problem of where to get the methanol in the long-term, and it does not solve the problem of sustainability across all sectors of the economy. Additional, expensive transitions will be required to solve these longer-term problems.

Traditionally, there are four "sources" of energy that could meet our long-term needs: conservation, renewables, nuclear, and coal.

THE SOFT PATH Advocates of the "soft" energy path argue that we might create a sustainable energy system by combining conservation with reliance on "soft" renewables, such as biomass, solar water heaters, and wind, hydro, and geothermal energy. Some conservatives have strongly endorsed this idea and argued that this kind of transition will occur easily and naturally, simply by relying on free markets and eliminating government "interference" (such as R&D on conservation and renewables).

As I will discuss later, there *are* some renewable technologies—like advanced solar cells—that *could* produce a very large amount of energy; however, the soft renewables are usually not defined to include these. In the past, when EIA published very long-term forecasts and documentation explaining those forecasts, the projections of supply from renewables were mainly based on carefully worked out estimates of the *upper limit* of potential supply. Hydroelectric supply is limited by the energy in our rivers, wind supply is limited by our supply of exploitable wind sources; and so forth. By and large, the *total* potential from these sources is something like one-tenth of present U.S. energy consumption. (EIA now predicts that renewable energy will *lose* market share from 1990 to 2010 because of a combination of limited potential and economic forces.)[16]

Advocates for specific soft technologies often argue for somewhat greater potential. For example, one report on biomass from the Office of Technology Assessment (OTA) began with an executive summary stating that wood alcohol might contribute as much as 10 quadrillion British thermal units (or 10 quads) of additional energy to our economy—

by itself about 12 percent of what we use.[17] But later volumes of that report warned that this assumed the widespread use of fast-growing evergreen monocultures to double production, and an avoidance of the soil conservation rules that the U.S. Department of Agriculture (USDA) has laid down for croplands (rules that many believe are still inadequate to prevent soil loss). A more objective estimate of the sustainable potential would be less than half of that 10 quads.

Most of these upper bounds are based on physical constants—such as flows of wind and water, that are independent of population. However, if population were reduced substantially, there would be a major increase in the potential supply of biomass energy, because there would be less competition from the food industry and other users of biomass. In the absence of truly comprehensive studies, it is hard to guess how large this increase would be. For example, if *all* the corn and wheat in the United States were converted to alcohol fuels (based on 2.6 gallons per bushel),[18] and if the U.S. crop were reduced in half to achieve sustainability (see Chapter 2) this would yield 10 billion gallons per year—only 1.5 quads of gross energy, and only 0.8 quads net. On the other hand, OTA has estimated that an additional 5 quads might be available from grasses and the like (*with* a smaller population),[19] and one might hope to achieve greater net efficiency by developing new conversion technologies. Personally, I incline toward conservatism here, but the uncertainties are large; I can imagine the possibility of a case for *doubling* the potential from soft technologies if population were cut very sharply. This would still only amount to about 20 percent of present U.S. energy consumption; that (together with a low-risk scenario for solar energy) explains the sixty million population figure in the overview. Again, I would not be surprised if a smaller figure showed up after more extensive analysis.

Serious advocates of the soft path have generally recognized these limits on soft energy supply and have argued that conservation can bridge the gap. But 80 percent of the end-use fossil fuel used in the United States lies in two sectors: transportation and industry.[20] The preceding section described how conservation, important though it is, is far from enough to create a sustainable economy. Fuelcell cars *would* allow a factor of two reduction in energy intensity, compared with the alternatives, but only at a price: The conversion losses in *making* methanol lead to only a marginal net improvement in efficiency.

The industrial sector is already going through a similar transition from fossil fuel to efficient electric technologies, without government intervention (aside from R&D). These technologies are relatively benign environmentally, and they enhance industrial productivity; however, if one accounts for conversion losses in generating the electricity, they often lead to greater energy intensity in production. The energy used per dollar of product may decline, because the quality and value of products goes up (for example, in the case of more effective drugs); however, this greater quality also leads to a greater total value of product (a qualitative growth in GNP), and the net effect on energy use is often positive.

Some economists have argued that higher energy prices should increase conservation in industry beyond the present trends; however, a recent comparison of the best in-depth models of industrial energy use shows that *all* of them report relatively low price elasticities.[21] This includes both econometric (or trend-based) models and engineering-based models. Earlier, more aggregated models showed larger elasticities because of apriori "consistency constraints," data bases ending in 1974, and failure to account for the detailed structure of industrial demand as it varies from time to time and place to place.

If population should grow much beyond present levels in the United States, there will probably be an additional energy demand for desalinization of water; some cities in California have already been getting into this technology. With anything like a population doubling, desalinization could provide a big part of our national water supply, and the additional energy requirements would be enormous.[22]

On balance, if one assumes some minimal level of growth in income per capita, it is hard to imagine a totally soft energy economy, without a drastic reduction of population. Given the difficulty of maintaining a complex economy on a small engineering base, I would question the feasibility of this scenario even if the reduction of population were possible. A dramatic improvement in international communications (requiring both advanced technology and cultural shifts) might increase our effective engineering base and compensate for the loss of labor supply, but there are so many obstacles here that I find it hard to visualize a way to overcome all of them at once. If there is any hope for this scenario, it would require drastic reductions in population growth, not only in the United States, but—for the sake of stability—worldwide.

COAL AND NUCLEAR The conventional wisdom in energy forecasting says that we will shift, first, to a coal-based economy, and then, as the coal grows more expensive, shift more to nuclear. Coal may be used more in the developed world and nuclear more in the developing world, for political reasons. (Public pressure has led to rising safety costs and restrictions on nuclear power in the developed world, while low-budget forms of nuclear power remain popular in nations more worried about poverty and military prestige.) Many long-range forecasting models simply assume that coal and nuclear are available in unlimited quantities.

The conventional wisdom may well be right. However, severe environmental problems with both fuels will make this transition less than automatic. There are also national security issues on the nuclear side that merit more serious action than we have seen as yet.

The environmental consequences of using coal have received a lot of attention. For example, many people associate coal with sulfur dioxide, which they associate with acid rain, which they associate with the massive recent die-back of trees in Germany, a true environmental disaster. Careful studies by the Germans, however, suggest that nitrogen oxides (NOx) may actually be the most important pollutant responsible for this damage (and for high ozone levels).[23] About 40 percent of the NOx emitted in the United States comes from motor vehicles, and about 50 percent from large boilers burning coal. Fuel-cell cars would eliminate the 40 percent, but conventional, affordable pollution control technologies would have only a marginal impact on the 50 percent. Fortunately, there has been great progress in clean coal research, which could solve this problem and probably even save money in the process, at least for new boilers.[24] What to do about existing boilers is a harder problem. The government is already spending billions on clean coal technology, and it is clear that strenuous efforts along these lines must be continued or expanded if we really want to clean up ozone and make a safe, economical transition to coal. Likewise, it is clear that a lot of private capital would be required to build the new plants and that the federal budget deficit will have a big effect on capital availability.

In the long term there are two other concerns about coal: (1) It contributes to greenhouse warming (more so than natural gas, but far less so than shale oil); (2) it is in finite supply. If the world relied *entirely* on coal, if we maintained economic growth, and if we avoided using environmentally questionable forms of coal or depending on undiscovered coal speculated on by officials in Communist countries, then coal might last somewhere on the order of six to ten decades.[25] This may seem like forever to some people, but the development of safe alternatives might also take many decades. In any case, the sooner we stop the accumulation of greenhouse gases, the better. It is not too soon to think about the transition away from coal.

Nuclear power has often been advocated as a sustainable alternative to fossil fuels. However, a huge amount of research would be needed, at a minimum, to make this technology acceptable to the public. Furthermore, it is clear that existing controls on nuclear proliferation have not been effective enough to prevent major emerging problems in the Mideast (Iraq/Israel and India/Pakistan) and elsewhere.* As recently as 1983, nuclear power accounted for only 3.3 percent of world energy supply.[26] Studies for the Second Report to the Club of Rome showed graphically how huge an increase in that industry would be required to supply all the world's energy needs, especially if one allows for population and economic growth in developing nations and the eventual need for breeder reactors.[27] The opportunity for nuclear weapons proliferation and terrorism is directly proportional to the availability of nuclear materials for diversion; a growth by orders of magnitude in civilian nuclear power would lead to a similar growth in the potential for diversion. If the number of political actors with access to nuclear weapons increased by orders of magnitude, and if the new political actors were more diverse in their motivations than the old ones (for example, included crazies), then the probability of a first use of a nuclear weapon would increase by orders of magnitude as well. There are many scenarios for what could happen after such a first use, ranging all the way from global horror and authoritarian repression to a greater willingness of other actors to use nuclear weapons. (Herman Kahn has described how many other weapons went through similar cycles in the past, starting from religious revulsion but ending in widespread use and death.) It is not clear whether high civilization and vigorous economic growth would be sustainable under any of these scenarios.

Some analysts hope that a new form of nuclear energy—controlled fusion—would solve all this. But after decades of research, the future of fusion as an affordable source of energy seems debatable, and major budget cuts have resulted from the debates. Known forms of fusion produce neutron radiation just as much as fission does, and the most economical form of fusion would probably be a hybrid fission–fusion reactor, leading to all the same national security problems. Breakthroughs

*Iraq initiated war in the Mideast after these words were written; unfortunately, despite the U.S. victory, arms control in the region still seems far off.

in fundamental nuclear science, such as neutron-free "cold-fusion," may yet be possible, but should certainly not be counted on.

From a forecaster's point of view, the nuclear path may well be the most likely one (after a short recess). Even with the present limited use of nuclear power, the hazards of nuclear proliferation have begun to yield serious consequences. These points, taken together, underline the need for more conscious effort and heavy investment to open the doors to any real alternative, for the sake of national security.

HIGH-TECH RENEWABLES Beyond coal and nuclear technologies, there is one family of technologies that does not face the tight upper limits that affect the soft technologies: high-tech renewables, such as direct solar. Simple physical calculations show that a modest fraction of the U.S. land area would be quite enough to sustain all our energy needs. Many years ago, DOE published a program plan for solar cells in which they would achieve economic competitiveness at least for peak power (for example, noontime in the summer) by the end of this century. For many years, actual price reductions actually exceeded the DOE plan, as one might expect from a solid-state technology that is a cousin to microchips and PCs; however, after drastic cuts in the DOE budget for solar cells and cuts in private research due to falling oil prices, the prices of solar cells flattened out. Progress is still going on, but it is very slow. Work is also going on on more direct solar technologies to produce methanol or hydrogen, through new programs at the Solar Energy Research Institute in Colorado.

In addition, there still remains the problem of what to do about baseline electric power, the bulk of our electricity use. All of the possibilities involve risk and, if they look good on a first evaluation, would still require enormous investments. It is essential to develop technologies that can compete economically with nuclear power, in order to persuade other countries to resist the nuclear path and to avoid domestic policies based on price shock (which killed synfuels). There is a vague hope that ground-based solar might become cheap enough somehow to compete with nuclear; however, base load power generally costs five to ten times less than peak power,[28] and it is questionable whether costs can be reduced much beyond the present projections. Still, there are new technologies to produce methanol or hydrogen directly using sunlight whose costs are difficult to project. There is also some hope that radically new forms of geothermal energy might work out, with more research. Some people have even hoped for vast amounts of primordial gas deep in the earth's crust, though recent assessments of this are not encouraging. Finally, it is still quite possible that one could generate electricity from solar cells in space and beam the energy down to earth at a marginal cost competitive with nuclear power. (This would be better for the environment than ground-based solar because the microwave-receiving zones would require less land per kilowatt-hour than would solar cells, in part because of twenty-four-hour operation. Also, low-level microwaves have only a higher-order effect on plant life, at the most, whereas cutting off light simply kills them.) From a sheer engineering point of view, the last of these alternatives is easy to visualize,[29] but it would require the development of cheaper space transportation systems, such as a second-generation National Aerospace Plane, and automated lunar mining technology; such technologies are within the range of what we now know, but would require an enormous amount of effort.[30]

In any case, when no *one* technology is guaranteed of success, the safest path is to fully explore a *variety* of them, even if it does cost more money to do so.

Even if we successfully switch to these advanced technologies, there will still be limits on the population that we can sustain comfortably and efficiently in the United States, because of land costs and water pollution.

The cost of high-tech solar energy will depend critically on the cost of land. The cost of land *near people* is a critical issue because of transmission and maintenance costs. Real estate costs in urban and suburban areas are already an economic burden to many people, and a doubling or tripling of population would make this phenomenon more pervasive across the country; this in turn would certainly raise the cost of land and thus the cost of solar energy. Reductions in population from the present level would reduce land prices in some areas, but the effect would not be so pervasive. (Perhaps a population reduction would allow more people to move to areas that receive more sunlight.)

On the environmental side, high-tech renewables are much more benign than the status quo, but they are not problem free. Even today, in California, there are major concerns about groundwater contamination, much of which has been traced to gasoline stations, chemical plants, and even computer manufacturers. Replacing gasoline with methanol would not change the overall magnitude of the problem (though methanol is more biodegradable), and a big increase in population density would presumably increase the concentration of pollutants. Likewise, high-tech renewables would not prevent undesirable by-products in most chemical plants or chip factories. Given that the problems today are already a concern, it seems very worrisome to imagine increases in population that could double or triple the scale of the problems.

Conclusion

This chapter has only touched the surface of some very difficult and complex issues.

The transition to sustainable sources of energy will require a whole series of major transformations in the economy, each costing billions of dollars, each entailing major risks and requiring serious attention now. Failure to make a timely or benign transition would lead to serious problems for national security, the environment, and longer-term economic growth. Successful transitions would require major government investment in accelerated R&D, stronger incentives to the private sector, and trillions of dollars in investments from the private sector. All three of these will be hard to come by in the coming years, if the present deficit environment persists. Any population policy that encourages investment and reduces the growth in the nonproductive population would have an *immediate* impact on the growth of the federal deficit, and help a great deal in increasing the probability of a successful transition away from oil. In the long term, the energy sector and the environment would probably be healthiest if the U.S. population were somewhere around 50 to 100 percent of the present level, in my view. If one were optimistic about biomass and international cooperation but pessimistic about high-tech renewables, then the optimum would be more like sixty million people.

If the issue of population growth is neglected, it may be difficult to avoid a doubling or even tripling of U.S. population (see Chapter 13), which would clearly pose problems for energy and the environment, due to higher land costs and water pollution.

BALANCING HUMANS IN THE BIOSPHERE

ROBERT COSTANZA

The question of technological optimism arises again in a broader conceptual context: If there is any hope that technical fixes can address all the resource and environmental problems we face, are we not justified in proceeding on that expectation?

Cultural evolution has allowed humans to change their behaviors and adapt to new conditions much faster than has biological evolution. It has also removed the inherently long-run bias of biological evolution and made us susceptible to several social traps. The most critical of these is the overpopulation trap, caused by the imbalance between the short-term incentives to have children and the long-term social and ecological costs of having too many. But the severe and very real uncertainty about the long-run costs of too many humans has hindered debate and action on this issue. We cannot wait for the uncertainty to be resolved, because by then it will be too late. What we must do is deal with the uncertainty in a more appropriate way. We should tentatively assume the worst and then allow ourselves to be pleasantly surprised if we are wrong, rather than assume the best and face disaster if we are wrong. A crude worst-case estimate of optimal U.S. population based solely on renewable resources and current consumption levels yields about 85 million people. An average resource consumption level of one-half current levels combined with a more equitable distribution of resources would yield a high-quality life-style for 170 million.

Cultural Versus Biological Evolution

Human beings, like all other animals, make decisions based on responses to local, immediate reinforcements. They follow their noses, with some mediation by *genetic* (and in the case of humans and some other species *cultural*) programming. To understand the human population problem, one needs to understand how this complex of local reinforcements and programmed responses interact over several different time scales with the ecosystem within which humans are embedded.

Biological evolution has a built-in bias toward the long run. Characteristics learned or acquired during the lifetime of an individual cannot be passed on genetically. Changing the genetic structure of a species requires the election and accumulation of characteristics (phenotypes) by differential reproductive success. Biological evolution is therefore an inherently slow process requiring many, many generations to significantly alter a species' physical characteristics or behavior.

Cultural evolution is much faster, and in recent years it has accelerated to hyperspeed. Learned behaviors that are successful can be almost immediately spread to other members of the culture and passed on in the oral, written, or video record. The increased speed of adaptation that this process allows has been largely responsible for *Homo sapiens'* amazing success at controlling the resources of the planet.[1] But there is a significant downside. Like a car that has picked up speed, we are in much more danger of running off the road or over a cliff. We have lost the built-in long-run bias of biological evolution and are susceptible to being led by our hyperefficient short-run adaptability over a cliff into the abyss.

The Overpopulation Trap

This process of short-run incentives getting out of sync with long-term goals has been well studied in the past decade under several rubrics,[2] but the one I like best is John Platt's notion of "social traps."[3] In all such cases the decision maker may be said to be "trapped" by the local conditions into making what turns out to be a bad decision viewed from a longer or wider perspective. We go through life making decisions about which path to take based largely on "road signs," the short-run, local reinforcement that we perceive most directly. These short-run reinforcements can include monetary incentives, social acceptance or admonishment, and physical pleasure or pain. In general, this strategy of following the road signs is quite effective, unless the road signs are inaccurate or misleading. In these cases we can be trapped into following a path that is ultimately detrimental because of our reliance on the road signs. For example, cigarette smoking has been a social trap because by following the short-run road signs of the pleasure and social status[4] associated with smoking, we embark on the road to an increased risk of earlier death from smoking-induced cancer. More important, once this road has been taken it is very difficult to change to another (as most people who have tried to quite smoking can attest).

The problem of overpopulation is a classic social trap, as has been pointed out by Garrett Hardin, Paul Ehrlich, and many others.[5] The biological and cultural incentives to procreate that are incumbent on individuals in the short run, combined with rapid reductions in mortality, which have changed the long-run ecological cost structure, have led us into the jaws of this most serious of traps. Cultural evolution has so far changed only the short-run half of the equation (lower mortality) and has put us on the path to unsustainable population growth. It is time for cultural evolution to change the other half of the equation to bring them back into balance.

Short-Term Benefits and Long-Term Costs of Human Population Growth

What are the major costs and benefits of human population growth? We can divide them into three broad groups: individual, cultural, and ecological.

Individuals make decisions about family size, so ultimately it is the costs and benefits that individuals *perceive* that will make a difference. Culture's role is to translate long-term ecological costs and benefits into individual behavior. Additional children provide benefit to parents chiefly as workers, caregivers in old age, and genetic carriers. The major costs are those for rearing children to a productive, independent age. In most of the world the benefits of children as workers and caregivers are still significant and the costs for raising children to a productive age are low since levels of education are low and children can start working productively at a very early age. In many countries children begin to "pay for themselves" by age ten or so. In the United States and other developed countries the situation is quite different. Children have little or no direct benefit to parents as workers, and because of social security systems, they are not absolutely necessary as caregivers in old age (although they are still desirable in this role). On the other hand, the costs to raise them to "productive age" are enormous. In highly industrialized countries "productive age" means after at least four years of college, and the costs to the parents are daunting. It is little wonder that middle-class family sizes in industrialized countries have fallen so dramatically.

But it is the long-term ecological costs of more humans that are now becoming critically important. These long-term costs are caused by our speeded-up cultural evolution and must ultimately be solved by the next wave of cultural evolution.

Cultural evolution also has an interesting effect on human impacts on the environment. By changing the learned behavior of humans and incorporating tools and artifacts, it allows considerable variation in resource requirements and human impacts on ecosystems. Thus it does not make sense to talk about the "carrying capacity" of humans in the same way that we speak of the "carrying capacity" of other species since, in terms of their carrying capacity, humans are many subspecies. Each subspecies would have to be culturally defined to determine levels of resource use and carrying capacity. For example, the global carrying capacity for *Homo americanus* would be much lower than the carrying capacity for *Homo indus*, because Americans individually consume much more generally than do individual Indians. In fact, the speed of cultural adaptation makes the analogy to species (which are inherently slow changing) misleading. *Homo americanus* could change its resource consumption patterns drastically in only a few years, while *Homo sapiens* would remain relatively unchanged. I think it best to follow the lead of

Herman Daly[6] in this and speak of the product of population and per capita resource use as the *total impact* of the human population. It is this total impact that the earth has a capacity to carry, and it is up to us to decide how to divide it between numbers of people and per capita resource use. This complicates population policy enormously since one cannot simply state an optimal *population*, rather one must state an optimal number of *impact units*. How many impact units the earth can sustain and how to distribute these impact units over the population is a very dicey problem indeed, but one that must also be included in our next round of cultural evolution.

The Importance of Uncertainty and How to Deal With It

One key element that has frustrated population policy is the enormous degree of uncertainty about long-term human impacts on the biosphere. The argument can be summarized as differing opinions about the degree to which technological progress can eliminate resource constraints. Current economic world views (capitalist, socialist, and the various mixtures) are all based on the underlying assumption of continuing and unlimited economic growth. This assumption allows a whole host of very sticky problems, including population growth, equity, and sustainability to be ignored (or at least postponed), since they are seen to be most easily solved by additional economic growth. Indeed, most conventional economists define "health" in an economy as a stable and high *rate of growth*. Energy and resource limits to growth, according to these world views, will be eliminated as they arise by clever development and deployment of new technology. This line of thinking is often called "technological optimism."

An opposing line of thought (often called "technological pessimism") assumes that technology will not be able to circumvent fundamental energy and resource constraints and that eventually economic growth will stop. It has usually been ecologists or other life scientists who take this point of view,[7] largely because they study natural systems that invariably do stop growing when they reach fundamental resource constraints. A healthy ecosystem is one that maintains a stable level; unlimited growth is cancerous, not healthy, under this view.

The technological optimists argue that human systems are fundamentally different from other natural systems because of human intelligence. History has shown that resource constraints can be circumvented by new ideas. Technological optimists claim that Malthus' dire predictions about population pressures have not come to pass and that the energy crisis of the late 1970s is behind us.

The technological pessimists argue that many natural systems also have "intelligence" in that they can evolve new behaviors and organisms (including humans). Humans are therefore a part of nature, not apart from it. Just because we have circumvented local and artificial resource constraints in the past it does not mean we can circumvent the fundamental ones that we will eventually face. Malthus' predictions have not come to pass *yet* for the entire world, the pessimists would argue, but many parts of the world are in a Malthusian trap now, and other parts may well fall into it.

This debate has gone on for several decades now. It began with Barnett and Morse's *Scarcity and Growth* and really got into high gear with the publication of *The Limits to Growth* by Meadows and associates[8] and the Arab oil embargo in 1973. There have been thousands of studies over the past fifteen years on various aspects of our energy and resource future, and different points of view have waxed and waned. But the bottom line is that there is still an enormous amount of uncertainty about the impacts of energy and resource constraints, and I doubt that the argument will ever be decided on scientific grounds.

In the next twenty to thirty years we may begin to hit *real* fossil fuel supply limits as well as constraints on production due to global warming. Will fusion energy or solar energy or conservation or some as yet unthought-of energy source step in to save the day and keep economies growing? The technological optimists say yes, and the technological pessimists say no. Ultimately, no one knows. Both sides argue as if they were certain, but the worst form of ignorance is misplaced certainty.

The optimists argue that unless we *believe* that the optimistic future is possible and behave accordingly, it will never come to pass. The pessimists argue that the optimists will bring on the inevitable leveling and decline sooner by consuming resources faster, and that to sustain our system we should begin to conserve resources immediately. How do we proceed in the face of this overwhelming uncertainty?

We can cast this optimist/pessimist choice in a classic (and admittedly oversimplified) game theoretic format using the "payoff matrix." In the

Real state of the world

	Optimists right	Pessimists right
Technological optimist policy	High	Disastrous
Technological pessimist policy	Moderate	Tolerable

Payoff matrix for technological optimism versus pessimism.

illustration, the alternative policies that we can pursue today (technologically optimistic or pessimistic) are listed on the left, and the real states of the world are listed on the top. The intersections are labeled with the results in combining of policies and states of the world. For example, if we pursue the optimistic policy and the world really does turn out to conform to the optimistic assumptions, the payoff is "High." This high potential payoff is very tempting, and since this strategy has paid off in the past, it is not surprising that so many would like to believe that the world conforms to the optimist's assumptions. If, however, we pursue the optimistic policy and the world turns out to conform more closely to the pessimistic technological assumptions, the result is "Disastrous": There is irreversible damage to ecosystems and technological fixes are no longer possible. If we pursue the pessimistic policy and the optimists are right, then the results are only "Moderate." But if the pessimists are right and we pursue the pessimistic policy, the results are "Tolerable."

Within the framework of game theory, this simplified game has a fairly simple "optimal" strategy. If we really do not know the state of the world, we should choose the policy that is the maximum of the minimum outcomes (that is in game theory jargon the MaxiMin strategy). In other words, we analyze each policy in turn, look for the worst thing (minimum) that could happen if we pursue that policy, and pick the policy with the largest (maximum) minimum. In the case stated above, we should pursue the pessimist policy because the worst possible result under that policy ("Tolerable") is a preferable outcome to the worst outcome under the optimist policy ("Disastrous").

Given this analysis, what can one recommend for population policy? Because of the large uncertainty about the long-term impacts of population growth on ecological sustainability, *we should at least provisionally assume the worst.* We must assume that the dire predictions of the Ehrlichs and Pimentels[9] are correct and plan accordingly. If they are right, we will still survive. If they are wrong, we will be pleasantly surprised. The consequences of provisionally assuming the best about the impacts of population growth, as Julian Simon would have us do,[10] are very different. If we assume Simon is right and he is not, we will have irreversibly degraded the planet's capacity to support life. We cannot rationally take that risk.

Optimal U.S. Population Under Prudently Pessimistic Assumptions

Given all this, what can be said about the optimal size of the U.S. (or any other country's) population? Obviously, it depends on the level of per capita resource consumption, the ability of technology to overcome resource constraints, and the long-term impacts of humans on the biosphere. These last two involve enormous uncertainties. But I have argued that in the face of this uncertainty we should be prudent until it can be proven otherwise. We should assume the worst. Then if cold fusion or some other technology comes in to save the day, we can be pleasantly surprised. But we should not bank on cold fusion, hot fusion, or anything else, since the costs of being wrong are disaster. "Don't count your solutions before they hatch" applies to fusion technology, population policy, and all other uncertain endeavors.

So if we make some prudently pessimistic assumptions, where do we end up? First, we should assume that technology will be no more effective at removing resource constraints than it is now, and that per capita resource consumption will remain at current levels. Actually, for a true "worst-case" analysis, we could assume consumption per capita would continue to rise, but we will leave a little optimism in the assumptions. Assuming the worst regarding the long-term impacts of humans on the biosphere leads us to conclude there are already far too many humans. Many authors have documented the potential adverse impacts of our current population on soil erosion, forest depletion, water and air pollution, and a host of other impacts. How many people could we sustain at current technology and consumption patterns if the worst of these impacts were true and unremediated? Certainly no more than we now have, but how many less?

I fall back on a rough energy calculation. In the worst case we must stop burning fossil fuels, both because we are running out and because the greenhouse effect is causing adverse climate changes. Assume also that in the worst case nuclear energy is too unsafe to use. The question comes down to how many people we could sustain at current technology and consumption patterns on renewable energy alone. This level is also consistent with the earlier recommendation to maintain the stock of natural capital at current levels to ensure sustainability. Remember that the worst case means no significant improvements in energy efficiency, contrary to what some technological optimists are predicting, but to balance this I will allow that all the renewable energy currently incumbent on the United States can ultimately be used.

The fossil and nuclear energy consumption in the United States in 1986 was 74×10^{15} British thermal unites (Btu). The U.S. population in 1986 was about 240 million. This gives an annual per capita fossil and nuclear energy consumption of about 300 million Btu per capita per year, which I will use to represent total current resource use.[11] The total solar energy captured by the U.S. environment (including near-shore waters) is about 100×10^{18} Btu per year.[12] But solar energy is much more dispersed and of lower quality than fossil fuel. It has been estimated to take about 2,000 Btu of solar energy to do the equivalent amount of *useful* work of 1 Btu of fossil fuel.[13] So the solar energy captured is equivalent to about 5×10^{16} Btu of fossil fuel. Assume that no more than half of this is available to drive human society directly, with the rest necessary for the ecological life-support system. Dividing this remainder of 2.5×10^{16} Btu by the 3×10^8 Btu per person per year energy needs of current U.S. citizens yields about 85 million people, or about 35 percent of the current population. But current U.S. per capita resource consumption is arguably more than what is required for a high-quality life-style and is not distributed very equitably over the population. Let us assume that with a more equitable distribution and a more "European" level of consumption per capita, we could support about twice the above estimate, or 170 million, at a high-quality life-style on renewable energy alone. This is admittedly a very rough calculation, and it is not the most pessimistic one possible. But I think it is a good general benchmark. One hundred seventy million people might be supportable on a sustainable basis at something approaching our current quality of life, but 240 million probably cannot be unless some major technical breakthroughs happen or we all reduce our standard of living significantly. Prudence requires that we target 170 million or fewer until the technical breakthroughs happen (if they happen). Otherwise our standard of living may go down to disastrous levels due to ecological deterioration from which we could never recover.

MANNING THE AMERICAN MILITARY IN THE TWENTY-FIRST CENTURY

Demographics and National Security

MARTIN BINKIN

One of the most frequently heard arguments for continued population growth is what might indelicately be called the cannon fodder argument: We need a large population of military-age youth for military security, particularly in light of the growth of third world populations. In this chapter Martin Binkin addresses that argument.

It is said that Josef Stalin, when cautioned against offending the Vatican, asked his advisers how many divisions the pope could field. Traditionally a nation's standing in the world has been determined by its military power and, for most of history, military power has been expressed in terms of division flags or the number of troops under arms. By the middle decades of the twentieth century, however, mass armies had become an anachronism, first, because of the introduction of thermonuclear weapons, and later, with the spawning of sophisticated military technologies that became substitutes for raw manpower. Even small nations, like Israel, have been able to prevail in military confrontations with enemies having much larger populations. More recently, the Japanese have demonstrated that economic power may be at least as important as military power in contemporary global relationships. Despite these trends, however, much of the conventional wisdom still holds that large armed forces are the sine qua non of national power. Thus the prospect that the population of United States may not continue to grow into the twenty-first century—moreover, depending on national policy choices, could decline markedly—has aroused some concern. These fears, however, are unwarranted.

This chapter examines whether a rising U.S. population is needed to meet our future military manpower requirements. In brief, I will argue that (1) U.S. military strength is not presently constrained by population size, (2) in the future a reduction in military manpower requirements is more likely than an increase, but (3) through efficient manpower management even a substantially larger military requirement could be sustained by the smaller population envisioned in the Census Bureau's lowest projections through the middle of the twenty-first century.

Demographics and Military Recruitment: Recent Experience

Dwindling birthrates in the United States—a trend that started in the late 1950s and brought the baby boom to an end in the mid-1960s—raised a host of public policy issues. As the children of that period (dubbed the birth-dearth generation) have grown older, the effects have already been felt, most notably by the nation's primary and secondary educational institutions. As the first cohorts of that generation completed high school in the early 1980s, higher education institutions and the civilian labor force began to notice the effects, while the armed forces braced themselves for the challenges expected to accompany the decline in the size of the pool of prospective volunteers for military service. The concern was somewhat similar to the alarm now expressed by some observers as they contemplate the prospect of an eventual turnaround in U.S. population growth.

At the turn of the decade, in fact, there was good reason to worry about the impact of demographic trends on the nation's ability to field a peacetime force of two million strong: During the latter half of the 1970s, when the number of Americans in the military-eligible population (eighteen- to twenty-two-year-olds) was at an all-time high, the armed forces compiled the poorest recruitment record in its history. In fiscal year 1979—the peak year for baby-boomers turning eighteen years of age and entering the military's prime recruiting pool, about half of the army's new recruits had standardized aptitude test scores in the lowest acceptable category (below the thirtieth percentile). Thus the prospect that the youth population would shrink by 25 percent over the next fifteen years and uncertainty about birth and fertility rates beyond that period set off alarms among defense manpower planners. If the armed forces were having trouble maintaining a force that comprised less than 1 percent of the U.S. population, some feared, how would the nation ever hope to raise an army large enough to win World War III, should that horrible prospect materialize? After all, at the peak of World War II the U.S. military establishment had under arms over eleven million men and women, or close to 10 percent of the total population.

Total Population Projections

Such concerns, however, can be readily discounted. First, even before recent events in the Soviet Union and Eastern Europe, a replay of World War II between NATO and the Warsaw Pact—that is, a protracted conventional conflict involving millions of troops—was considered an extreme long shot. The betting among serious analysts was that any conventional military confrontation between the two sides would be measured in terms of days or weeks, rather than months or years, ending early either in negotiations or in escalation to nuclear conflict. In any case, few envisaged any situation that would require tens of millions of Americans to serve in the armed forces.

But even if, against all odds, the nation were to get involved in a protracted war of attrition that would require a substantial expansion in the size of the armed forces, full mobilization would be ordered, conscription would be reinstituted and some eighteen million American men in the eighteen-through-twenty-six year cohorts would provide the initial pool of draftees, followed, as necessary, by men in the older age groups, and opportunities would be expanded, perhaps, for American

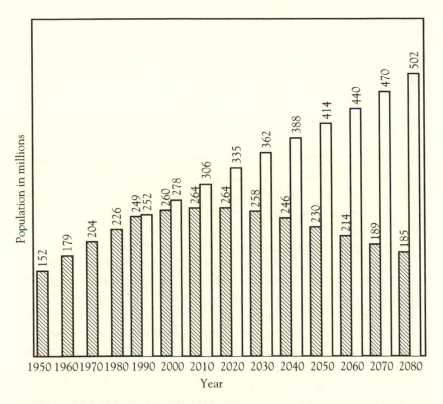

U.S. population, past and projected. The lower projections are from the Census Bureau's lowest series (number 19), assuming net annual immigration of 300,000 and fertility (TFR) converging at 1.5 in 2080. The highest series (number 9) assumes annual immigration of 800,000 and ultimate TFR of 2.2. There is in fact a lower series in which immigration and emigration are in balance, but the Bureau does not consider that a serious possibility. The projections are conservative; immigration and fertility are presently outrunning the "high" scenario. Sources: 1950–80, Census data. 1990–2080 projections from Gregory Spencer, *Population Projections of the United States, by Age, Sex and Race: 1988 to 2080*, Series P-25, no. 1018, Washington, D.C.: Bureau of the Census, 1989).

women to serve or, indeed, be conscripted into military services. In the extreme, a U.S. military force equal to that of World War II (eleven million) would now constitute less than 5 percent of the total population, not the nearly 10 percent in that conflict. In short, the current size of the American population is more than adequate to support worst-case scenarios, provided that the nation is willing to reinstitute conscription. And, as the graph of U.S. population numbers from 1990 to 2080 shows, even at the "lowest" projections by the Census Bureau, total population size would not be an issue in the foreseeable future. The population projected for 2080, for example, while substantially smaller than the current figure, would still be larger than the population that sustained our armed forces during World War II.

The "Qualified and Available" Population

The more relevant issue is the requisite population to sustain U.S. military forces under voluntary peacetime conditions. The key consideration here is not so much the size of the total American population, but rather the size of the relevant-age youth cohorts that form the supply pool of prospective volunteers.

The magnitude of the challenge can be seen in the table calculating the proportion of "qualified and available" males who would have to volunteer for military service before reaching age twenty-three if the military services were to attain their projected active and reserve manpower needs.[1] This calculation follows one age group through time, excluding those who, because they are on a college track, are *not likely* to volunteer and those who, because they would be mentally, physically, or morally unqualified, *cannot* volunteer.[2]

As the table depicts, during 1984–88, an average of about 1.8 million males turned eighteen each year. Based on past experience, about 525,000 of them were considered "dedicated" college students (those who would remain in college at least into the third year), with a low propensity for enlisted military service. (This group, of course, provides the bulk of military officer candidates, but the military officer corps represents such a small fraction of the relevant age cohorts that the size of those cohorts is not an important consideration in staffing the officer corps.) Another 526,000 would fail to meet the minimum physical, moral, or aptitude standards for entry into the armed forces.

To maintain an active military force of about 2.1 million and a reserve force of roughly 1.0 million, about 376,000 males had to be recruited annually (278,000 active and 98,000 reserves), or about 50 percent of the "qualified and available" pool of eighteen-year-old males. Daunting though this task might appear, recruiting goals were met with relative ease, at relatively modest cost, and without compromising the quality of the forces. In fact, the armed forces faced the formidable task of meeting these recruitment goals over a period during which the youth popula-

Proportion of Qualifed and Available Males Required Annually for Military Service, Fiscal Years 1984–1988 (Thousands unless otherwise indicated)

Item	1984–1988
Total noninstitutionalized 18-year-old males[a]	1,800
Nonavailable college students (adjusted for dropouts)[b]	525
Unqualified males	526
Mental[c]	337
Physical or moral[d]	189
Total: qualified and available male pool	749
Total male recruit requirement	376
Active forces	278
Reserve forces	98
Percent of pool required	52

[a] Assumes 1.5 percent of the male population aged 18 to 24 is institutionalized.

[b] Estimates based on 1980 participation rates: In 1980, 74.4 percent of the youth cohort that had entered the fifth grade in 1972 completed high school, and 46.3 percent of the initial group enrolled as full- or part-time students in programs creditable toward a bachelor's degree. Assumes that 25 percent of first-time enrollees leave during the first year and 12.5 percent during the second year.

[c] Based on 1981 military aptitude requirements, 2 percent of males with one or more years of college would be expected to be unqualified, 10 percent of high school graduates without college experience would not meet minimum standards, and 60 percent of non-high school graduates would not qualify.

[d] Assumes that 16.3 percent of the male youth population meeting minimum aptitude requirements would be disqualified on physical grounds, and 3.9 percent would fail to meet moral standards.

Sources: Total 18-year-old male population from Bureau of the Census, *Current Population Reports*, series P-25, no. 704, "Projections of the Population of the United States: 1977 to 2050" (Washington, D.C.: GPO, 1977), pp. 44–48, 51–55. Institutionalized population estimates based on preliminary data from the 1980 census provided by Bureau of the Census. First- and second-year dropouts based on estimates provided by National Center for Educational Statistics. Mentally unqualifed derived from data contained in special tabulations provided by Office of the Assistant Secretary of Defense for Manpower, Reserve Affairs, and Logistics. Physically and morally unqualified derived from unpublished data provided by Office of the Assistant Secretary of Defense for Manpower, Reserve Affairs, and Logistics. Male recruitment requirements compiled from Department of Defense, *Manpower Requirements Report, FY 1984*, vol. 3: *Force Readiness Report* (Washington, D.C.: DOD, 1983), pp. III-12, III-20, III-21, IV-10, V-7, VI-6, VI-9, VI-10. Projections of Navy and Marine Corps reserve requirements based on fiscal 1983 recruitment data.

tion was in decline. As matters turned out, they not only survived a 15 percent dip in the youth population that occurred during the 1980s, but positively thrived, attracting recruits with record-setting levels of education and aptitude test scores. By the close of the decade, close to 90 percent of all new military recruits had earned their high school diplomas, compared with just over 70 percent in the late 1970s. Likewise, fewer than 5 percent of the new recruits in 1989 scored in the lowest acceptable category (below the thirtieth percentile) on the standardized military aptitude test, compared with close to 30 percent a decade earlier.

A variety of factors contributed to this seeming paradox, including an economic recession that led to diminished employment prospects for U.S. youth, substantial military pay increases, an improved educational benefits package, and a growing popularity of the military among America's young, attributed partly to the replacement of President Jimmy Carter's characterization of U.S. "malaise" with President Ronald Reagan's "standing tall" jingoism.[3] In any event, the message should be reassuring for those concerned that a decline in the size of the U.S. population over the long term might preclude the nation from fielding adequate military forces.

Youth Population Projections

For the near term, the size of the youth population will continue to shrink until the middle of the 1990s, when the effects of the "birth-dearth" will run their course. While the size of the eighteen- to-twenty-one-year-old male population will dip to 6.66 million in 1994, the number of young U.S. males will still be large relative to the pre-baby-boom era, making it unlikely that the armed forces will run into any difficulties in attracting a sufficient number of volunteers. Cohort sizes will begin to increase again after 1995, an upturn that can be expected to last at least until 2010,[4] after which estimates are uncertain, depending on assumptions about immigration and fertility rates. As the graph on U.S. male population figures from 1948 to 2038 indicates, the differences between the U.S. Census Bureau's highest and lowest projections are substantial; by 2038, the size of the eighteen- to-twenty-two-year-old cohort is expected to range from a low of about seven million to a high of close to thirteen million. At the low end, the size of the cohort would be about 20 percent smaller than now exists, but it would still surpass the size of the similar-aged cohorts of the 1950s and early 1960s.

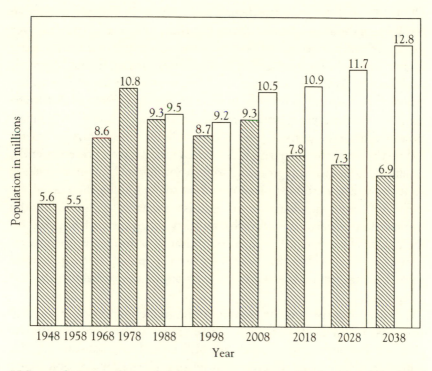

U.S. population: males aged eighteen to twenty-two. All cohorts have been shifted from 20-24 age cohorts by advancing them two years; this does not affect the numbers at this level of rounding.

Future Prospects

What are the chances that the armed forces can continue to meet their manpower needs under the lower population projections? The answer depends on a variety of factors that become more uncertain the further in time that one projects, but the conclusion here is that the nation could field requisite military forces under the "lowest" population scenario, especially if current prospects for reducing the size of the military establishment do in fact materialize and if a variety of manpower policies—many legacies of the conscription era—were remodeled to meet the needs of the contemporary military establishment. It is convenient to separate these policies into those that affect the demand for "qualified and available" males and those that affect their supply.

DEMAND OPTIONS   On the demand side, the most important variable is the size of the armed forces. Obviously, the smaller the forces, the fewer personnel will be needed out of the youth cohort, all other things being equal. Given the recent changes in the Soviet Union, Eastern Europe, and Central America, the prospects have brightened for sizable reductions in the U.S. armed forces. Indeed, it does not seem premature to speculate that the large standing forces maintained by the world's superpowers during the years of the cold war will become an anachronism. While the ultimate size of the U.S. armed forces, given present trends, is difficult to predict with precision, some knowledgeable observers believe that the military establishment could be cut in half by the end of the century.[5] Under those circumstances, it is reasonable to assume that the annual flow of personnel into the military could be cut from close to 400,000 to fewer than 200,000. Should that situation transpire, any remaining concerns about the adequacy of the population to support the armed forces, even under a low-growth population trajectory, would evaporate.

But even if the current trend toward greater superpower stability is reversed, and if cuts in the size of the armed forces do not occur, the demand for new male recruits can still be reduced substantially by substituting women or civilian personnel for uniformed males. Some steps have already been taken toward this end. In fact, the role of women in the military has been expanded appreciably over the past two decades: In 1972 women constituted less than 2 percent of the force; today they account for close to 11 percent of the total. This expansion has leveled off in recent years, primarily because of laws and policies that prevent them from filling a range of "combat" positions. This expansion can be resumed if recent efforts to relax the combat exclusions are successful.[6]

The demand for young male Americans to perform military service could also be reduced by staffing more of the jobs now filled by uniformed personnel with civilians. The ground rules that govern the relative numbers of military and civilian employees in the armed forces are imprecise, and the rationale underlying the determination of the current composition is unclear. Whether combat forces—for example, army or marine infantry, naval destroyer crews, and air force strategic bomber crews—should be military or civilian is obviously not at issue. And few would doubt that those who directly support the combat forces and are expected to operate in a combat zone should be uniformed personnel.

Even when agreement is reached on this obvious point—that combat forces should be composed of military personnel—a question remains: what constitutes "combat forces"? The distinctions are not as sharp as they appear. Must crews flying and servicing airlift aircraft similar in configuration to those used commercially, such as the C-5, be military? Must naval support ships, such as oilers and tenders, be manned by uniformed sailors? In fact, some civilian contractor employees routinely deploy with the combat fleet. And drawing the line between military and civilian personnel combat support functions becomes more difficult when it is recalled that U.S. combat forces currently deployed rely on foreign national civilians for certain forms of support.

The retention of a larger proportion of military personnel beyond one term of service would also reduce turnover and hence the annual requirement for new recruits. For example, to sustain a force of, say, of 500,000 enlisted personnel of which 36 percent are careerists (that is, serve beyond an initial tour of four years) would require an annual input of about 80,000, while the same size force with 44 percent careerists would need only 70,000 new recruits per year. Thus, to the extent that the military services retain a larger proportion of their personnel, they could substantially control the demand for new volunteers while continuing to meet total manpower needs. Arguably, this would be a prudent course to follow in any event, since modern military technology places a higher premium on an experienced workforce.[7]

SUPPLY OPTIONS   Turning to the supply side of the issue, the "qualified and available" male population, as defined above, excludes certain categories of individuals. Changes in recruitment policies and entry standards could bring some of these categories into the supply pool, thus increasing the number of potential volunteers.

Since college students have typically not shown an interest in serving in the enlisted ranks, the armed forces understandably dedicate few recruiting resources to the campus market. Although it is unreasonable to expect that the military services could attract large numbers of graduates of four-year colleges and universities into the enlisted force, it is appropriate to consider programs designed to attract graduates of two-year junior or community college programs. Just how many of the approximately 525,000 youths in each cohort might be attracted is difficult to predict, but the success of the Army College Fund program during the 1980s, which offered extra educational benefits to certain classes of volunteers, suggests that incentive programs could be devised to increase the propensity among the college-bound to serve in the armed forces and thereby expand the supply of those who would be "qualified and available" for military service.

Another approach for expanding supply is to adjust educational and test score entry requirements. Actually, specifications concerning the quality mix of recruits are arbitrary; there are no hard-and-fast rules for judging how smart or how well-educated individuals must be to function effectively in the armed forces. As indicated in the table on qualified and available males, about 29 percent of each eighteen-year-old cohort can be expected to fail to meet current standards for entrance into the armed forces. Relaxation of these standards, which has been done periodically in the past, depending on supply and demand, would give the services access to a larger supply pool within cohorts of the same size. Furthermore, an adjustment in physical standards along the lines of those adopted during World War II, which allowed people who were not "combat fit" to fill limited-duty billets, could enlarge the pool even more.

Conclusion

The United States has been able to field armed forces of sufficient size to support its national security strategy under challenging conditions—declining youth cohorts and an all-volunteer recruitment system. The force of the evidence indicates that total population growth is neither a necessary nor a sufficient condition to ensure that the nation is able to protect its security interests.

At bottom, it is becoming increasingly apparent in the closing years of the twentieth century that military strength is not necessarily synonymous with national security. Other elements—the availability of energy and food at reasonable cost; the natural resource balance, the skill levels of the population, and the degree of popular identification with the system—also deeply influence a nation's security.

I do not profess to expertise in these areas. In Chapter 2 the Pimentels argue that a smaller population is essential to the maintenance of living standards as the country moves into a solar-based energy system with changes in agricultural practices to save its resource base. In Chapter 6 Vernon Briggs argues for the importance of better education and less job competition at the unskilled level to avoid generating an alienated underclass overrepresented with ethnic minorities. If the lower Census projection would in fact contribute to the pursuit of these and other elements of national security, I am confident that future military manpower requirements will not stand in the way of a national decision to take that course.

POLITICAL CONFRONTATION WITH ECONOMIC REALITY

Mass Immigration in the Post-Industrial Age

VERNON M. BRIGGS, JR.

As has already been pointed out, differential fertility is very close to a tragedy: The most children are born to parents with the least prospect of providing the nurture and education to help their children move up the economic ladder. Immigration tends to make the problem worse by increasing competition for the less-skilled jobs. Policies that would be of immediate benefit in breaking the cycle of poverty also have long-term demographic consequences.

As the United States enters its post-industrial phase of economic development, its labor market is in a state of radical transformation. There has been a marked break away in the nation from evolutionary patterns of employment growth, along with changes in the composition of the labor force. The introduction of new and extensive technological advances means that more output can be produced with fewer labor inputs.

Major shifts in consumer tastes have altered the character of the demand for labor by contributing to the meteoric growth of the service sector and the decline of the goods sector.

The coexistence of labor shortages and vacant jobs is becoming the operative challenge for policy makers. In such an environment, labor force policies must focus on the qualitative aspects of the supply of labor rather than on its mere quantitative size. The nation does not need more workers per se; it does, however, desperately need specific types of labor to meet the emerging requirements of its postindustrial economy.

On the supply side, major changes have occurred in the expectations of minorities and women concerning their participation and their status in the labor force. If we combine these trends with greatly enhanced foreign competition and rapidly changing population demographics, we find that unprecedented demands are being placed on the U.S. economy and government to nurture and educate the nation's citizens and to help them find employment opportunities.

Because mass immigration has reemerged during this period of extreme flux, it is essential that the nation's immigration policy be consonant with the pursuit of these economic and social goals. At present, it is not. Instead, policymakers perceive immigration policy as essentially political, to be manipulated without any serious concern about its economic impact.

All advanced industrial nations—to varying degrees—are experiencing similar changes in their employment patterns. Only the United States, however, is experiencing such major simultaneous alterations in its labor force. Of the multiple influences on the size and composition of the U.S. labor force, the revival of mass immigration is by far the most distinctive. Indeed, a recent comprehensive study of U.S. society conducted by an international team of social science scholars concluded that "America's biggest import is people." It added that "at a time when attention is directed to the general decline in American exceptionalism, American immigration continues to flow at a rate unknown elsewhere in the world."[1]

The Phenomenon of Mass Immigration

The revival of mass immigration began in the mid-1960s when the nation's existing immigration laws were overhauled. The reform movement of that era sought to purge the system of the racism associated with the "national origins" admission system that had been in place since 1924. Modest increases in the level of immigration were envisioned. No one, however, anticipated what subsequently occurred. The ensuing mass immigration flow has been the cumulative result of the tyranny of seemingly small, politically motivated policy decisions, as well as the product of a massive dose of political indifference to the ensuing policy outcomes.

Of all the factors that influence population and labor force growth, immigration is the one component that public policy should be able to control. To date, however, policymakers in the United States have been unwilling to view immigration policy in this light. Unguided in its design, immigration policy is dominated by the pursuit of purely political objectives. It has yet to be held responsible for its sizable economic consequences.[2]

Prevailing immigration policy primarily promotes the migration of relatives of recent migrants and provides little room for immigration to supply those persons who already possess needed skills and experience. Less than 8 percent of the immigrants and refugees who are legally admitted to the United States each year are admitted on the basis that the skills and education they possess are actually in demand by U.S. employers. The percentage is considerably less if illegal immigrants are included in the total immigrant flow.

Each successive immigration "reform" since the 1960s has increased the annual level of immigration. Furthermore, the failure to enforce the existing laws has permitted the largely unfettered influx of illegal migrants from less economically developed nations to compete with this country's poor and to aggravate their collective poverty. Immigrants constitute a rising portion of the total growth of the labor force, and at current U.S. fertility rates and immigration levels they will lead within a century to a U.S. population one-half again as large as would occur with natural increase alone.[3]

In all its diverse forms, the immigrant flow has accounted for anywhere from one-quarter to one-third of the annual growth of the U.S. labor force during the decade of the 1980s. The presence of a considerable number of illegal immigrants complicates efforts to be precise. It is highly probable that, when the rising female labor force participation rate eventually stabilizes (as it soon must) and as the influence of the baby-boom generation on the size of the work force ebbs (as it is beginning to do), immigration could, by the turn of the century, account for all the annual growth of the nation's labor force. Immigration, therefore, is already a vital determinant of the nation's economic welfare; it can only be expected to become more so.

Public Unawareness of Policy Consequences

Public recognition that immigration has once again assumed a prominent role in the U.S. economy has, unfortunately, been slow to develop. Immigration significantly declined in importance from World War I through to the mid-1960s. As officially measured, the foreign-born percentage of the population had steadily fallen from 13.2 percent in 1920 to 4.7 percent in 1970. The foreign-born population in 1980, however, rose to 6.2 percent of the U.S. population, a 46 percent increase over the decade. Given immigration developments during the 1980s, the figure for 1990 should easily approach 9 percent, or about one of every eleven persons in the U.S. population. Even these percentages are widely suspected of being far too low because a significant undercount of illegal immigrants by the 1980 Census and the anticipation of similar problems in the 1990 Census. Given policy obligations already built into existing immigration laws and prevailing congressional tendencies to incrementally expand immigration without regard to overall policy consequences, the percentage should again approach or exceed the high level of 1920 by the year 2000.

The effects of the resurgence of mass immigration have not aroused greater public attention chiefly because the impact is geographically concentrated. Six states—California, New York, Florida, Texas, New Jersey, and Illinois—account for 38.4 percent of the U.S. population but for 71.4 percent of all immigrants admitted to the United States in 1987. The additional flows of illegal immigrants, nonimmigrants, and refugees have followed similar settlement paths. Moreover, within these states, immigrants have overwhelmingly settled in urban areas.[4] In 1980, 92 percent of their foreign-born population that was actually counted that year by the Census lived in metropolitan areas, compared to only 72 percent of the native-born population. Thus, the magnified effects of mass immigration are largely manifested in the urban areas of a handful of states. They are, however, the largest labor markets in the U.S. economy (for example, New York, Los Angeles, Chicago, Houston, and

Miami). Hence, there is still a pronounced national as well as a clear local significance to these developments.

In 1981 a presidential commission, the Select Commission on Immigration and Refugee Policy, bluntly stated that U.S. immigration policy was "out of control," and it urged policymakers to confront "the reality of limitations."[5] Subsequently, on two occasions Congress attempted to adopt legislation that would address the nation's immigration policy in a comprehensive manner. Both efforts failed. A new tactic was next pursued: piecemeal reform. The immediate consequence was the adoption of the Immigration Reform and Control Act of 1986, targeted largely to the issue of illegal immigration. But even this policy thrust was watered down. Its provisions failed to adequately address the issue of worker identification. Congress, in a period of fiscal constraint, has been unwilling in the years since its enactment to sufficiently fund the enforcement mechanisms required to make the law effective. Moreover, as Congress has turned its attention to the remaining areas of policy reform (those pertaining to legal immigrants, nonimmigrant workers, and refugees) it has encountered well-organized special interest groups who have placed selfish and shortsighted goals ahead of any consideration for the national welfare. These groups focus their power on each of the separate policy components that Congress takes up. There is apparently no one interested in the cumulative outcome. The consequence is that Congress is in the process of making a mockery of the Select Commission's informed plea for a policy of "limitations." If anything, immigration policy is now more out of control than it was when the reform process began almost a decade ago.

The Changing Nature of the Labor Market

Paralleling the return of mass immigration, the years since the 1960s have also witnessed a dramatic restructuring of the nation's industrial and occupational patterns. The goods-producing industries, the country's dominant employment sector at the founding of the nation, have rapidly declined. As late as 1950, over half the labor force was employed in this sector; by the late 1980s, it accounted for only about 26 percent of all employed persons. It is projected to decline even further in the 1990s. Moreover, the largest employing industries in the goods-producing sector have sustained the most significant contractions. Agricultural employment which has declined annually since the late 1940s, accounts now for only about 3 percent of all employed workers. Manufacturing, which in the mid-1950s provided jobs for over one-third of the labor force, now does so for less than one-fifth. Mining has also had a steady decline. Only the construction industry has shown moderate growth, but it is characterized by significant cyclical fluctuations in any given year.

The rapid fall-off in employment in the goods-producing sector has been caused by the confluence of several broad economic forces. First, there has been the shift in consumer spending patterns that is the hallmark of the coming of a postindustrial economy. The maturing of the mass consumption society is symbolized by shifts in expenditures away from goods and toward services. It is a truism in economics that where spending increases, employment increases (as in the service sector), and where spending falls, employment declines (as in the goods sector). Second, in addition to spending shifts, the advent of computer-controlled technology has created self-regulating production systems that have reduced the demand for unskilled and semiskilled workers in the goods-producing section.[6] Finally, of course, the intrusive effects of international competition in the past two decades have exceeded any such previous pressures in U.S. economic history. The manufacturing sector in particular has been hit hard by the tide of foreign imports (and the inability to export) associated with the largely unilateral pursuit of a free trade policy by the U.S. government.[7]

In the wake of the sharp declines in employment in the goods-producing sector, there have been dramatic increases in the service-producing industries. Responding to the shifts in consumer spending patterns, 70 percent of the U.S. labor force is now employed in services. The U.S. Department of Labor projects that 90 percent of the new jobs that will be created in the remainder of the twentieth century will be in the service industries and that the service sector will account for 75 percent of all employment by the year 2000. Thus, the demand for labor is being radically restructured.

The supply of labor is slowly adapting, but the adjustment process is not as easy or as automatic as it was in earlier eras when the goods-producing sectors dominated. The displaced workers from the agricultural sector in the early twentieth century had little difficulty qualifying for newly created jobs in the burgeoning manufacturing sector. They only had to relocate, and when immigration flows were sharply reduced between the 1920s through to the 1960s, they tended to do so. But the emergence of the service economy has imposed an entirely different set of job requirements on the actual and potential labor force. While the technology of earlier periods stressed physical and manual skills for job seekers, the service economy stresses mental, social, linguistic, and communication skills. As a consequence, the shift to services has meant declining job opportunities for those who lack a quality education and skills. As former Secretary of Labor William Brock succinctly said in 1987, "[T]he days of disguising functional illiteracy with a high paying assembly line job that simply requires a manual skill are soon to be over. The world of work is changing right under our feet."[8] Tragically, a disproportionate number of those who are presently vulnerable to these adverse employment effects are racial minorities, women, and youths.[9]

Directly associated with these dramatic industrial trends are the derivative changes in occupational patterns. Over one-third of the growth in employment since 1972 has occurred in the professional, technical, and related worker classifications. Other broad occupational groups experiencing substantially faster-than-average growth over this period have been managers, administrators, and service and sales workers. The greatest decline in employment has been among operatives, farmers, farm laborers, and private household workers. The U.S. Department of Labor projects that the occupations expected to experience the most rapid growth in the 1990s are those that require the most highly educated workers.[10] These include executives, administrators, and managers; professionals; and technicians and related support workers. Collectively, these three occupational categories accounted for 25 percent of total employment in 1986 but are expected to constitute 40 percent of the nation's employment growth for the remainder of the century.

The Changing Composition of the Labor Force

The composition of the U.S. labor force is also experiencing major changes. Since the mid-1960s Blacks, Hispanics, and Asians, as well as women from all racial and ethnic groups, have dramatically increased their proportions of the total labor force. As shown in the table on labor force characteristics, the Bureau of Labor Statistics projects that these trends will continue. Women will account for two-thirds of the annual growth in the labor force, and Blacks for about 25 percent in the 1990s.

Selected Labor Force Characteristics, 1986–2000
(Millions of Persons)

Group	Labor Force Total in: 1986	2000	Absolute Change 1986-2000	Percent Change 1986-2000	Share of Total in: 1986	2000
Total	117.8	138.8	20.9	17.8	100.0	100.0
White	101.8	116.7	14.9	14.6	86.4	84.1
Black	12.7	16.3	3.7	28.8	10.8	11.8
Hispanic	8.1	14.1	6.0	74.4	6.9	10.2
Asian	3.4	5.7	2.4	71.2	2.8	4.1
Women	52.4	65.6	13.2	25.2	44.5	47.3
Men	65.4	73.1	7.7	11.8	55.5	52.7

Note: The race/origin subgroups overlap and therefore do not add to total. Hispanic figures are included in both the White and Black classifications.

Source: U.S. Department of Labor

In the 1980s the Hispanic population grew five times faster than the population as a whole, and Hispanics are projected to account for 15 percent of overall growth in the labor supply during the 1990s. The same general pattern also holds true for Asian Americans.

Presently, the incidence of unemployment, poverty, and adult illiteracy are much higher and the labor force participation rates and educational attainment levels are much lower for Blacks and Hispanics than is the case for non-Hispanic Whites (comparable data for Asians are unavailable). It is also the case that Blacks and Hispanics are disproportionately employed in the industries and occupations that are already in sharpest decline (that is, in the goods-producing industries and in blue-collar occupations).[11] Thus, those groups in the labor force that are most rapidly increasing are precisely those most adversely at risk because of the changing employment requirements. Unless public policy measures are addressed to human resource development needs, both these and other vulnerable groups have dim prospects in the emerging postindustrial economy.

If mass and unguided immigration continues, it is unlikely that there will be sufficient pressure to enact the long-term human resource development policies needed to prepare and to incorporate these groups into the mainstream economy. Instead, it is likely that the heavy but unplanned influx of immigrant labor will serve, by providing both competition and alternatives, to maintain the social marginalization of many citizen Blacks and citizen Hispanics. As a result, the chance to eliminate once and for all the underclass in the U.S. economy will be lost—probably forever.

The Impacts of Immigration

Immigration policy, by definition, is capable of influencing not only the quantitative size of the labor force but also its qualitative composition. As matters now stand, there is virtually no synchronization of the immigrant flows with the demonstrated needs of the labor market. With widespread uncertainty as to the number of illegal immigrants, refugees, and nonimmigrant workers who will enter, it is impossible to know in advance how many actual persons from foreign countries are actually entering the U.S. labor force each year. Moreover, whatever skills, education, linguistic abilities, talents, or locational settlement preferences most immigrants, refugees, and nonimmigrants have is purely incidental to the reason that they are admitted or enter the country. The legal immigration system that was in effect from 1965 through 1991 reserved 80 percent of the 270,000 visas issued each year for various adult family reunification purposes. The immediate relatives (spouses, minor children, and parents) of each of these visa recipients—an additional 217,514 persons in 1989—are admitted automatically and, of course, are also exempt from meeting any labor market standard. Only 20 percent of the visas were issued on a basis of work-related needs. As of October 1, 1991, a new immigration system goes into effect, but despite the political rhetoric associated with its passage, which spoke of greater responsiveness for meeting labor needs, it does not change the prevailing family domination of entry priorities. The new law, the Immigration Act of 1990, increases total annual immigration to a ceiling of 700,000 persons—an approximately 35 percent increase a year in total legal immigration. The new law reserves 140,000 visas for immigrants who will be admitted for work-related reasons. But 140,000 is still 20 percent of 700,000, so there is really no percentage change in policy focus from the old law. Moreover, the 140,000 work-related visas also *include* the visas for all "accompanying family members" of those admitted for work-related reasons. Hence, the actual number of immigrants admitted for work-related reasons will be far fewer than the 140,000 visas. Likewise, the number of refugees admitted each year is the result of a determination by the president (it is about 125,000 persons at present levels); they are, of course, not subject to any labor market test, nor are the estimated 200,000 to 500,000 illegal immigrants who continue to enter the United States each year. The vast preponderance of the illegal immigrants and refugees of the 1980s have had very few skills, little formal education, and limited (if any) literacy in English. In addition several hundred thousand nonimmigrants are admitted each year to work in the United States for various lengths of time after only minimal checks as to whether citizen workers are available or could be trained to do the work.

The labor market effects of the current politically driven immigration system are twofold. Some of the immigrants do have human resource endowments that are quite congruent with the labor market conditions currently dictated by the economy's needs. In fact, they are desperately needed due to the appalling lack of attention given by the nation to the adequate preparation of many citizen members of its labor force. But most do not, and they must seek employment in the declining sectors of the goods-producing industries (for example, agriculture and light manufacturing) or the low-wage sectors of the expanding service sector (for example, restaurants, lodging, or retail enterprises). Unfortunately, many of the nation's citizens who are in the underclass are also in these same employment sectors. A disproportionately high number of these citizens are minorities, women, and youth. As these citizen groups are growing in both absolute numbers and percentages, the logic of national survival would say that they should have the first claim on the nation's available jobs. The last thing they need is more competition from immigrants for the limited number of existing jobs and for the scarce opportunities for training and education.

The postindustrial economy of the United States is facing the real prospect of serious shortages of qualified labor. It does not have a shortage of actual or potential workers: No advanced industrial nation that has twenty-three million illiterate adults (some say the figure is now twenty-seven million) and another forty million adults who are marginally literate need have any fear about a shortage of unskilled workers in its foreseeable future.[12] Immigration is a contributing factor to the growth of adult illiteracy in this nation. As a consequence, immigration, by adding to the surplus of illiterate job seekers, is serving to diminish the limited chances of many poorly prepared citizens to find jobs or to improve their employability. It is not surprising therefore, that the underground economy, with its culture of drugs, crime, and gangs, is thriving in many of the nation's urban centers. The nature of the immigration flow is also contributing to the need to expand remedial education, training, and language programs at a time when such funds are desperately needed to upgrade the human resource capabilities of much of the citizen labor force.

The popular notion of the need for labor force growth for growth's sake is obsolete. It is doubtful that the idea was ever completely valid since it is, in essence, the deadly theory of the cancer cell. It is a general principle that can distort normal adjustment processes. With respect to the labor market, shortages are a wonderful issue for society to confront. Shortages force public policymakers to look at how society is using and preparing its human resources. It is no accident that issues such as education, health, housing, transportation, training, rehabilitation, poverty prevention, and antidiscrimination measures have only recently come to the fore. Labor shortages should compel policymakers to resolve these domestic needs before they turn to the placebo of mass immigration. It is the quality of life that is the key to the achievement of a fully employed economy and an equitable society in the postindustrial era.

The prospect of shortages of qualified labor offers to this country a chance to improve the lot of the working poor and to rid itself of its large underclass. It can force public policy to focus on the necessity to incorporate into the mainstream economy many citizens who have been left out in the past. It was in this precise context that William Aramondy, president of the United Way, said in 1989, "We have the biggest single opportunity in our history to address 200 years of unfairness to blacks. If we don't, God condemn us for blowing the chance."[13] The major threat to the "opportunity" he correctly identified is the perpetuation of the nation's politically dominated immigration policy. It is long past time for immigration policy to cease being a contributor to the problems of the U.S. labor force. Instead it must become accountable for its economic consequences so that it can be part of the answer to the nation's pressing needs in an increasingly competitive world economy.

Labor Force and Population Size

The preceding discussion (and, indeed, my professional experience) is focused on the size, composition, and change of the U.S. labor force. Other authors in this volume have much greater professional expertise to address the question of optimum population in the sense of an overall number. There are, however, close connections between the policies I have advocated here and the nation's demographic future.

As to immigration, the current pattern of mass immigration of primarily unskilled people is a direct threat to the nation's well-being. We do require the immigration of certain skills and professional expertise, but not in such numbers as to discourage our national effort to produce professionals and skilled workers in those categories.

The nation's requirements could possibly change again in the future, and we should retain the flexibility to examine immigration policies in the light of changing realities. For the foreseeable future, however, I suggest immigration policies involving a movement far smaller than at present and from economic strata that tend in most countries to have fewer children than the poor and unskilled. This, of course, means that their contribution to U.S. population growth after their arrival would be smaller than for the average present immigrant.

As to the character of the indigenous labor force: we need skilled labor, not mass labor. There is already a substantial population of functional illiterates who have great trouble entering the labor force. We have let educational standards slide: our graduates, by and large, are neither literate nor (in Garrett Hardin's phrase) numerate. Our national policies and social behavior have constituted a nearly total mismatch with our needs.

In the first chapter Lindsey Grant points out that fertility among the affluent and the educated is far below replacement level. It is about twice as high among the poorest and least educated, however. This difference is geometric as the generations progress: four times as many grandchildren, eight times as many great-grandchildren, and so on. Those who are able and who want to educate their children are having fewer of them; the population growth is occurring among those who cannot educate theirs. At present, the poor are in a vicious circle, their poverty often perpetuated by their ignorance. Social policies to reduce this discrepancy in fertility would lead to fewer poor children and greater availability of high-quality education for those whose parents lack the wherewithal.

In a society like ours, one is on delicate ground even to suggest that there is a public interest in fertility levels. Our view of the role of government would certainly preclude any very large government role in any effort to change the national mindset about them. One can, however, posit a happy situation wherein the poor have about the same number of children as the more educated and prosperous, and in which those children—precisely because their parents and society can better afford to rear and educate them—will escape the vicious cycle of poverty and, having escaped it, adopt the fertility habits of their new economic condition.

In Chapter 13 Leon Bouvier sketches several demographic scenarios drawn from Census Bureau projections. What I have said here about immigration and fertility would lead me somewhere close to or below his "hard" path—a total fertility rate of 1.5 and net immigration of 300,000. That scenario yields a slight rise in population from the present 250 million to 278 million in 2020 and then a gradual decline to 218 million in 2080. I find this prospect rather attractive. Immigration, education, and the size and composition of the labor force and population should be seen as interconnected and with fundamental consequences for the national well-being. Our politicians must work themselves out of the illusion that immigration is simply a political issue and a way of rewarding vociferous interest groups. It is an important determinant of our future.

Optimal City Size and Population Density for the Twenty-First Century

Alden Speare Jr., and Michael J. White

P roponents of population growth have argued that economic efficiency is a product of urban size and that the larger cities provide a higher quality of life. The weight of evidence suggests otherwise.

The United States, like many other parts of the world, has several large cities that seem to be constantly beset with problems of crime, conges- tion, pollution, and mismanagement. At times the population size of these areas alone seems to make them unmanageable. The City of New York, for example, had a population of about 7.3 million within 302 square miles in 1990. Los Angeles had over 3.5 million within 465 square miles, and Chicago had 2.8 million within 228 square miles. Each of these cities is surrounded by smaller cities and densely settled suburban area, bringing the total in these metropolitan areas to 18.1 million for New York, 14.5 million for Los Angeles, and 8.1 million for Chicago.[1] Are these cities, and others like them, merely the product of outdated agglomeration economies and continued population growth, or is their current size still justifiable in terms of greater efficiencies in the production of goods and services and the amenities offered to their inhabitants?

We will reexamine the old arguments that larger scale leads to greater efficiency, reduced costs, and a better quality of life. We will also look at the environmental and social costs associated with different scales of settlement. Finally, we will look at how people's perception of the desirability of a particular place and the perceived problems of that place vary with size. We will question the common view that population decline has negative consequences for cities.

There is much disagreement on the subject of optimal city size, and we do not expect to arrive at a single type of urban settlement that is optimal or ideal for all people. In a 1989 Gallup Poll, New York City received the largest number of votes both for the best city and for the worst city in the United States.[2] Its supporters pointed to the number of job opportunities, the shopping, and the cultural activities, while its detractors mentioned the high cost of living, the crime, and the pollution. Which of these advantages and disadvantages are likely to continue into the next century, and how is technology changing the relative advantages of large versus small cities? Before addressing this question, we will briefly summarize the history of city growth.

Current Population Distribution as a Result of History

The current distribution of population in the United States reflects the history of national settlement. The vast variations in population density are largely the result of the location of past economic opportunities and the establishment of self-perpetuating migration streams. If the United States were being settled today, the distribution would probably be quite different.

Eight of the ten largest metropolitan areas in the United States have central cities that developed in the nineteenth century.[3] These cities were primarily dependent upon water transportation and were located at major ports for sea transportation (for example, New York, Boston, and

San Francisco) or at the junction of major rivers or lakes (for example Detroit and Chicago). These cities were all settled before automobiles and buses were available; businesses and houses had to be close together to permit most people to travel on foot between them. The rivers along which they are located often divide the land and create barriers to land transportation.

Newer cities, such as Dallas, Los Angeles, and Phoenix, were designed for automobile transportation and have fewer water barriers, although they can still have traffic jams due to population growth beyond what was anticipated in the design of highway systems. With the development of land transportation, fewer people need live near sea ports, and high residential densities are not needed. Metropolitan areas developed in the past decade, such as Bradenton, Florida, and Naples, Florida, have much lower densities and are almost entirely suburban in character, lacking a dense core.

While the earlier history of the nation was one of growing population concentrations, the trends of the 1970s were in the direction of population deconcentration. John Long of the Bureau of the Census shows that population growth was greatest in the lowest-density states and in the smallest places.[4] What caught people's attention were two observations: first, that nonmetropolitan growth exceeded metropolitan growth during the decade and, second, that the largest metropolitan areas, those with over one million people, experienced absolute population decline during the decade. While central city decline had been observed in some cities since the 1930s, this was the first time that both cities and suburbs lost population in several areas. Since 1980 growth has been more even across size categories, although still favoring states with lower population densities.

One reason for the continued growth of some of the larger and older cities during the 1980s was the flow of immigrants from abroad to these cities. The recent upsurge in immigration, both legal and undocumented, has found its way disproportionately to larger urban areas. For example, in the 1980 Census 94 percent of the immigrants who arrived between 1970 and 1980 lived in metropolitan areas of one million or more, whereas only 75 percent of the general population did.[5]

During the 1970s immigration accounted for one-third of the growth of all metropolitan areas; it represented a larger fraction in some of the largest areas.[6] Los Angeles, which grew 14 percent in the 1970s, would have lost population had there been no immigration and had internal migration remained the same. Immigration also kept population growth from declining or significantly reduced the decline in Boston, Chicago, New York, and San Francisco. In the Washington, D.C. area, immigration accounted for almost all the net growth.

In the 1980s this urban concentration continued. For the approximately 600,000 immigrants legally admitted to the United States in fiscal year 1987, the three largest metropolitan areas (New York, Chicago, and Los Angeles) accounted for about 30 percent of intended destinations (places of residence), whereas only about 10 percent of the general population lives in these places.[7] Nonmetropolitan destinations accounted for 7 percent, compared to 24 percent of residences for the population as a whole. Illegal immigration is also concentrated in urban areas (New York, Los Angeles, Houston, Miami), although there is substantial movement to rural agricultural areas, too. In sum, the admission of immigrants to the United States (as well as their unauthorized arrival) has served to make the distribution of population more concentrated than it would otherwise be.

Agglomeration Economies— Do the Old Arguments Hold?

One argument for the existence and development of cities rests on the notion of agglomeration economies. These economies are advantages in production that derive from the spatial proximity of producers of goods and services. By agglomerating, producers reduce the transportation costs of moving goods from one firm or stage of the production process to another.

The agglomeration economy notion goes a long way toward explaining the development of the great industrial urban centers in the United States and elsewhere during the late nineteenth century and early twentieth. In the production of durable goods (automobiles, appliances, and the like) it was advantageous for producers to congregate; indeed, the growth of Chicago, Detroit, and Pittsburgh seems to bear this out.

Such agglomeration economies were also viewed to be operating in the service sector, where, again, face-to-face contact through physical propinquity served to cut costs and foster the more rapid spread of ideas. The archetype here is the very dense clustering of financial services in the Wall Street area of lower Manhattan.

Throughout the twentieth century technological advances have chipped away at agglomeration economies, however. Improvement in roads, with the shift from railroad to truck transportation, and most recently the development of high-speed electronic communication have worked in this direction, promoting suburbanization and then enabling movement to even lower density settings, including smaller metropolitan areas and rural communities. Now an organization far from a major metropolis can have access instantly through telephone lines to the financial markets and other sources of news and information, just as it can deliver that information quickly through electronic networks. It is for this reason that the so-called back offices of major financial institutions move out of the high-rent downtown areas to suburban or exurban locations.

In addition to economies of agglomeration, there also exist *dis*economies of agglomeration—increased costs or disadvantages associated with higher density and proximity. Congestion costs are the most frequently mentioned. (Pollution is another; it is discussed in the next section.) Whereas proximity should reduce the cost of delivering goods and services by decreasing the length of transport needed, traffic has become the bane of the urbanite's daily travel routine; it is perhaps the most obvious congestion cost. Indeed, data from U.S. censuses indicate that workers in larger metropolitan areas spend a longer time getting to work than do those in smaller metropolitan areas. Much of this difference is due to congestion; the remainder is due, ironically, to the greater physical distance to be covered in a larger, more agglomerated urban area.

These are the ideas, but what is the evidence? Is there an optimal city size? There appears to be no consensus on an exact optimum value for city population, but social scientists have tried to estimate the magnitudes and effects of agglomeration economies and diseconomies. As one might imagine, it is very difficult to disentangle the "true" effects of agglomeration on industrial productivity, congestion, and pollution.

One attempt to estimate recent changes in agglomeration economies focused on those industries that have provided one-third of employment in production industries.[8] It found that the productivity advantages of large cities have declined. In a study using industrial data from the United States and Brazil, economist Vernon Henderson found that economies of scale in manufacturing were more due to localization (being near a related activity) rather than to urbanization (size of place), per se.[9] Productivity improvement rose with size of place but then declined. If technological change continues along the same line as it has in recent years, then any productivity advantage of large urban areas will continue to dissipate. Even so, one recent review of a number of empirical studies concluded that "despite these shortcomings and potential biases, the message from the empirical literature is clear: economies of proximity exist and exhibit considerable quantitative strength."[10]

We can see, then, that both economies and diseconomies of agglomeration are operating, and an accurate assessment of their overall effect requires the difficult task of estimating each. The question to ask for policy is whether the markets for goods and labor as currently constituted are adequate to maximize well-being, balancing the positive and negative aspects of urbanization. It is probably accurate to say that the market does much to promote an optimal location of firms and households, with each weighing individually the costs and benefits of agglomeration. If so, the movement of the most mobile—large corporations and prosperous families—from the cities to their suburbs in recent decades would seem a judgment against high density.

It is also probably the case that the market does not capture all of these influences. Many people do not have a wide range of choice in the type of place where they live. They are restricted by the need to be within commuting range of an acceptable job based on their skills and interests, and they must be able to afford housing.

The Environmental Costs of Large Population Concentrations

Pollution of the environment results both from the concentration of population and from the way in which individuals and businesses act toward controlling potential sources of pollution. Even in low-density rural areas, certain processes of mining and manufacturing can result in serious environmental problems. While the growth of population and incorporation of territory into townships or other political units can sometimes facilitate action to control pollution, as population growth continues, it more often increases the environmental problems.

Large population concentrations usually require higher costs per person for the maintenance of clean water and the safe removal of garbage. Air quality, in particular, may be difficult to maintain at high population densities if there is not a natural flow of air through the area. Some cities, such as Los Angeles, have particularly difficult problems dealing with air quality because air is often trapped.

It is somewhat difficult to measure the quality of the environment in different metropolitan areas because of the lack of sufficient monitoring sites or the lack of common means of measurement from one area to another. Air quality, for example, is often measured at only one site, and the location of that site affects the level of the measurement. If measures from that site indicate poor air quality, there is no way of telling whether all persons in the metropolitan area breathe poor air or only those close to the monitoring site. According to one study, single-site measures appeared to be adequate for small particle pollution but not for larger particles, which varied more across metropolitan areas.[11]

The staff at Zero Population Growth has constructed an index of environmental pollution that combines measures of air quality, water quality, sewage treatment, and hazardous waste.[12] This index shows that the environment in larger cities is poorer than that in smaller cities. There is a significant dividing line between central cities of 250,000 or more and smaller ones.

Smaller cities have two advantages in dealing with the environment. First, because of smaller size and typically lower density, they have less concentration of pollutants to deal with, other things being equal. Second, because they have a smaller and often more homogeneous population, they may have an easier time mobilizing support for programs to regulate and reduce pollution.

The Social Effects of Urban Scale

Although much of the attention in the scholarly literature on the costs and benefits of urbanization focuses on economic criteria, the social side presents other important aspects of those costs and benefits. These include the relative distribution of income (or more generally resources) for urban areas, crime, antisocial behavior, and racial and ethnic conflict. In a sense these are externalities of agglomeration diseconomies seen through a sociological or psychological lens. Although many ad hoc theories exist, however, solid empirical evidence linking city size to these social disamenities is hard to come by.

Are the rich richer and the poor poorer in large cities compared to smaller ones? The statistical evidence is weak and mixed. Using data on income distribution for the seventy-nine largest U.S. metropolitan areas,[13] we found that a 10 percent increase in metropolitan population was associated with a 0.2 percent increase in income inequality. This is quite a modest relationship, but it does suggest that the distribution of income is more unequal in larger metropolitan areas. Up to about 1980, income inequality in the United States declined, despite increasing urbanization over much of this period.[14] It has risen since then. In 1980 the mean income deficit—the average amount of additional income needed for poor households to move out of poverty, was $3,075 in the United States as a whole and $3,014 for rural areas. New York, Los Angeles, and Chicago, the three largest metropolitan areas, recorded mean income deficits higher than the national average, but the deficit was lower than the national average in Boston, Cincinnati, Buffalo, and Detroit.[15]

Whether the poor are worse off in large urban areas than in other places is more difficult to ascertain. Costs of living are higher, so an equivalent amount of money may provide less in terms of goods and services compared to a rural area. For the individual poor person to be better off in the large city, there must be some factors that compensate, such as the chance of getting a better-paying job (and moving out of poverty), other social services provided "in kind," lower transportation costs (no need to own a car), and the like. It is very difficult to get an accurate estimate of the net balance of these factors because so many components are unmeasured.

Casual observation of the news media would suggest that large cities are the sites of more crime, personal danger, and other deviant behavior. The statistics bear this out. The rates of robbery and crimes against property show the sharpest rise with urban size.[16] Certainly the recent wave of drug-related violence has been heavily concentrated in large cities. Historically, however, urban areas have not been appreciably disadvantaged with regard to murder rates; rural areas have higher rates than small metropolises.

Crime is one indication of social alienation. There are several others, including school dropout, suicide, and teenage pregnancy rates. These problems are often worse in urban areas, particularly central cities. Among younger never-married women (eighteen to twenty-four years of age), for instance, the fertility rate of central city residents was nearly 45 percent above the national rate, although it was still lower than the rate for corresponding women living in nonmetropolitan areas.[17] We also find that people aged twenty to twenty-four residing in central cities are much more likely than their suburban counterparts not to be high school graduates, and the incidence of dropping out is slightly higher than for nonmetropolitan residents.[18] While in both of these cases some of the apparent central city–suburb-nonmetropolitan difference could be due to compositional influences (and movement out of the cities after the change in behavior), it is consistent with the notion that cities, particularly inner cities, do not foster mainstream behavior.

Another place to look for social differences is in the infant mortality rate, a statistic often quoted (and lamentably so for the United States) as an indication of level of development. While infant mortality rates do not tell us directly about behavior, they do provide a window on how adequate the social service delivery system is. They also reflect some differences in social behavior. Maternal drug use, teenage parenthood, and so on, all put infants at higher risk. In 1987 the United States had an infant mortality rate (IMR) of 10.1 deaths in the first year of life per 1,000 live births. Most but not all of the top ten metropolitan areas showed higher IMR in 1987. For the New York metropolitan area the figure was 11.7 (Brooklyn, 13.9); Los Angeles, 9.8; Chicago, 12.5 (Cook County, 13.8); San Francisco, 7.6; Philadelphia, 11.7 (City of Philadelphia, 17.3); Detroit, 12.1; Boston, 7.2 (Suffolk County, 11.9); Dallas, 9.4; Houston, 9.3; Washington, D.C., 11.0 (D.C., 19.3).[19] Clearly central city (county) areas show higher rates than their suburbs. Children born in more urban areas are disadvantaged for survival through childhood.

Racial and ethnic conflict is pronounced in cities, for urbanization brings into close proximity those of disparate backgrounds. We also observe that larger metropolises exhibit higher rates of segregation.[20] Certainly ethnic antagonism becomes manifest in big-city politics, where the race of the candidate matters greatly. It is important to note that urban areas also provide advantages to minorities. One theory even argues that immigrant ethnic groups in particular form enclave economies, garnering local resources that tend to bolster the well-being of the group in the long run. In less diverse, less urbanized areas, a majority group may exert virtual hegemony over the minority in politics and economic life. As the history of race relations in the U.S. South reminds us, moreover, ethnic conflict and violence are not limited to large urban areas.

Despite the evidence of an association between city size and crime, income disparity, and ethnic conflict, we must ask whether changes in the scale of living would produce changes in these outcomes. In other words, we must determine whether these outcomes are simply the result of the composition of cities or whether urbanization itself generates these phenomena. A subcultural theory of urbanism developed by urban sociologist Claude Fischer argues that there is an urban effect, which builds upon differences in composition. Because urban areas are large, they contain a critical mass of individuals who share a common disposition. Organized crime is one example of commonly disposed individuals; the arts provide another. Urban residence also allows one to achieve a greater degree of anonymity, facilitating socially deviant behavior.

Would decreases in urbanization reduce some of these negative social externalities? Probably yes, but only insofar as the differences were due to agglomeration per se. Compositional differences between urban and rural areas, and among cities of different sizes, are not likely to be removed merely by changes in the scale of living.

Where Would People Live if They Had a Choice?

The wide-scale population deconcentration of the 1970s touched off a lively debate on whether or not people were giving up the higher incomes and other benefits of large cities for the perceived higher quality of life in small towns and rural areas. Studies of residential preferences over the past forty years have consistently shown that many people who live in large cities would prefer to live in smaller cities, towns or rural areas. However, most of those wishing to live in rural areas preferred them to be within thirty miles of a city of over 50,000.[21] What seems to be preferred is a relatively small scale for one's immediate residential surroundings, and, at the same time, the availability of shopping, services, cultural, and recreational opportunities associated with a metropolitan area.

The preference for smaller urban settlements can also be seen in the degree to which people in different-size places are satisfied with the neighborhoods in which they live. The 1985 American Housing Survey asked a representative sample of Americans about their satisfaction with their neighborhood and perceived neighborhood problems. The results, shown in the accompanying table, indicate that satisfaction is greater in smaller and more suburban places and that residents of these places perceive fewer problems than do those in cities. The differences are particularly strong for the perception of crime as a problem. While cities are often thought to offer better services in exchange for putting up with

Satisfaction and Problems by Type of Place:
American Housing Survey, 1985
(Percentages)

Type of Place	Neighborhood Satisfaction	Any Problem	Crime	Noise	Traffic	Litter	Poor Service
City, large MSA	75	47.5	25.1	22.9	17.6	16.1	5.4
City, small MSA	78	41.3	11.6	21.2	19.3	14.1	3.8
Suburb, large MSA	82	39.1	9.3	20.4	23.6	11.5	4.8
Suburb, small MSA	84	35.7	6.7	16.8	17.8	11.5	5.7
Other urban place	82	34.7	5.3	20.9	17.4	13.5	3.5
Rural	87	28.3	42	14.4	14.3	10.8	4.5

Note: Large MSAs are Metropolitan Statistical Areas or Consolidated Metropolitan Statistical Areas with populations of one million or more.

other problems, few people in any areas noted services as a problem and there was little difference by type of area.

While race is often discussed in relation to city–suburb differences, Blacks shared the same relative evaluation of satisfaction and problems as whites. With the exception of rural areas, which they did not rate better than small urban areas, Blacks were also more satisfied in smaller and more suburban places than they were in larger places and central cities. While there is some tendency to associate the problems of large cities with the racial or ethnic composition of these cities, members of minority racial or ethnic groups appear to suffer at least as much as others from the problems in these areas. It would appear that all races would be better off with smaller-scale settlements.

Although data on preferences for different size communities would seem to suggest that we should be involved in a continuing process of population deconcentration, we have not been in one since around 1980. While the process of suburbanization continues within most metropolitan areas, there is no longer a net flow from metropolitan to nonmetropolitan areas.

To some extent the nonmetropolitan movement of the 1970s was self-defeating. First, it redistributed people to counties adjacent to metropolitan areas. Then, as a result of growth, these areas got redefined as metropolitan. Second, nonmetropolitan population movement resulted in sufficient growth in and around small cities to give them metropolitan status.

Consequences of City Decline

In the past, the decline of population in cities and metropolitan areas has often been judged negatively. In a Brookings Institute book, Bradbury, Downs, and Small, for example, list a host of problems associated with urban decline.[22] In their Census monograph on metropolitan change, Frey and Speare show that metropolitan areas that declined between 1970 and 1980 had increasing proportions who were poor, increasing unemployment, and declining house values.[23] They also found less satisfaction among residents of declining areas. However, not all consequences of past decline have been negative. The Pittsburgh Metropolitan Area, which has experienced population decline over the past four decades, was rated as the top city in the *Places Rated Almanac* in 1985 and in third place out of 333 metropolitan areas in 1989 (see Chapter 1).[24] This rating was based on a combined set of ratings of jobs, housing, living costs, health, environment, education, arts, recreation, and climate. In contrast, Houston, which has been touted as a success in free enterprise–induced growth, had a score of 66. Feagin, who did a careful case study of Houston's growth, concludes that while growth may have satisfied business interests, the city now has serious problems of air, water, and hazardous waste pollution, an inadequate education system, and other serious problems.[25]

The perception that urban shrinkage leads to negative consequences is due to two facts that are usually associated with such declines. First, declining cities have usually experienced a loss of jobs and relatively high unemployment rates. Second, those who leave for better opportunities elsewhere are often younger workers with above-average education and skills. While unemployed persons are somewhat more likely to move than are those who are employed, they comprise only a small part of the migration stream from declining places, and in general these cities end up with a population that has a lower average educational level, a lower proportion of skilled workers, and a lower per capita income. This makes it harder for the city to compete for new jobs or to find tax revenues to pay for services for a population that has increased needs.

The cause of the problem is not population decline per se, but the loss of jobs and the selective out-migration of younger, more educated, and more highly skilled people. Since the natural increase rate has always been greater than zero, population decline has occurred only when there has been substantial out-migration. We have not been able to observe the consequences of a decline due to a negative rate of natural increase, that is, a birth rate lower than the death rate. That would be a very different type of decline, one that would not change population composition, except in terms of average age. Since incomes tend to rise with age, the effects on the tax base ought to be positive, and the demand for some of the most expensive urban services, schools and police to deal with teenage offenders, would be reduced.

8

THE PLIGHT OF THE CHESAPEAKE

STEPHEN E. TENNENBAUM AND ROBERT COSTANZA

A pattern of smaller urban clusters is not likely to be a viable alternative to megalopolis. It generates its own problems. The Chesapeake serves as an example and an important case history in its own right.

The Chesapeake Bay, the largest estuary in North America, has been the subject of more scientific study and political wrangling than any other body of coastal water in the world. It has become clear that what happens in the bay is in large part a function of activities in the drainage basin, but the focus of most past studies has been rather narrow. We are only now beginning to develop a comprehensive picture of the bay and its connections to its drainage basin.

Population increases in the Chesapeake Bay watershed have led to changes in land use and agricultural practices resulting in increasing volumes of wastes that impact natural terrestrial and aquatic systems, and ultimately lead to the deterioration of the bay itself. Regulation of human activities may slow these effects, but the only long-term cure is a stable or declining population ensconced in a healthy and likewise stable economy.

In this chapter we develop an historical and spatial perspective of human activities in the Chesapeake Bay drainage basin. Fundamental to gaining this perspective is the conceptualizing of the Chesapeake Bay *system* as the combination of the drainage basin and the bay itself. Accordingly, we have assembled and mapped past and present human activities in the Chesapeake Bay drainage basin in order to gain this perspective.

Background

The Chesapeake Bay is an ecological system whose beauty and vitality have led to high human population growth rates. These high population growth rates have directly and indirectly caused its infirmity, including declining fisheries, receding wetlands, vanishing seagrasses and a devastated oyster industry. In this chapter we look at the larger scale terrestrial trends within the entire Chesapeake Bay watershed that have produced these impacts and have led to a decline in the quality of human life. Traffic congestion, disappearing natural and agricultural areas, swelling landfills, and overtaxed water treatment facilities are some of the effects.

The Chesapeake Bay is a mosaic of estuaries that, taken together, comprise the largest single estuary in the United States. It was formed from Atlantic waters eroding and drowning the mouths of the rivers that feed it. It is 193 miles long, 3 to 25 miles wide and with its tidal tributaries covers an area of 4,400 square miles and has 8,100 miles of shoreline.[1] The drainage basins that feed it comprise 64,000 square miles in six states, and three major cities lie on the banks of its tidal system.

There are complex factors affecting the bay that have manifested themselves as substantial changes in water quality and the structure of the biological communities. Many of these changes have been observed for some time due to the importance of the Chesapeake Bay as a commercial fishery. The Chesapeake Bay Program has documented some

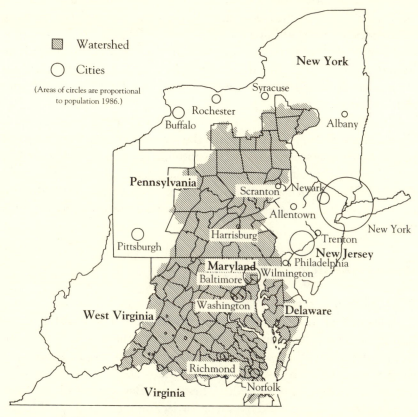

Location of Chesapeake Bay Watershed and some major cities within 200 miles. Adapted from a map compiled by S. Tennenbaum and R. Costanza, Chesapeake Biological Laboratory, University of Maryland, Solomons, Maryland.

of these trends.[2] For example, increased levels of nutrients in the upper reaches of the bay and its tributaries have contributed to eutrophication, with increasing blue-green algae and dinoflagellate blooms. Concentrations have increased as much as 250-fold in the past thirty years. Areas of the bay that have experienced oxygen depletion have increased fifteen-fold in the same period. There are high concentrations of toxic organic compounds and metals in the water column and sediments near industrial facilities and river mouths, such as the Patapsco and Elizabeth rivers. Submerged aquatic vegetation (SAV) is rapidly disappearing in all but a few areas. Commercially important fish that spawn in freshwater and whose young use SAV for refuge and as feeding areas, such as alewife and shad, have decreased substantially as well, replaced in part by marine breeding species such as bluefish and menhaden. Oyster harvests have declined from over 100 million pounds annually in the late 1800s to only around 20 million pounds in the latter part of this century. And there are increasing worries about the sustainability of the blue crab population because of these problems, along with the ever-increasing crabbing pressures. In spite of all this, the Chesapeake fishery has for over thirty years provided an average of 10 percent of the total U.S. fishery catch and employment for 14 percent of the nation's fishermen.[3]

Watershed Demographics

Population changes in the watershed are shown in the maps for 1940 and 1986. The number of dots is proportional to population in each county and distributed randomly within each county. Between 1940 and 1986 the population of the watershed increased 87 percent. About 20 percent of this increase was due to net migration into the watershed, the majority of it to areas in Maryland and Virginia surrounding Baltimore and Washington. The population of the watershed grew at an average annual rate of 1.6 percent between 1952 and 1972, almost the same as the U.S. average for the same period, 1.5 percent. But the growth was concentrated in the Maryland and Virginia portions of the watershed, which averaged 2.6 percent growth compared to the remainder of the watershed which grew more slowly, at only 0.4 percent.

The most striking changes were in three areas: Richmond, the Norfolk–Virginia Beach area, and the Baltimore–Washington corridor. Growth can be attributed to increases in industry related directly and indirectly to the expanding U.S. Government, and also to the increasing fashionableness of the Chesapeake Bay as a recreation area. The latter forces are amplified by the high immigration rates to the area.

These areas also illustrate the "urban flight–suburban sprawl" phenomenon that has at once undermined the more natural and rural atmosphere that many originally left the city for, and at the same time removed businesses and middle- and upper-income residents who served as a revenue base for the cities. The resulting deterioration of services and infrastructure worsens as people move further and further out. Increasing travel time to reach work, with the concurrent degeneration of traffic conditions, and soaring property values are among the resistive forces that quell the further spread of suburban development.

Totals for portion of states within
the watershed:

District of Columbia	636,235
Delaware	84,559
Maryland	1,706,959
New York	495,710
Pennsylvania	3,006,638
Virginia	1,530,935
West Virginia	118,617
Total	7,579,653

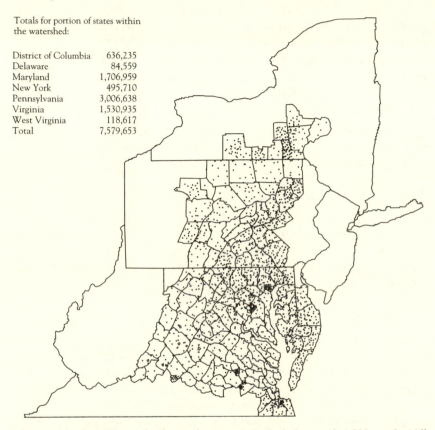

Chesapeake Bay Watershed population 1940. Each dot equals 1,000 people. (All
maps compiled by S. Tennenbaum and R. Costanza, Chesapeake Biological Laboratory,
University of Maryland, Solomons, Maryland.)

It appears that these forces may be approaching an equilibrium, at
least for the time being. Between 1972 and 1986 the growth rate of the
Maryland watershed population slowed to an annual rate of 0.9 percent,
and that in Virginia to 1.8 percent, and emigration rates from the cities
have slowed. For example, Washington's emigration rate decreased from
an annual average of 1.3 percent in the 1960s to less than 0.8 percent
in the early 1980s. In addition, the spatial extent of the sprawl appears
to be presently limited to the counties immediately surrounding the cities
in question. However, the information contained in the population maps

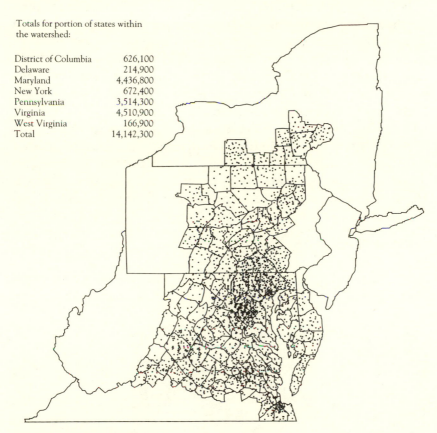

Totals for portion of states within
the watershed:

District of Columbia	626,100
Delaware	214,900
Maryland	4,436,800
New York	672,400
Pennsylvania	3,514,300
Virginia	4,510,900
West Virginia	166,900
Total	14,142,300

Chesapeake Bay Watershed population 1986. Each dot equals 1,000 people.

in this chapter is only suggestive. Demographic trends can be the result of any number of factors. Variation in birth rates, cultural heritage, local versus long-distance moves, political climate, and zoning laws muddy the waters. In addition, as sprawl and growth occur simultaneously, secondary economic centers inevitably spring up, initiating their own cycles.

Patterns of settlement and resettlement broadly affect land use in other ways as well. For example, there has recently been a slight but noticeable increase in woodland in the New York portion of the watershed. The fact that there was a concurrent loss of cropland and pasture only indicates that there were net changes from one type to another, but there is no indication as to the reason for these changes. The marked differences in changes in agricultural and forested acreage from one state to another strongly suggest that they are due to differences in state agricultural policies and tax laws. On the other hand, as shown in the land-use map, the pattern of urbanization is more straightforward in light of the population changes discussed above.

Increases in evidence of human activity accompany the increases in population in both magnitude and distribution. Maps of manufacturers, energy consumption, housing units, water use, solid waste production, and air pollutants closely resemble the maps of population. However, changes in life-style have caused accelerated increases in con-

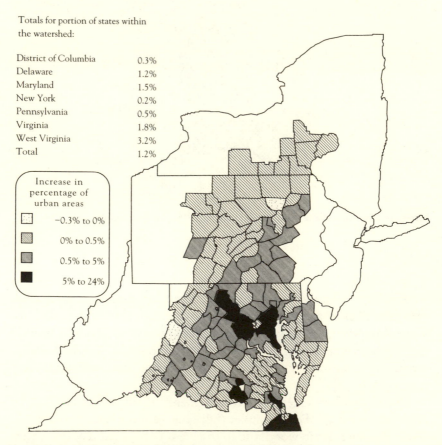

Totals for portion of states within
the watershed:

District of Columbia	0.3%
Delaware	1.2%
Maryland	1.5%
New York	0.2%
Pennsylvania	0.5%
Virginia	1.8%
West Virginia	3.2%
Total	1.2%

Increase in
percentage of
urban areas

-0.3% to 0%

0% to 0.5%

0.5% to 5%

5% to 24%

Land Use in Chesapeake Bay Watershed, 1978–1985.

sumption and waste production. From 1952 to 1986 we have seen the following increases in the watershed: per capita energy consumption has gone from 567,000 British thermal units (Btu) per day to 744,000 Btu per day. Nitrous oxide emissions by vehicles have gone from 1.0 pounds per week per person to 1.7 pounds per week per person, and per capita solid waste production has risen from 2.2 pounds per day to 3.7 pounds per day. In contrast, public and industrial per capita water use for the watershed as a whole has decreased in the same period from 334 gallons per day to 278 gallons per day. This is due in large part to the decline in total use in Pennsylvania during this period from 1.46 billion gallons per day in 1952 to only 1.18 billion gallons per day in 1986. In the Maryland and Virginia portions of the watershed, the per capita use rate held nearly constant at about 237 gallons per day. This suggests that changes in energy consumption, toxic emissions, and waste production may be due to changes in heavy industry in Pennsylvania; the constant per capita public demand for water occurs in a region that is primarily residential and light industry.

Agriculture

Changes associated with agriculture are tied to increases in population in their overall magnitude, and to cultural and historical practices in their distribution and local magnitude. Heavily populated areas necessarily exclude agriculture. Some of the best agricultural land in the country, the basis for the initial local growth, is rapidly being converted to residential developments, industrial parks, and shopping malls as rising property values make farming unprofitable. It is not clear, however, whether agriculture itself is more benign than urban and surburban development to an ecosystem such as the Chesapeake Bay. Both load the system with wastes and nutrients while consuming "natural" areas that could have absorbed some of that load.

While total farm acreage in the watershed decreased from 23.2 million acres in 1954 to 14.4 million acres in 1987, cropland only decreased from 10.5 million acres to 9.0 million. Meanwhile, from 1954 to 1987 the average farm size increased from 126 to 190 acres. This means that larger percentages of farms are devoted to crops (64 percent versus 45 percent), while less lies fallow, pastured, and wooded. Operations are larger and more intensive. Irrigation has increased from 40,000 to 180,000 acres,

Totals for portion of states within
the watershed (in tons):

Delaware	240
Maryland	939
New York	166
Pennsylvania	985
Virginia	1,108
West Virginia	132
Total	3,570

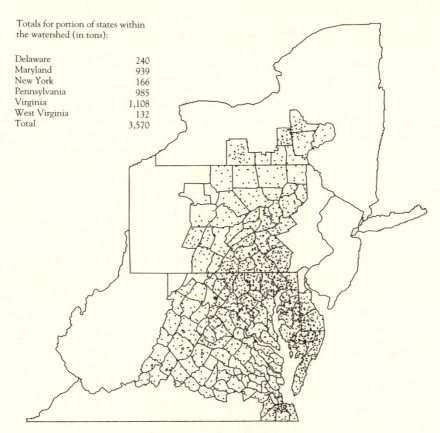

Pesticide use in Chesapeake Bay Watershed, 1954. Each dot equals 1 ton.

and fertilization rates have increased from about 210 to 250 pounds per cultivated acre. As the maps for 1954 and 1987 show, pesticide use, which was almost nonexistent in the early 1950s, peaked in the 1970s and subsequently decreased from 15,000 tons in 1974 to 13,000 tons in 1986. This reflects the greater specificity of the pesticides used in 1986.

If we examine the application of fertilizer nitrogen, shown in the next map, we see a pattern that follows the general distribution of farmland, but with an overall increase in the intensity of use.

The nutrient loading rates for the mainstream Chesapeake Bay are 78,700 tons per year nitrogen and 3,600 tons per year phosphorus.[4] If

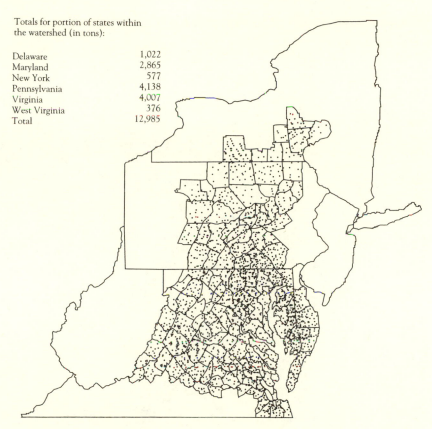

Totals for portion of states within
the watershed (in tons):

Delaware	1,022
Maryland	2,865
New York	577
Pennsylvania	4,138
Virginia	4,007
West Virginia	376
Total	12,985

Pesticide use in Chesapeake Bay Watershed, 1987. Each dot equals 1 ton.

one assumes that the loading rate is proportional to the amount of nutrients applied within the watershed, then this implies that phosphorus loading has increased around 4 to 10 percent and that nitrogen loading has increased somewhere between 34 to 125 percent since 1954. This would not only be a great change in the amount of nutrients but (and this may be even more crucial) a great change in the relative proportion of nutrients. The increased concentrations of nutrients in specific localities, such as Lancaster County, Pennsylvania, may intensify this problem.

Totals for portion of states within
the watershed (in tons):

Delaware	4,341
Maryland	18,247
New York	4,724
Pennsylvania	23,558
Virginia	25,504
West Virginia	1,356
Total	77,730

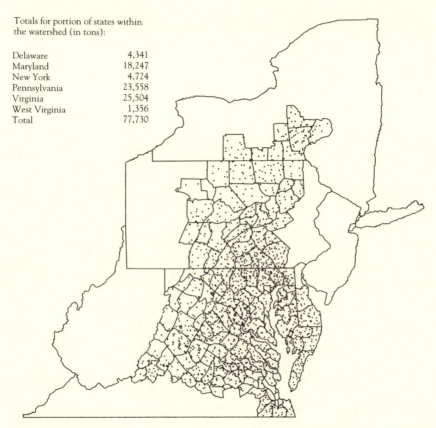

Nitrogen content of fertilizer in Chesapeake Bay Watershed, 1954. Each dot
equals 25 tons.

Conclusion

The Chesapeake Bay has undergone very rapid population growth with
associated environmental impacts. We have mapped some of these
changes as they are reflected in the characteristics of the bay's watershed. The impacts of these activities in the watershed on the bay itself
are known to be large, but their specific interconnections are only now
being investigated. The Chesapeake Bay has 835,000 people living in
its drainage basin for every cubic mile of water in the bay (the Baltic Sea
has 17,000 people per cubic mile, and the Mediterranean has 355 people

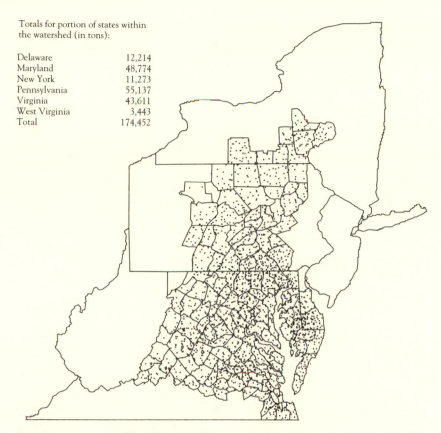

Totals for portion of states within
the watershed (in tons):

Delaware	12,214
Maryland	48,774
New York	11,273
Pennsylvania	55,137
Virginia	43,611
West Virginia	3,443
Total	174,452

Nitrogen content of fertilizer in Chesapeake Bay Watershed 1987. Each dot
equalt 25 tons.

per cubic mile, by way of comparison). Even if all of these people were
minimizing their environmental impacts (which they are not), their sheer
numbers are daunting to a system as sensitive as the Chesapeake. If these
numbers continue to increase as they have in the past, the prospects for
America's largest estuary seem bleak.

YOU CAN'T GO WEST
Stress in the High Country
DENNIS BROWNRIDGE

To those who believe that there is plenty of room for more population in the wide open spaces of the West, we propose a closer look.

Journalists and travel brochures often portray the American West as a vast and underpopulated land of virgin forests, boundless wildlife, and empty deserts. The usual cliches are "unspoiled," "remote," and "wilderness." But this view is a romantic illusion. The West has been thoroughly surveyed, mapped, tramped over, prospected, and inventoried. All of it has been allocated to some use. The frontier is gone; there is no virgin, idle land waiting to be discovered. Forests, water, rangeland, and amenities are being consumed at a rate that cannot be sustained, certainly not without sacrificing other resources. Pollution of air and water is widespread. Indeed, resource conflicts and environmental problems dominate politics and headlines throughout the region.

The West has long been the fastest-growing part of the country. In 1900 it held four million people—5 percent of a nation of seventy-five million. A lifetime later, in 1990, it had fifty million—20 percent of a nation of 250 million.[1] It has the most populous state, California, and several of the biggest and fastest-growing metropolises. Nevertheless, much of the West remains thinly populated, the "wide open spaces" of lore. The phrase "rural West" is almost an oxymoron. The dense networks of rural farmsteads and villages typical of the East or of Europe are rare in the West. The great majority of westerners have always lived in cities and towns. So, to a New Yorker or midwesterner, the nonmetropolitan interior West must seem empty indeed.

But sheer living space does not limit population. All the cities and towns of the United States would fit into Utah with room to spare, but there would be nothing for people to do, no way to make a living. Most of the West is thinly populated for good reason: It has little or no economic use.

Geographic Constraints

There are three things, besides funny hats and pointy-toed boots, that distinguish the West from the rest of the country:

1. **Mountains.** The shifting crustal plates have rippled it with range upon range of rugged mountains. From the Rocky Mountain front to the Pacific Coast, mountains are almost always in sight. There is lots of flat land between the mountains, of course—the land you see from the highways. But most of it is high plateau, averaging 1500 meters (5000 feet) above sea level. High altitude means cold winters and short growing seasons.

2. **Aridity.** Thanks in part to the rainshadow effect of the mountains, most of the West is also dry. It is either steppe (a semiarid climate that can support short grass) or full-fledged desert. With minor exceptions, it is too dry to farm without irrigation. A good many homesteaders discovered that the hard way. You can still see their decaying cabins dotting the landscape. Only a narrow coastal strip of the Pacific Northwest is both wet and warm enough to support eastern-style farming. It is no coincidence that Oregon was the original destination of settlers trekking west in the 1840s.

In short, nine-tenths of the West is too dry, too cold, too steep, or too rocky for crop farming. And it is farming that sustains large rural populations.

3. Public Land. Mainly because it is useless for farming, half the West was never claimed under the various nineteenth-century land grant laws. Since the nation is now full, the land giveaway laws have been repealed (except for the controversial 1872 Mining Law). The land that no one wanted remains in public ownership, freely accessible to all, the last vestige of a public domain that once stretched from the Appalachians to the Pacific. The public lands include:

Bureau of Land Management (BLM)	23% of Western land
National forests	18% of Western land
National parks and monuments	1.5% of Western land
National wildlife refuges	0.7% of Western land
National recreation areas (mainly reservoirs)	0.4% of Western land

Another 2 percent of the West is government land, used for bombing, war games, and weapons development. The military says it needs much more and is currently trying to appropriate another half percent (14 000 square kilometers or 3.5 million acres) from the public lands.[2] Several additional percent is owned by the states and might be considered public. Since the public lands have no permanent inhabitants, they appear empty on a population map. But they are by no means unused. Their resources are open to private commercial exploitation and they serve tens of millions of recreational visitors a year.

The Great Plains are sometimes included in the West, dividing the country at the hundredth meridian. While the Plains lack the mountains and public land of the "real" West, they satisfy the high-and-dry test. The figures in this chapter are for the eleven western states, the West of the statisticians, which roughly splits the differences between these two geographic definitions.

Forests

The West supports the finest coniferous (softwood) forests in the world. They include the tallest trees (Redwoods), the most massive trees (Sequoias), and the oldest trees (Bristlecone pines) found anywhere on Earth. The Pacific Northwest (coastal Washington, Oregon, and northern California) has magnificent rainforests rivaled in lushness and beauty only by the hardwood rainforests of the tropics.

But some perspective is in order. Seventy per cent of the West is un-forested, and half the nominal forestland is so dry or cold that it sup-ports only brushy, stunted, or slow-growing trees with no commercial use, valuable only as watershed and wildlife habitat. Only 15 percent of the West is commercial forestland, capable of growing timber.[3]

Nevertheless, western forests supply 60 percent of the nation's soft-wood (construction) lumber. Half of that comes from the great Douglas-fir, cedar, and Redwood forests of the Pacific states. Ponderosa pine, a large and beautiful tree of the drier interior, supplies another fifth. The trees of the high Rockies—lodgepole pine, spruces, true firs, and aspen—are relatively unimportant. The South produces three times as much lumber as all eight Rocky Mountain states put together.

For three centuries the United States was self-sufficient in wood. But since the 1940s we have been a net importer, and the gap is widening rapidly. We export a large volume of irreplaceable old-growth timber, mostly to Japan, but we import much more. The United States cuts more wood than any other nation—more than half a cubic kilometer (20 billion cubic feet) per year, a veritable mountain of wood. We are cutting more than ever before, yet we now consume 13 percent more wood—and 30 percent more lumber—than we produce.

Can we blame this on increasingly profligate consumption? Not at all. We use only half as much wood and lumber per person as Americans did in 1900. There has been an explosion in pulp products (paper and cardboard), but it has been offset by a corresponding decline in barrels and boxes and countless other products once made of wood. Many have been replaced by petroleum-based plastics, metals, and other nonrenewable materials. Lumber consumption has dropped per capita because we build smaller and plainer houses; we use more stucco, con-crete, and aluminum; we use trees more efficiently; and we get along with inferior products like particleboard (a miserable, ersatz wood made of glued sawdust).

But if we use much less wood per person and are cutting more from our forests, how did we go from being a net exporter to the world's big-gest importer? The answer is simple: U.S. population has more than tripled since 1900. In a single lifetime, we have added 175 million people.

Almost all of our wood shortfall is imported from Canada. Canada's forests are not as fine as our own. Its vast taiga forest in its subarctic North is a stunted, slow-growing spruce/fir forest, with little value other than for pulp. Canada cuts only 40 percent as much wood as we do. Canadians use wood the same way we do. Yet Canada is the world's greatest *exporter* (44 percent of world lumber exports), while we are the biggest importer. How is this possible? Again, the answer is simple: the United States has ten times more people than Canada.

Much western timber is still cut from virgin forest. The trees are often hundreds and sometimes thousands of years old. In little more than a lifetime, 90 percent of the virgin, old-growth forest in the Pacific Northwest has been destroyed.[4] Only small patches remain and they are currently being logged at 250 square kilometers (100 square miles) a year. At that rate all that is not protected in parks or Wilderness areas will be gone in a decade or so. In the interior, the great stands of old-growth Ponderosa pine are also virtually gone. Somewhat more virgin forest survives in the Rockies, but it contains only small pockets of old growth, since most Rocky Mountain species are small and short-lived.

Of course, trees grow back. In fact we are growing wood at a faster rate than in the past, simply because small, immature trees grow faster than big old ones. However, while we may appear to be getting more "interest" out of the forest, the wood is of much lower quality, and our "capital" is rapidly being eroded. Since 1952 the net volume of softwood sawtimber standing in western forests has declined about 20 percent. This represents a per capita decline of 50 percent (since U.S. population has mushroomed during the same time). For each American, there is only half as much sawtimber standing in the western forests as there was a generation and a half ago. The decline is obvious to anyone who drives the backroads of the Pacific Northwest. Clearcuts—large, completely deforested patches—are everywhere to be seen. Huge stumps remind you of the forest that once was, like the ruins of a great civilization.

Large virgin trees bring high prices because the wood is superior and because more of the tree is usable as lumber. When a tree matures, its lower limbs drop off and growth slows, producing a stronger, finer-grained, straighter-grained, and knot-free ("clear") wood. The deep, rich colors that give Redwood and yellow (Ponderosa) pine their names also develop only in old trees.

Aesthetically, there is no comparison between diverse old-growth forests and the dreary tree farms that replace them. Old-growth forests are verdant, multicanopied, cathedral-like places, with huge trees and an astonishing complexity of life. Managed forests are monotonous, even-aged monocultures of uniform small trees, their interiors tangled with dead lower branches. There is no match for old-growth timber, alive or dead. But once these ancient forests are gone, they and whatever organisms depend on them are gone forever.

But haven't we saved a lot of old-growth in national parks and wilderness areas? Unfortunately not. Reserves where logging is prohibited are mostly rock, ice, desert, or noncommercial forest. Productive timberlands were usually excluded when boundaries were set. National parks are often confused with the much larger national forests that surround them. National forests did function as preserves for half a century, but when private timberlands were exhausted in the 1940s the national forests were attacked with vigor. Today they are managed primarily for timber production. However, the Forest Service is very good at public relations (witness Smokey the Bear). Since the 1960s the agency has left thin screens of trees along major highways—like stage sets or Potemkin villages—to give motorists the illusion of driving through primeval forest. But step off the road for a stroll in the woods and you are surrounded by stumps and rusting logging cables.

As I write this, environmental groups are engaged in a last-ditch battle to save as much of the remaining old-growth as possible. Daring activists are dangling from ropes high in the treetops or chaining themselves to trunks in a desperate attempt to forestall the loggers and convince Congress to protect what little is left. There are no really big chunks; it is all bits and pieces.

It is clear that western forests will supply a declining fraction of our wood. In 1970, they held almost 90 percent of the country's standing softwood sawtimber. Now only 75 percent is in the West, partly because old growth is disappearing and partly because the pine forests of the South have come back after generations of abuse. It is also clear that the annual cut from western forests will have to be reduced. It will have to be reduced substantially if we want to save what little virgin forest remains and if we want to manage the rest in a genuinely sustainable way that does not diminish fish, wildlife, water quality, biodiversity, or other resources.

What about conservation? We do consume an astounding amount of wood: two and a half cubic meters (3.3 cubic yards) per person, per year—a ton and a half for every American. Half of that is lumber, the most critical use because it requires quality wood and mature trees (you can not make 12-inch boards out of 10-inch trees). Most lumber goes for housing. We could use more substitute materials, but they have many drawbacks (expensive, not renewable, take a lot of energy to manufacture, hard to work, poor insulators, unsafe in earthquakes, toxic, ugly, and so on). A much simpler way to reduce per capita lumber consumption is to have a stable population. Lumber is not consumed in the usual sense, since buildings do not wear out. A well-maintained wooden house can last for centuries. But a growing population means that new housing is constantly needed just to maintain the status quo. More subtly, it means that many buildings are razed unnecessarily, long before their time. In a growing city, rising land values mandate that buildings be replaced with higher-density structures. The condition of the buildings does not matter; even the finest structures are destroyed. But in a city with a stable population, buildings last much longer and there is much less waste. Indeed, one can usually reconstruct the population history of a place just by looking at its architecture. Curiously, western cities and towns that were stable or lost populaton in the past are among the most prosperous and desirable today because they have retained the ambience of fine old buildings (Portland, San Francisco, Santa Fe, Aspen, and Telluride, to name some well-known examples).

More than a quarter of our wood is pulped for paper and cardboard. Much of that is undeniably wasted, since paper makes up 40 percent of the mass in our landfills.[5] Newspapers and magazines are two-thirds advertisements. If we could finance them some other way, we might reduce paper consumption significantly—but how can we do that without making reading matter prohibitively expensive? An easier target is overpackaging, especially the absurd American habit of giving out paper bags with every purchase. Recycling should also be stepped up, of course. But even if we slashed paper consumption in half, we could not be self-sufficient and maintain healthy forests, given our present population. Nor would paper conservation necessarily help the lumber shortage.

A fifth of our wood is burned as fuel, for heat and some electricity. A generation ago, use of fuelwood was almost negligible, but since the oil crises of the 1970s it has jumped six-fold. We now burn almost as much wood as we did at the turn of the century, when wood and coal supplied nearly all of our energy. Per person, we burn only a quarter as much, but the population is so much bigger that total consumption is back at historical levels. Even so, wood supplies only a tiny fraction of the nation's energy.

Most fuelwood comes from logging culls, mill waste, thinning projects, and noncommercial forest. Supply is not yet a problem, although firewood cutting has decimated rare mesquite bosques and some ancient juniper/pinyon stands in the Southwest. But commercial energy projects using forest biomass would run into supply problems and conflicts with other uses. Today the limiting factor on wood fuel seems to be air pollution. Many western towns have had to restrict wood stoves because of severe winter pollution problems.

Wood is one of our few genuinely renewable raw materials. As petroleum runs out, wood could supply more of our needs, as it did in the past. But it certainly cannot do so with our present population, much less an expanding one. Nor can we expect Canada to supply us with unlimited wood, since the Canadians are becoming increasingly concerned about the destruction of their own forests.

Water

Humans use far more water than all other resources combined, except air. Water is the lifeblood of the West, the limiting factor for almost every activity. Land without access to water is virtually worthless. Western history is filled with political and legal battles, and even shooting wars over water.

Since the turn of the century, the federal government has been subsidizing massive water projects in the West, with the express purpose of increasing population—agricultural population at first, later urban populations as well. Water development has followed a familiar pattern. First, population grows where there is a good natural supply. Eventually population growth outstrips the supply, but by then the place has enough political and economic clout to import water from afar. The infusion of new water stimulates rapid new growth as worthless land becomes valuable overnight. In two or three decades, population growth again precipitates a crisis, and another heroic project is conceived to bring water from still more distant sources. In some areas this vicious circle has repeated itself several times. Many western politicians have built their entire careers around water.

Modern water engineering was invented in the West, where the world's first big dams were built. Aqueducts hundreds of kilometers long carry water across deserts and mountains. Vast quantities of energy are consumed to pump water out of the ground and over mountains. But the limits are being reached. Virtually every river has been dammed. Some are little more than a chain of reservoirs, stretching for hundreds of kilometers (like the Columbia and lower Colorado). Others have been literally sucked dry (like the Owens in California, the Gila and Santa Cruz in Arizona, and the Arkansas). The once mighty Colorado, which carved the Grand Canyon and drains a fifth of the West, no longer reaches the sea. On a typical day, every drop is diverted for human use before it reaches the Gulf of California. Indeed, the Colorado is over-subscribed. Because hydrologists overestimated its flow, more water was allocated in law than exists in the river.

A quarter of the West's supply is groundwater, much of which is nonrenewable, or "fossil" water, stored during the Ice Age when the climate was wetter. In many places, groundwater is being "mined"—pumped much faster than nature can recharge it. In southern Arizona, for example, water tables are dropping one to two meters (3 to 7 feet) a year.[6]

The combination of diverted rivers and falling water tables is drying up the wetlands even where they are not being deliberately drained for agriculture. This was prime waterfowl and wildlife habitat, but the wildlife populations are crashing.

In recent years, water quality has proved to be as serious a problem as water quantity. Western surface and ground waters are being polluted by a variety of nonpoint sources: heavy metals leached from old mine tunnels and tailings; logging sediments; sediments and nutrients from livestock grazing; nutrients and pesticides from agriculture; and oils, metals, and solvents in the cities. But paradoxically, the most widespread cause of water pollution seems to be water development itself. Salts are concentrated when water evaporates from reservoirs, canals, and ir-rigated fields and can reach toxic levels. Irrigation also leaches salts from the ground. Most irrigated land in the West is underlain by sediments with high concentrations of toxic salts, left when ancient seas and Ice Age lakes dried up. Long-term irrigation dissolves out these salts, which either percolate down and contaminate the groundwater or are carried off by field drains and end up in a river or in the sump lakes and marshes that occupy many of the closed basins in the West. Most of these lakes and marshes are wildlife refuges, critical habitat for migratory birds and endangered fish, but they are rapidly becoming cesspools of poison. Of greatest concern is selenium, which deforms and kills fish and water-fowl at very low concentrations and may be passed up the food chain to humans. In California's Kesterson National Wildlife Refuge, selenium poisoning has caused the greatest incidence of wildlife deformity ever recorded. Similar disasters are occurring in at least three other refuges, and high levels of selenium have been discovered in dozens of other refuges throughout the west, all associated with large irrigation projects.

A related problem is salinity in irrigation water, which can stunt or even kill crops if concentrations are high enough. Salinity is an acute problem in the Colorado River and in California's rich San Joaquin Valley.

Ninety per cent of the West's developed water is used for irrigation. Western farms tend to be very large and productive. They also tend to be very profitable, thanks to numerous subsidies—cheap water, cheap power to pump the water, and price supports. Yet only 11 percent of the West is farmed, since there is far too little water to irrigate it all. In many areas, further population growth can only occur at the expense of farming. "Water ranching"—buying up distant farms and abandoning them for the water rights—is increasingly popular. Since the 1930s, thousands of square kilometers of productive farmland have been abandoned to tumbleweed and sagebrush as the water has been carried off to distant cities. Owens Lake, one of the largest and most picturesque lakes in California, has been reduced to a salt flat—the victim of population growth in Los Angeles. Mono Lake, equally large and beautiful, is now meeting the same fate. Current efforts by Phoenix, Denver, and Las Vegas to secure distant water rights are precipitating bitter struggles between urban and rural communities. Cities do not waste water; they use much less, for a given area of land, than farming. And cities as well as farms in the arid West are making strenuous efforts to conserve water and recycle sewage effluent. In Tucson, Arizona, per capita use has declined sharply as lawns and shade trees have given way to cactus and rock gardens. But population growth inevitably wipes out any conservation gains.

Many western dams were built for hydroelectric power, not for water supply. In fact, excessive damming reduces water yield because so much is evaporated from the surface of the reservoirs. For example, Utah's Lake Powell wastes enough water by evaporation to supply a million people. Yet the reservoir supplies no water; its only function is to generate power to finance other water projects. And in the process, it has destroyed Glen Canyon, one of the world's most beautiful canyons.

Dams produce half the West's electricity, almost an exajoule per year, although they pale in comparison to the total U.S. energy consumption of 90 exajoules. If the West had twenty million people (as it did in 1950), it could presumably generate all of its electricity with existing dams. Hydropower is clean and renewable, at least until the reservoirs silt up, but that can take centuries. Theoretically, we could double western hydropower, but it would mean the utter destruction of remaining rivers and would further reduce the water supply because of evaporation. The best sites have long since been dammed. There were plans at one time to dam the Grand Canyon at both ends and divert the rest of the river through a tunnel, but an outraged public quashed the idea. A battle is now raging to reduce generation at Glen Canyon Dam (at the head of the Grand Canyon) because the fluctuating flows are devastating the park's beaches and fish. Fish, incidentally, are the most endangered class of native animals in the West, thanks to massive water engineering.

Proposals have been made to transport water from the Columbia River (the only drainage with a significant surplus) or even from the Yukon in Canada. While technically possible, these projects would be astronomically expensive and would require equally astronomical amounts of energy to pump the water over mountains. They would also be enormously destructive of the natural environment. And to get the Yukon water we would probably have to conquer Canada. Desalinization of seawater is another possibility, but, again, expense and energy are limiting factors.

Grazing

Almost all of the land in the West that can possibly support a cow or a sheep and is not otherwise developed is used for commercial grazing. Even wilderness areas, wildlife refuges, military reservations, and some national parks are open to commercial grazing. Yet western rangelands produce an almost insignificant fraction of our meat. The public lands (the bulk of the range) grow less than 2 percent of the nation's beef. Their main function is producing calves, although only a tenth of the country's cattle are born there.[7]

Most of our beef is grown in the East, on irrigated pasture, or in feedlots. Although beef consumption per capita has declined, we are no longer self-sufficient, consuming 3 percent more than we produce. In fact, the United States is the world's largest net importer of beef. Again, it is instructive to compare Canada, which has the same beef-eating habits we do and much less pasture land. Canada is a net exporter, simply because it has a tenth as many mouths to feed.

Despite the cowboy mythology ingrained in our culture, the western range is not a very good place to raise livestock. Forage is produced at a slow rate. Animals can only be grazed part of the year. In drier regions it may take a square kilometer (about 250 acres) to support a single cow (compared to 500 cows per square kilometer [two per acre] in Missouri). All the public lands—half the West—support only 30,000 ranchers. For most of them ranching is a part-time occupation, pursued more as a lifestyle than as a livelihood. Although public lands ranchers are heavily subsidized, paying grazing fees far below market value, ranching is not a lucrative business for most of them.

A century of commercial grazing has taken a heavy toll on the land. Large cattle-like animals are not native to most of the West, so the vegetation is not adapted to them. Bison (buffalo) were mainly a plains animal and generally did not range west of the Rockies. The BLM estimates that 68 percent of its rangeland is in "unsatisfactory" condition ("poor" or "fair"). Only 2 percent is rated in "excellent" condition.[8] The virgin steppes of a century ago supported far more livestock than they do today. In an effort to increase grass and water for livestock, thousands of square miles of juniper/pinyon woodland have also been deforested.

Commercial grazing competes directly with wildlife. At the behest of ranchers, the government spends millions of dollars a year to poison and trap wildlife deemed a threat to livestock. Grizzly bears, wolves, and jaguars have been all but eliminated. Ranchers generally oppose attempts to reintroduce native carnivores or to build up herds of native herbivores. In my own county, for example, a rancher was recently convicted of slaughtering a large number of elk, out of fear that his grazing allotment would be reduced if elk numbers grew. Drinking water, not forage, is often the limiting factor for livestock, as well as for wildlife. While wells and catchment basins developed for livestock can benefit wildlife, livestock have a serious impact on riparian (streamside) environments. In the arid West, riparian habitat is of critical importance, harboring most of the rare and endangered species of plants, fish, and wildlife.

One might argue that grazing is the best use for land with no other commercial value. Growing cattle feed is certainly an inefficient use of prime eastern farmland, which might better be employed growing human food for a hungry world. With careful management, western rangelands could probably support some commercial grazing without diminishing other resources. But current livestock numbers will certainly have to be reduced, and the rangelands—the least productive lands in the West— will never support significant numbers of people.

Amenities

For many people, the West's most valuable resources are open space, natural beauty, wildlife, and the physical freedom offered by the public lands. This is not just a value judgment; tourism is the biggest industry in many western states. Chambers of commerce invariably list the natural environment as a major asset. But amenities and freedoms diminish in direct relation to the number of people trying to enjoy them. It is clear, for example, that most national park visitors today are cheated of the natural experience they presumably seek. They spend most of their time jostled by crowds, fighting traffic, or struggling to find a place to stay. It has become fashionable to blame the problem on cars, but shuttlebuses, bicycle paths, raftable rivers, and foot trails are often crowded, too. It is hard to escape the conclusion (though managers try) that there are just too many people in the parks. Nor is the problem much better in national forest campgrounds. Even the open desert is becoming crowded. In the winter months, tens of thousands of sun-seeking retirees from colder states camp on the public lands of the Southwest. Whole cities of trailers and motor homes spring up, stretching as far as the eye can see across the fragile desert plains. It is still easy to car-camp in solitude, at least if you do not mind cowburnt rangeland or cutover forest. But overuse—too many people—is certainly the number-one problem threatening the natural areas of the West.

Earlier in this century, human activity had decimated most large native animals. Several were on the verge of extinction. Since then wildlife agencies have brought many of them back, at great expense and with much artificial manipulation. But would-be hunters and fishers outnumber the game and fish, so increasingly complex restrictions are necessary. On many streams, fish must be released after they are caught. Hunting permits are often rationed, using lotteries and auctions. In my own state of Arizona, a hunter recently paid $60,000 for a permit to shoot a bighorn. He missed.

The greatest freedom of all is found in wilderness—a place to experience the world without being manipulated by other humans. The idea of preserving land in its natural state is an American invention that author Wallace Stegner has rightly called "the best idea we ever had." It is an idea that has been admired and copied by more than 120 nations around the world. The modern wilderness movement, which culminated in the landmark 1964 Wilderness Act, began in the 1920s after the national parks had been opened to automobiles and the national forests were earmarked for logging. Its aim was to keep small parts of the country free of the sights and sounds of humans and their machines—places big enough to assure solitude and absorb a two-week trip on horse or foot. But wilderness is rapidly disappearing as logging, grazing, mining, oil and gas development, off-highway vehicles, resort development and urbanization saturate the land with roads. Only 4 percent of the West is protected as designated Wilderness.[9] At this writing, another 9 pecent or so survives as de facto wilderness. Environmental organizations are engaged in prolonged political battles to save as much of it as they can. They will not be able to save it all, since competition for other uses is intense.

Few wilderness areas remain that are big enough for a two-week trip. There are so many people and so little wilderness that visits are often rationed with computerized permits. It is ironic that wilderness, which survives mainly because no one wanted it in the past, is the only place where the government has tried to determine an optimum population and enforce it with fines. In some areas you must reserve space months in advance. To raft some rivers you must apply years in advance. Because of overuse, onerous restrictions have become necessary. Campfires are often prohibited. Lakes and streams are often polluted. Solitude is difficult to find. And it is almost impossible to escape the noise of aircraft. Many wilderness areas, national parks, and wildlife refuges have been designated Military Operating Areas (MOAs), used for aerial war games. Others are deluged by tourist planes, helicopters, and commercial jets. It might be honest to say that there is no real wilderness left in the West, as the authors of the Wilderness Act envisioned the concept.

It is important to distinguish sustainable population from optimum population. Optimum population is reached when adding more people does not improve the quality of life. Of course, what one regards as optimum population density depends on one's background, age, and many other personal factors. Residents of Wyoming, our least populous state, like to say that "Wyoming has more antelope than people, and that's the way it should be." On the other hand, many people are content to spend their entire lives in teeming cities. So I suggest that an optimum population would offer the greatest freedom of choice, the greatest diversity of experiences. It is clear that the West has long since passed that point. There is no shortage of high-density experiences, but low-density experiences are increasingly at a premium. The Rural Renaissance that began in the late 1960s is hard evidence that we have passed what people regard as the optimum population. For the first time in history, the flow of people from rural to metropolitan areas reversed. Western cities are still growing rapidly, partly by natural increase and partly by immigration from other regions or countries. But at the same time, waves of urban refugees are filling up the hinterlands.

I should point out that the energy schemes discussed in other chapters in this volume—coal, natural gas, oil shale, nuclear, direct solar, wind, and biomass—would all have devastating effects on the natural environment of the West. Vast expanses of land would have to be sacrificed. We saw a small example of this devastation during the Rocky Mountain energy boom of the late 1970s and early 1980s. Other areas will be affected as well. For example, tapping our uranium reserves will wreak havoc on the scenic Colorado Plateau. Grand Canyon National Park is already ringed by thousands of uranium claims, waiting for the price to rise. In the fragile western environment, where the tracks of a single vehicle can last a generation, the scars left by mining usually last forever. And renewable energy sources can destroy even more land than mining because the energy density is so low. For example, the wind farms in California's San Gorgonio Pass have blighted San Jacinto Peak, one of the most dramatic mountainscapes in the nation, while generating only a minuscule fraction of our energy.

Conclusion

In the American West, the limiting factors for sustainable population are water (both quantity and quality), altitude and topography, and energy. The fifty million people now in the West certainly exceed these limits. But sustainable population is not the same as optimum population. Optimum population allows the highest quality of life, provides the greatest diversity of experiences, and permits the greatest freedom of living styles. Optimum population for the West has also long since been exceeded, perhaps by a factor of two or three. Forests, rivers, grasslands, wildlife, scenic beauty, quiet, solitude, and freedom have been drastically diminished by the impact of too many people.

10

THE MOST OVERPOPULATED NATION

PAUL R. AND ANNE H. EHRLICH

Demographers in recent years have focused most of their attention on the third world, on the assumption that that is where the population problem is most intense. A broader perspective would suggest that the impact of humankind on the Earth's biosphere is a product of sheer numbers and our consumption habits. Perhaps demographers should look homeward.

Those of us who deal with population issues all the time are frequently confronted by people who believe the population problem belongs to someone else. It traces, in their view, to poor Indians who do not understand how to use condoms, or to Mexican peasants who invade our country to steal our jobs, or to the Catholic hierarchy, which persists in its irrational opposition to the use of effective birth control methods. But Indian peasants mostly *want* the children they have; they know how to use condoms. And at the moment Mexican immigration is probably a net benefit for the United States, although in the middle term it could become a disaster. And relatively few Catholics pay attention to the Vatican's position. After all, Italy has the smallest family sizes in the world!

The view that overpopulation is not our problem just does not wash. Yes, poor nations have serious population problems, but in many respects rich nations have worse ones. Nothing recently has made the degree of overpopulation in the United States more obvious than George Bush's confrontation with Iraq. If the United States had stabilized its population in 1943, when it was in the process of winning the largest land war in history, today it would just have 135 million people. Assume that per capita energy consumption nevertheless had grown to today's level; that is, our smaller population was still using sloppy technologies: gas-guzzling automobiles, inefficient light bulbs and pumps, poorly insulated buildings, and so on. Even if its citizens were just as profligate users of energy as we are, the 135 million Americans could satisfy their energy appetite *without burning one drop of imported oil or one ounce of coal.*[1]

Of course, if we had been smart, we also would have become energy efficient and would have made a transition to some form of solar-hydrogen economy. It has been estimated that an energy-efficient U.S. could have the goods now supplied by energy use at an expenditure of about one third the energy now employed. For the environmental health of the globe as a whole, and for that of the United States itself, a drastic reduction in the use of energy technologies that place greenhouse-enhancing carbon dioxide into the atmosphere is clearly mandatory.

$I = P A T$

The impact of a population on the environment can be roughly viewed as the product of three factors: the size of the population (P); the level of per capita consumption, or affluence (A); and the measure of the impact of the technology (T) used to supply each unit of consumption. This provides the shorthand equation $I = P \times A \times T$, which, although oversimplified (because the three factors P, A, and T are not independent), provides a basis for comparing the responsibility of different nations or groups for environmental deterioration.

Using the $I = P A T$ equation, one can see that the population problem in the United States is the most serious in the world. First of all, the P factor is huge: With 251 million people, the United States is the fourth largest nation in the world. And compared with other large nations, the A and T factors (which, when multiplied together yield percapita environmental impact) are also huge—their product being on the order of one-and-a-half times that of the Soviet Union; twice that of Britain, Sweden, France, or Australia; fourteen times that of China; forty times that of India; and almost three hundred times that of a Laotian or Ugandan. In percapita energy use, only Luxembourg, Canada, and a few oil-producing nations in the Middle East, such as Qatar and Bahrain, are in our league, and all those nations have comparatively tiny populations. When the population multiplier is considered, the *total* impact of the United States becomes gigantic, several hundred times that of Bangladesh.

Those multipliers are based on percapita commercial energy consumption, which is the best surrogate for $A \times T$ that is readily found in government statistics. The contributions of very poor countries to environmental deterioration are underestimated by these statistics, since they do not include the impacts of use of "traditional" energy sources (fuelwood, dung, crop wastes), which comprise 12 percent of energy use globally but a much larger component in poor countries. Including those sources would not change the U.S. position as the planet's primary environmental destroyer, though.

That preeminence makes sense intuitively, too. Few Laotians drive air-conditioned cars, read newspapers that transform large tracts of forest into overflowing landfills, fly in jet aircraft, eat fast-food hamburgers, or own refrigerators, several TVs, a VCR, or piles of plastic junk. But millions upon millions of Americans do. And in the process they burn roughly a quarter of the world's fossil fuels, contributing carbon dioxide and many other undesirable combustion products to the atmosphere, and are major users of chlorofluorocarbons, chemicals that both add to the greenhouse effect and attack Earth's vital ozone shield.

We have destroyed most of America's forest cover (replacing a small fraction of it with biologically impoverished tree farms) and are busily trying to log the last of the old-growth forests in the Northwest, threatening the long-term prosperity of the timber industry, in part to service the junk bonds of rich easterners. The western United States is one of the largest desertified areas on the planet due to overgrazing by cattle and sheep—not because we need the meat (only a small portion of our beef comes from the arid West) but because of the political power of ranchers in the western states and a nostalgic view of western history. And Americans have contributed mightily to the destruction of tropical forests by purchasing products ranging from beef to tropical hardwoods derived from the forests.

Furthermore, each additional American adds disproportionately to the nation's environmental impact. The metals used to support his or her life must be smelted from poorer ores at higher energy cost or transported from further away. The petroleum and water he or she consumes, on average, must come from more distant sources or from wells driven deeper. The wastes he or she produces must be carried further away, and so on. Activities that created little or no environmental burden when the United States had a small population, such as putting carbon dioxide into the atmosphere by burning fossil fuels, increase that burden with every additional individual when the population is large.

Consuming Our Capital

Basically, like most of the rest of the world, the United States has been consuming environmental capital—especially its deep, fertile soils, ice age groundwater, and biodiversity—and calling it growth. Furthermore, directly and by example, it has been helping other nations to do the same. It would not be remotely possible for Earth to support today's 5.4 billion people on humanity's "income" (which consists largely of solar energy) with present technologies and life-styles—even though for billions their life-style is living in misery, lacking an adequate diet, shelter, health care, education, and so on. And in the past decade the United States has retarded the worldwide movement towards population control because of the brain-dead policies of the Reagan and Bush administrations.

The key to civilization's survival is reduction of the scale of the human enterprise and thus of the impact of human society on our vital life-support systems. This can be achieved most rapidly by reducing all of the P, A, and T factors. In rich nations, this means immediate and rapid conversion to much more efficient use of energy and an immediate press toward population *shrinkage*. Fortunately, rich nations have the kind of age composition that makes the transition to negative population growth (NPG) a relatively simple matter; a few European countries have already achieved it.

The Holdren Scenario

The best overall strategy has been divised by John P. Holdren, professor of energy and resources at the University of California at Berkeley. The Holdren scenario shows how energy use per person could be adjusted over the next century without over-straining Earth's life-support systems.[2] As shown in the table, total worldwide rate of energy use today is almost 14 terawatts (tera $= 10^{12}$) produced by the combination of a relatively small population of rich people, each using a great deal of energy, and a huge population of poor people, each using relatively little energy. The essence of Holdren's scenario is that rich countries would become much more energy efficient, reducing their percapita use from almost 8 kilowatts to 3 kilowatts (this means a reduction in the United States to less than one third of current use, but this clearly is technically feasible, with no loss in quality of life). In poor countries, percapita use would increase from slightly more than 1 kilowatts to 3 kilowatts, so at the end of a century everyone would basically have the same standard of living (at least as measured by access to energy).

The Holdren Scenario for More Equitable Energy Use Worldwide

Year	(A) × Population (billions = 10^9 people)	(B) = Energy/Person (kilowatts = 10^3 watts)	(C) Total Energy Use (A × B) (terawatts = 10^{12} watts)
1990			
Rich	1.2	7.7	9.2
Poor	4.1	1.1	4.5
Total	5.3		13.7
2025			
Rich	1.4	3.9	5.4
Poor	6.8	2.2	15.0
Total	8.2		20.4
2100	10	3	30 (□ 2 × now)

If population shrinkage in rich countries and population control in poor countries limited the peak size of the human population to ten billion, the Holdren scenario would result in a total global energy use at a rate of about 30 terawatts. Whether or not that would be sustainable for even a short time would depend, among other things, on whether the poor countries repeated the mistakes of the rich countries in development or concentrated on using more environmentally benign energy technologies—in particular, some form of solar power and the use of hydrogen as a portable fuel. Our guess is that it might be possible to run a world temporarily on 30 terawatts, but to prevent long-term deterioration, it will be necessary to reduce population size substantially below ten billion. Indeed, the population eventually should be reduced to the vicinity of one or two billion with an aggregate energy use of, say, 5 to 7 terawatts, if the health of ecosystems is to be restored and a substantial safety margin provided.

The U.S. Role

A large part of the responsibility for solving the human dilemma rests on the rich countries, and especially on the United States. We are the archetype of a gigantic, overpopulated, overconsuming rich nation, one that many ill-informed decision makers in poor nations would like to emulate. Unless we demonstrate by example that we understand the horrible mistakes made on our way to overdevelopment and that we are intent on reversing them, there seems little hope for the persistence of civilization.

The first step, of course, is for the United States to adopt a population policy designed to halt population growth and begin a gradual population decline. Such steps can be taken without immediately targeting an eventual optimum population size, since that optimum is far below 251 million. With leadership at the top, say, a president who kept pointing out that patriotic Americans stopped at two children *maximum*, we could probably achieve NPG in the United States within a couple of decades.

Americans would also, of course, have to recognize that for every immigrant who arrives in the United States and is not balanced by an emigrant, a birth must be forgone. We can never have a sane immigration policy until we have a sane population policy. The ideal mix of births and immigrants is a difficult question that must be solved by public debate. Our own view is that immigration adds important variety to our population and permits the United States to give refuge to people who really need it. So our preference would be to maintain a reasonable level of immigration and compensate for it with fewer births. But many others would consider the small family sizes thus required too high a price to pay, or they simply do not like "foreigners" (or are outright racists) and would prefer much stricter limits on immigration. Throughout this debate, it must be kept in mind that from a global environmental perspective, immigration into the United States is not neutral. Immigrants from poor nations, often among the brightest and most ambitious members of their societies, are frequently very successful financially, and even the less well-off quickly acquire American superconsuming habits. They tend to bring with them the reproductive habits of their societies, moreover, so they also produce larger families of superconsumers than those of us whose families immigrated earlier. Thus, even though immigration to the United States does not produce a net increment to the global population.[3] it does produce a net increment in total environmental impact.

The immigration issue is extremely complex and ethically difficult,[4] but it must be faced. Equally daunting, after a decision on levels of immigration has been made, will be monitoring the flow and enforcing the quotas. Badly needed now is a wide-ranging discussion, first, of population policy and then of immigration within the context of that policy.

Optimum U.S. Population

Which brings us finally to the question of an optimum population for the United States. What can be said about it in light of the foregoing discussion? About the only thing that is certain is that the optimum will depend upon the scale of the A and T factors. And with a quality of life that more or less resembles today's or is superior to it, and with present or foreseeable technologies, the optimum would be far below the present population.

Calculating an optimum size for any human population today is no easy task. First of all, the optimum will depend on the standard of living of the average individual. A population of vegetarian Gandhis can be much larger than one made up of superconsuming Trumps. It also depends on the environmental impacts of the technologies used to support the life-style. An optimum population that uses light, highly fuel-efficient vehicles for personal transportation can be larger than one that drives gas-guzzlers. And one that uses commuter trains, buses, carpool vans, or even redesigns its cities to eliminate most commuting can be even bigger. On this interdependent globe, the optimum size depends as well on the population sizes, technologies, and life-styles adopted by other nations.

Of course, optimum population size depends upon the answer to the question: "How long will it be sustained?" With a Reaganesque program of consuming all natural resources for the exclusive benefit of people now alive, the optimum will cetainly be much higher than one that gives importance to the long-term maintenance of society.

Finally, optimum population depends upon the aggregate of life-style choices of individual citizens. A United States in which nearly every family wanted to live on at least a five-acre parcel of land would have a much lower optimum population size than one populated with people who loved crowded living in action-filled cities.

With all these caveats, we offer some personal opinions on an optimum population for the United States. No sensible reason has ever been given for having more than 135 million people. The putative reason for choosing that number is that the United States fought and won (with lots of help from others) the greatest war in history with that number of people. But there is no sign today—indeed, there was none during World War II—that brute numbers led to victory. The Germans and Japanese, with tiny populations compared to the total of the Allies, almost won the war—thanks to a combination of, on average, better military leadership, better weapons, better interior lines of communication, and, often, superior troops. The struggles of Germany with the Soviet Union and Japan with China highlighted these factors. Clearly, if the other Allies had not been involved, David would have mopped up Goliath in both cases. Today, of course, Israel puts permanently to rest the notion that a large population is essential for military power.

Our personal preference would be to design a nation with a maximum of life-style options. If forced to make an estimate of the optimum population size of the United States, we would guess around seventy-five million people. That was about the population size at the turn of the century, a time when the United States had enough people for big, industrial cities and enough wilderness and open space that people who wanted it could still find real solitude. With about that number, we believe, a permanently sustainable nation with a high quality of life could be designed—if it were embedded in a world that was similarly designed.

The critical point, though, is that views of an optimum are going to change as society and technology change and as we learn more about the environmental constraints within which society must operate. It is fun to make guesses now, but those guesses may be far from the consensus view of our society a century hence (when, for example, the concept of solitude may be well-nigh forgotten). Unless there is a disaster, it will probably take a century or more even to approach an optimum—plenty of time for research and discussion. It suffices today to say that for our huge, overpopulated, superconsuming, technologically sloppy nation, the optimum was passed long ago. And because of decades of destruction of natural capital, the optimum will surely be lower the second time we approach it, and lower still for every year we postpone the turnaround. For our own sakes, and that of humanity as a whole, a rapid move to NPG is essential.

THE CORNUCOPIAN FALLACIES

In a book devoted to "optimum population," some space should perhaps be given to rebutting the argument that humankind should not pursue an optimum, or that bigger is better, more or less forever.

This chapter is taken from a paper written before Herman Kahn's untimely death.[1] He headed the Hudson Institute and generated or assembled most of the argumentation presently used against any deliberate effort to influence population growth.

Julian Simon is my other adversary in this environmentalist's critique of "cornucopians," who do not believe in limits to growth. Dr. Simon was cited briefly in the preface to this book. He is Professor of Marketing in the College of Business Management, University of Maryland, and an adjunct scholar with the Heritage Foundation.

An intense if intermittent debate has been under way between environmentalists and "cornucopians." The environmentalists warn of threats to the ecosystem and to renewable resources, such as cropland and forests, caused by population growth and exploitative economic activities. The cornucopians say that population growth is good, not bad (Julian Simon), or that it will solve itself (Herman Kahn), that shortages are mythical or can be made good by technology and substitution, and generally that we can expect a glorious future.

The debate has strong political overtones. If things are going well, we don't need to do anything about them—a useful argument for laissez faire. If something is going wrong, the environmentalists usually want the government to do something about it. The debate thus gets mixed up in the current reaction against "petty government interference" and a generalized yearning to return to earlier, more permissive economic and political practices.

Although there are substantial differences between their views (as we shall see later in this chapter), both men are identified with a simple message of reassurance to a society that does not seem to want to be told about problems. The message is best exemplified in the title of the article in *Science* magazine that brought Simon to prominence: "Resources, Population, Environment: An Oversupply of False Bad News."[2]

For the employer seeking assurance of cheap labor or the businessman hoping for larger markets, it is comforting to be told that more immigration and population growth are good things. The idealist, eager to help hungry fellow humans and fearful that pleas for lower fertility are a cover for racism, is just as likely to be beguiled by the message, unless he or she has come to realize that laudable purposes sometimes conflict with each other.

One could hardly object to a couple of cornucopians urging people to be of good cheer and stout heart, were it not for the danger that they may convince some citizens and policy makers not to worry about some pressing problems that urgently need attention. The cornucopians' argumentation, however, is seriously flawed as a tool for identifying the real and important present trends.

There is an asymmetry in the nature of the arguments of the environmentalists and the cornucopians. The environmentalist—the proponent of corrective action—is (or should be) simply warning of consequences if trends or problems are ignored; he or she does not need to predict. The cornucopian, on the other hand, must predict to make his or her case. He must argue that problems will be solved and good things will happen if we let nature take its course. Since nobody has yet been able to predict the future, cornucopians are asking their listeners to take a lot on faith. They say, in effect, "Believe as I do, and you will feel better." Simon says explicitly that his conversion to his present viewpoint improved his state of mind.

The cornucopians have made assumptions and chosen methodologies that simply ignore or dismiss the most critical issues that have led the environmentalists to their concerns:

- The cornucopians pay little attention to causation and project past economic trends mechanically.
- They casually dismiss evidence that doesn't "fit."
- They employ a static analysis that makes no provision for feedback from one sector to another.
- They understate the implications of geometric growth.
- They base their predictions on an extraordinary faith in uninterrupted technological progress.

We will look into some of these cornucopian fallacies, the reasoning processes and omissions that characterize Simon's and Kahn's analyses.

Extrapolating Past Growth: The Wrong Methodology

Simon argues that the past is the best guide to the future. Perhaps, but much depends on what part of the past you look at. He devotes most of his effort to demonstrating in various ways that humankind's economic lot has improved in the past century or so, which is not an issue.

Simon bases much of his argument on an econometric study of past correlations between the number of children and economic growth.[3] This approach leaves unanswered the question: Which, if either, phenomenon caused the other one? The mathematics may simply obscure the commonsense proposition that family size grows in a period of prosperity.

That 1977 study presumably remains the basis for Simon's views, but his line of argumentation has shifted somewhat. He shows graphs of long-term trends in the prices of certain minerals and foodgrains to show price declines that suggest that things are getting better.

If one selects the right series (aluminum, for instance, but not lumber), the graphs can be made to show the desired downward curve. They reflect a long-term improvement in the efficiency of production, and to some extent they are a product of the fossil fuel era through which we have been passing, which has made energy very cheap. The graphs do not address the questions "The prices to whom? Expressed in what currency?"

They are not adjusted for the buying power of different groups, or the lack thereof. Perhaps more fundamentally, this line of argumentation addresses only one small aspect of the many implications of population growth that have been raised in preceding chapters of this book.

Kahn is more nimble polemically. He extrapolates mid-twentieth-century growth trends with a line of reasoning that comes very close to economic vitalism. His specialty is impressive graphic presentations of the future, but examination suggests there is more of the airbrush than of intellectual discipline in those graphs. In one of his major works, *The Next 200 Years*, he projects per capita "gross world product" at $20,000 in A.D. 2176, but one is uncertain whether these are constant dollars, current dollars, or imaginary ones. As best one can gather from the text, this projection is based on a freehand plot of logistic or "S-curves" (slow/fast/slow) of GNP growth for different categories of countries, drawn roughly from the U.S. and European experience.[4]

There are two problems with this method. First, analogy can be a dangerous process. To predict the future performance of the poor countries based upon the past performance of the rich countries may involve too loose an analogy to justify the faith put in it. The analogy assumes that the underlying factors are substantially similar. They are not. In contrast to Europe when it industrialized, poor countries today tend to have faster population growth rates, no colonies in which capital can be mobilized, lower incomes (probably), extreme foreign exchange problems, no technological lead over the rest of the world, and no empty new worlds to absorb their emigrants.

Second, and even more important, gross national product—or "gross world product"—is not tangible and exists only in people's minds. It has no life of its own. It is simply a way of giving a numerical abbreviation to a sum of economic activities. It is determined by underlying realities: the availability and quality of land, water, industrial raw materials, and energy; technological change; the impact of population change on production and consumption; the productivity of the suppporting ecosystems; labor productivity; and so on. However, Kahn simply projects GNP, without analyzing the forces that generate it.

Proof of past success is no assurance of future well-being, and the mechanical projection of economic curves is hardly a reliable guide to the future.

In general the human condition has been improving for a sustained period—at least it was doing so until the 1970s. Indeed, the scale of the growth is a new thing on Earth, and the very magnitude of the growth of population and of economic activity is the source of the issue. For the first time, population and economic activities have grown so sharply as to bring them into a new relationship with the scale of the Earth itself.

The hallmark of recent history has been this explosive growth, supported by and supporting an extraordinary burst of technological change and humankind's first intensive exploitation of fossil fuels. The central question for the future is not "Did it happen?" but rather: "Can such growth be sustained, or does it generate dynamics that will bring the era to an end? If the latter, what will the changes be, and what if anything should we be doing to forestall them or to shape them in beneficial directions?"

Ignoring Climate Change

As a single example, let us take the question of carbon dioxide in the atmosphere. It takes little imagination to recognize that CO_2-induced rainfall and temperature changes, rising sea levels, and perhaps the necessity to curtail fossil fuel use could influence future economic activities. The fact that human activity is changing the very chemical composition of the air we live in would seem adequate justification to bring the issue into any consideration of current trends affecting the well-being of our species.

A particular target of the cornucopians in the early 1980s was the *Global 2000 Report to the President*,[5] which was the most serious effort to date within the U.S. Government to relate resource, environmental, population, and economic issues to each other. "Global 2000" devoted fourteen pages to human-induced effects on the climate, focusing primarily on CO_2 but dealing with other issues as well. It concluded that agreed-upon climate projections are not currently possible to make, but it called attention to the problem: "The energy, food, water and forestry projections [in the report] all assume implicitly a continuation of the nearly ideal climate of the 1950s and 1960s. The scenarios are reported here to indicate the range of climatic change that should be analyzed in a study of this sort."[6]

Simon seems to have ignored the carbon dioxide issue.

Kahn discusses the problem along with other possible causes of a warming trend. He concedes that a warming trend might raise the level of the oceans but argues that "this would hardly mean the end of human society. Major shifts might be forced in agricultural areas and in coastal cities." He concludes: "It seems unlikely now that the carbon dioxide content will ever double unless mankind wants it to happen."[7] Thus, he cheerfully dismisses this problem and thereby illustrates the curious inversion of his logic.

Why does he dismiss substance for "prediction"? He dismisses the real issues for fear they would lead his readers to lose faith in the future he has promised them. Would he not better join the environmentalists and concentrate on telling his audience that, if they want that future, they may need to take the carbon dioxide problem seriously?

Which intellectual approach is the more valid way of attempting to understand current trends affecting human welfare? If you seek a sense of what will shape the future, examine the issues generated by population and economic growth; do not simply extrapolate the growth. Economic changes cannot be studied in a vacuum.

Doctoring the News

One cannot escape the feeling that some of the Simon/Kahn rebuttals of "bad news" are directed more by polemical ends than by an effort to get at the truth. Such casual hip-shots are more likely to generate doubts about the writer's credentials than to convince readers that bad news is false.

For example, Simon makes points by using gross totals rather than per capita figures. He sometimes shifts sources to manufacture trends. On world population, for example, to show that "U.N. and other standard estimates" have been steadily lowering their projections of anticipated population in 2000, he starts with a 1969 UN worst-case scenario, higher than their "high" series, then moves down to a later UN "low" series projection, and winds up with a 1977 Worldwatch Institute figure, justifying his inclusion of the Worldwatch figure by saying that Worldwatch is UN supported. Through these devices, he manages to show the projection declining from 7.5 billion to 5.4 billion. In fact, the UN projection for 2000 has remained remarkably constant, the median projection having fluctuated between 6.1 and 6.5 billion since 1957. And Lester Brown points out that his Worldwatch figure was not a projection but a proposed target.

Also, to prove that *world* air quality is improving, Simon, in *The Ultimate Resource*, cites statistics on U.S. air quality in the early 1970s.

His figures are dated and limited, but they are neverthelesss gratifying. He pays the environmentalists whom he excoriates the ultimate compliment of appropriating their work. If U.S. air quality has stabilized or improved in some ways since then, it is at least in some measure the product of environmental efforts like the Clean Air Act.

Kahn generally takes a subtler line. He, too, points to improvements in air quality, but he is quite willing to accept the need for some expenditures on air quality and other environmental measures, and he includes "possible damage to earth because of complicated, complex and subtle ecological and environmental effects" among eight "real issues of the future." In effect, his technique is to admit the possibility of environmental problems but to avoid focusing on them or attempting to measure their importance; he quickly moves on to extolling the brightness of the future and attacking those he deems pessimistic.

In short, the cornucopians slight the resource and environmental issues that the environmentalists consider the most important questions to be examined.

The Lack of Feedback

The cornucopians stand breathless on the edge of wonderful new expectations. Simon writes: "Energy. . . is the 'master resource'; energy is the key constraint on the availability of all other resources. Even so, our energy supply is non-finite. . ."[8]

He makes this remarkable claim just as the nation is discovering that the fossil fuel era is a passing phase and that petroleum, on which we principally rely, will go first. The U.S. Geological Survey estimates that exploitable U.S. resources are equal to about sixteen years' consumption, even at current rates of use (which, with a growing population, means diminishing use per capita).[9] There are serious environmental penalties to the use of fossil fuels, in any case. Coal is the most abundant remaining fossil fuel, but the most polluting.

Simon asserts that we will "dig deeper and pump faster" and find more oil. One wonders why the oil geologists hadn't thought of that, as U.S. production goes down and reserves decline. He expects oil to be derived from "coal, shale, tar sands and the like," without a word about the costs or the environmental implications. He expects oil substitutes from biomass; he does not consider the trade-offs with forestry or with an agriculture that is already pressing hard on its soil and water resources. He expects fission energy to become cheaper. (He thinks it "already costs less than coal or oil"; this will come as a surprise to the power industry.) Despite the sobering things we have learned about nuclear power since 1945, he entertains no doubts that this is a good thing. He looks forward to nuclear fusion.[10]

These expressions of faith (for they are only that) reflect a belief in infinite substitutability that Simon probably acquired from the academic economists. The assumption is not based on any systematic rationale, nor is it buttressed by any evidence other than the fact that the industrial world has been doing pretty well, so far. It is simply an assumption required by the economists to run their models. Biologists and ecologists have been trying, without success, to persuade the economists that the assumption is terribly dangerous in a finite world on which human economic activity is pressing ever more heavily. There are no practicable substitutes for clean air and water or a functioning ecological system. Energy itself can be dangerous, and the evidence (as distinct from one's hopes) suggests that it will become more expensive, rather than less, as Paul Werbos discusses in detail in Chapter 3.

Any projection for continued expansion in the use of energy must ask the questions: What are the implications of developing the energy for the environment and for resources, and what are the likely consequences of its use? The same question should be asked about projections calling for continuing expansion in the use of chemicals, or indeed of any physical resource. *Global 2000* undertook to carry out as much of this kind of interactive analysis as possible. Although it found that the state of current knowledge did not permit analysis to be carried very far, it undertook the examination of hundreds of such interactions.

The agricultural projections, for instance (themselves central to other major projections such as population and GNP) require certain assumptions about intensification of agriculture: a doubling or trebling of chemical fertilizer inputs (to a point where artifical introduction of nitrogen compounds into the biosphere will exceed the natural production), parallel increases in herbicides and pesticides, and reliance upon monocultures. These assumptions, in turn, generate questions concerning desertification, the conversion of forest and loss of forest cover, the effect of intensive agriculture on soil productivity, the impact of increased fertilizer application on watercourses and fisheries and perhaps on climate, and the risks associated with pesticides and monocultures—all of which affect the initial assumptions about agricultural productivity and GNP and population. The degree of confidence concerning different interrelationships is made clear, and reference is made to the technologies that can help forestall or mitigate the harmful interactions foreseen.[11]

There is nothing remotely approaching this sort of interactive analysis in the works of the cornucopians. Kahn simply projects economic growth assuming that the necessary inputs will be available and that environmental problems will be surmounted. Simon does not address these questions in any integrated fashion. I would argue that they are not even addressing the real issues.

The speed at which technology is changing, the demands for economic growth posed by population growth, and the effort to raise living standards in developing countries are combining to force change at an unprecedented rate, which makes the study of the future more important than ever. The principal purpose of future studies should be to look as far ahead as possible, to study the implications of current and projected activity, to see how different sectors and issues interrelate. This process is anything but static. It should be a continuing process of probing and testing the potential consequences of different activities and directions of growth, of identifying the issues that need attention and the potential directions for beneficial change.

It was the lack of and the need for this capability that *Global 2000* high-lighted. A follow-up study made specific recommendations for improving the capability within the U.S. Government. Simon and Kahn, standing aside and reassuring everybody that the future looks good, seem strangely irrelevant to this entire process.

The Infinite Earth Fallacy

Neither Kahn nor Simon sucessfully deals with the simple facts that the Earth is finite and that no physical growth can be indefinitely sustained. Three mathematical examples of the power of geometric growth should be illuminating (bear in mind, however, that they are not predictions):

- Even if the entire mass of the earth were petroleum, it would be exhausted in 342 years if pre-1973 rates of increase in consumption were maintained.[12]

- Assume that we have one million years' supply of something— anything with a fixed supply—at current rates of consumption. Then increase the rate by just 2 percent per year (very roughly the current world population growth rate). How long would the supply last? Answer: 501 years.

- At current growth rates, how long would it take for the world's human population to reach the absurdity of one person on each square meter of ice-free land? Answer: about 600 years.

These things will not happen. Resource use will not rise in a geometric curve until a resource is exhausted, then plunge suddenly to zero. There will be changes in real prices, adjustments, and substitutions—the whole pattern of constantly shifting realities that makes prediction impossible. The population will never remotely approach such a level. Long before then, birth rates will fall sharply, death rates will rise, or both will happen.

However, the examples dramatize that the outer limits to current growth patterns are not so very far away. Indefinitely sustained growth is mathematically impossible on a finite earth. Populations have exceeded the carrying capacity of local environments many times and have sometimes paid the price of a population collapse, but human geometry for the first time requires that we think in terms of the relationship of population and economic activities to the entire Earth. World population has risen from about one billion to about over five billion in about six generations. The demand for resources and the environmental impacts have been more than proportional, because per capita consumption has also risen. This is not a mathematical fantasy or a projection for the future. It is a description of current reality. Kahn and Simon offer several responses to this point, none of them satisfactory.

- They fudge the problem by shifting the calculations. They project the potential longevity of the supply of raw materials based on current demand rather than on increasing demand.[13] Since they are also assuming rising populations and rising per capita consumption, this is not an argument—it is a moonbeam. The calculations above should have disposed of it permanently. A more sophisticated variant is to say that GNP will rise, but not resource consumption, because we will be more efficient and we will be consuming more intangibles, such as culture. This is very likely, within limits. However, nobody has yet drawn a model of sustained growth relying upon the consumption of operas to feed the multitudes.

- They suggest that the problem is so far away as to be irrelevant to those living now. Simon, in a bit of sophistry that he has probably come to regret by now, says: "The length of a one-inch line is finite in the sense that it is bounded at both ends. But the line within the end points contains an infinite number of points . . . [T]herefore the number of points in that one-inch segment is not finite." He then extends the analogy to copper and oil. He argues that we cannot know the size of the resource "or its economic equivalent," and concludes: "Hence, resources are not 'finite' in any meaningful sense."[14] This kind of argument is really pretty shocking. An inch of string is finite, even if it can theoretically be cut into infinitesimal pieces. The Earth is finite, even though we may differ endlessly about how much of a given resource may be available.

• Kahn says that population and consumption levels will stabilize in two centuries. He projects population stabilization at fifteen billion but allows himself a margin of error of two—that is, the population may be somewhere between 7.5 and 30 billion. Most of us suspect that population will stop growing *somewhere* within that range. He does not attempt to explore whether the resource base would support the fifteen billion population he posits, or what the ecological and environmental effects of such population and consumption levels would be; he simply announces that we can handle them. He thinks that prosperity will lead to lower fertility, but he does not ask whether the population growth itself will in some countries preclude the prosperity he expects. He offers no capital/output analysis to suggest how world consumption levels will progress from where they are to where he hopes they will be. In short, he states a dream without attempting to explore how it will be realized or what the effects of its achievement will be.

• Simon says different things at different times. Sometimes he advocates population growth without limits of time or circumstance, and he speaks of resource availability and population growth "forever," without recognizing the crudest of barriers: lack of space. Elsewhere he advocates "moderate" population growth. Still elsewhere he urges that we not worry about the effects of geometric population growth, since it has never been sustained in the past, and he documents his remark with graphs showing that population growth has periodically been reversed by pestilence, invasion, and famine. Is this the man who professes such warm feelings toward his fellow humans?

Most environmentalists agree that population growth will eventually stop, if only through the operation of the Four Horsemen. The hope is that it will be stabilized by limiting fertility rather than through hunger and rising mortality. It is this goal that leads many environmentalist to advocate conscious efforts to limit fertility. Kahn thinks that fertility will be limited automatically, but he does not show how. Simon, apparently, is not dismayed by the alternative.

Technology as a Faith

Technology is knowledge. It is very difficult to predict increases in knowledge; technological trends are among the least predictable of the forces that will shape our future. The cornucopians are justified in reminding us forcefully of the effects of technology. A lot of people from Malthus on have underestimated it, and some environmentalists still ignore it.

Let us agree on one point: The world has been experiencing a burst of remarkable technological growth.

Although Kahn and Simon seem to have missed this point, *Global 2000* assumes that this rate will continue to the end of the century. This approach may be faulted as too sanguine, but it is perhaps the safest projection, given the relatively short time frame. From this modest projection, however, we move to an article of faith among the cornucopians that the more pragmatic among us do not share—that the recent high rate of technological growth will continue *indefinitely*. Simon's advice to use the past as a guide argues against too much faith: Human history has been characterized by spurts of technological growth alternating with periods of slow growth, dormancy, or retrogression. Technology may continue its recent phenomenal growth, but it is an act of faith to assume that it will.

In addition, technology is not necessarily benign. It shapes us as we shape it. Right now, while it may be making communications cheaper, it makes unemployment worse. It helped to generate the spurt in population growth that now concerns the environmentalists. New industrial and agricultural technologies have created many of our present environmental problems. Other technologies will almost certainly help us to correct our mistakes, but a sensible observer with a feeling for history would be justified in assuming that those solutions will in turn generate new problems to be addressed.

If one chooses *not* to stake human welfare on unsupported faith in technology, a certain caution is in order. Humankind will not have suffered if population growth is less than the advance of technology makes possible, but it may suffer very seriously if hopes for technology prove too high and if populations outrun the ability of science to support them.

No Limits to Debating

If this article reflects a jaundiced view of the cornucopians' methods, it is not meant to discourage the debate. We can learn from each other.

We are all—cornucopians and environmentalists alike—trying to understand and describe a world in vast change. The technological growth on which the cornucopians pin their hopes is itself part of that change, as are the population growth and the environmental by-products of technological growth that concern the environmentalists.

We are all—except for a few nuts who enjoy human misery—interested in seeing the modern improvement in human welfare continue.

Cornucopians by their nature tend to emphasize *solutions* where environmentalists emphasize *problems*. An interchange can be useful. Do the environmentalists overstate difficulties and fail to recognize new directions that can be helpful? Have we explored the opportunities presented by the oceans, by recent breakthroughs in biology, and by electronics and data processing as thoroughly as we have explored the dangers from desertification, deforestation, and acid rain? Have we pressed for the elimination of legal and administrative impediments to benefical change as eagerly as we have pressed for restrictive legislation?

If we urge the cornucopians to recognize the problems, we should share their interest in promoting technological change that will help to address the problems.

Those of both persuasions should remember that this is no single battle at Armageddon. Solutions will create their own problems, and problems their solutions. Everyone should recognize that only change is constant. And change right now is very fast.

We would ask of the cornucopians that they accept as much. Growth such as we have witnessed cannot be indefinitely extended. We must all seek a sustainable relationship between people and the Earth. Most particularly, we must work out the implications of population growth. The issue cannot be "should it stop?" The questions are, when should it stop, and how?

12

TOO MANY OLD PEOPLE?

The Dependency Ratio

On a more down-to-earth and visceral level, it has been argued that more young people are needed to take care of the growing number of old people in the United States. Proponents of that argument do not look at the demographic consequences, but all those young people, of course, would mean accelerated population growth. Aside from that unmentioned consequence, the argument itself is highly questionable.

The aged are not the only dependents. Children make demands upon society that may be higher than those made by the old. To make a somewhat imprecise comparison: Total school expenditures (excluding kindergartens, nurseries, and creches) in 1986 were estimated at $270 billion—spent overwhelmingly, of course, on the young. This is 66 percent more than total Social Security payments to the aged in that year, and it is almost identical with the estimate of total federal benefits to the aged that year, including their share of Social Security, Medicare, Medicaid, all federal military and civilian retirement programs, food stamps and subsidized housing. Beyond these statistics, there is another point to be made for the old: By and large, they are living on their savings, while the support of the young is a direct charge on parents and society.

There are about twice as many young people (depending upon how you define young) as old ones, and the cost of rearing them is a major element of the economy. An Urban Institute study suggests that, in 1981 dollars and depending upon the education provided and whether the mother was working, it cost roughly $75,000 to $125,000 to raise a child. With seventy million children that year, this translated very roughly into something like 10 to 16 percent of GNP. A maturing population will mitigate these costs, as it increases the expenditures by and for the old.

As a first step, we should compare the total working-age population with the total population of the young and the old—a comparison somewhat loosely called the dependency ratio. The proportion of the population in the working ages has been rising and, barring another baby boom, it will continue to rise for another generation. The working-age population, defined rather arbitrarily as fifteen to sixty-four year olds (a convention popular with demographers), has constituted the following percentage of the total population in recent decades:

1940	65 percent
1950	65 percent
1960	61 percent
1970	62 percent
1980	66 percent
1985	66 percent

If fertility stays about as it is now, that proportion is expected to rise to 69 percent by 2010 and then begin to decline to 63 percent in 2025.

The point is that the dependency ratio has moved down and up, without any clear correlation with economic well-being. One might take comfort in the fact that the nation faces a long period with an improving ratio. In a stable population, by the way (with low mortality and after the demographic wobbles had been sorted out), about 61 percent of the population would be fifteen to sixty-four.

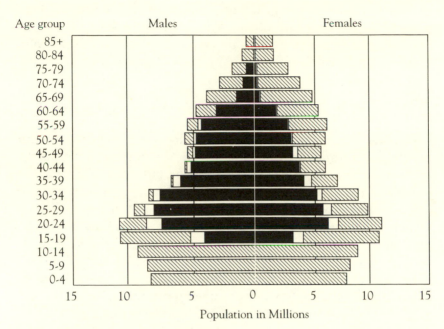

Population, labor force, and employment.

The Trouble with That Ratio

Such an analysis offers a rather simple version of the world, in which those of working age are supporting those who are not. A look at the above figure should make clear that it is not that simple.

The people in the central black area are working. Those in the white stubs are unemployed—and unemployment compensation totals more than $20 billion each year. At the gray ends of the bars are other dependents: students, discouraged workers no longer looking for work, the idle rich, housewives, retirees and family members and widows or widowers of those on retirement programs. Some of them are on aid to families with dependent children (AFDC), which costs the nation $16 billion per year. There are disabled workers receiving, in total, $55 billion per year.

The real proportion of working to non-working is much lower than the "dependency ratio" would suggest. At present, about 45 percent of the total population works. This is the true measure of dependency. Every worker supports about 1.2 non-workers. If indeed we need more workers, there are ways of improving the ratio. Bring unemployment down. Find ways of bringing labor and jobs together. Improve job safety. Find ways of enlisting discouraged workers. Encourage more women to seek jobs. Employ the elderly through programs such as shared jobs.

How Much Labor Do We Need?

Those who worry about dependency ratios may be worrying about precisely the wrong problem. Now and for the foreseeable future, the problem seems to be, not a shortage of labor, but rather a redundancy of labor of the wrong types, in the wrong places. Along with the rest of the industrial world, this country is in the midst of a technological revolution. Computerization, automation, genetics, the systematic organization of production—all of these are multiplying the productivity of labor, assuming only that there is capital to mobilize the technology. There are immense gains from this process. There are also two very apparent penalties. One of them is unemployment, which inched up from 4.5 percent of the labor force in the 1950s to 7.3 percent in the 1980s. The other result is the reappearance of the sweatshop: the disenfranchised accepting third world employment conditions to compete with the better-capitalized firms. One sees an image, as in multiple mirrors, of millions of John Henrys struggling to win their races against the steam hammer.

This country and the "American dream" were built on a degree of labor scarcity that meant that a worker could expect a decent wage for his or her work. The scarcity encouraged experiments with labor-saving approaches and technologies, which in turn led to higher productivity, higher wages, and a mass market that is still the center of the world trade. However, those technologies also helped to shrink the market for unskilled labor, of which there is now a chronic surplus.

The potential supply of labor from third world is, for practical purposes, inexhaustible, and the United States is a powerful magnet. If we continue to raise immigration quotas and wink at the illegal immigration of laborers willing to work at the bottom of the economic ladder, wages may be driven down to the subsistence level. The United States would then come to resemble a third world country, with perhaps half our people at the ragged edge of survival. Is that what we want?

There is a conflict of moral issues here: We are right to feel sympathy for the world's poor, but our first obligation is to our own society. We cannot solve the problem of third world population growth by attempting to absorb the surplus. The scale of the problem is much too big.

The United States a generation ago, in rare unity, launched perhaps its greatest moral crusade: to eliminate racism and to bring Blacks into the economic mainstream. Since then, we have inadvertently allowed our immigration policies to do the one thing that could most effectively sabotage that crusade: we have allowed the almost unfettered competition for entry-level jobs. Those jobs should have constituted the point of entry for poor Blacks into the economy.

It is not enough to argue that the immigrants, hungry and perhaps fearful of deportation, will work harder than most Americans. Poor Blacks are Americans, too. How do we help bring this increasingly isolated, alienated, and restless group into the system?

The second graph shows the disparity between employment levels of Blacks and other Americans. Partly as a consequence, Blacks comprise almost exactly half the prison population in the United States, although they represent only 12 percent of the total population. The issues raised by Dr. Briggs in Chapter 6 are real and very serious.

The nation that gave the American dream to the world should look to its own tradition. Too much labor means cheap labor, and cheapened

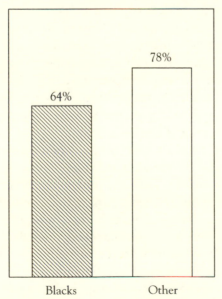

Proportions of U.S. Blacks and Whites employed, aged 20–29, 1989.
Sources: Bureau of Labor Statistics; Census.

labor may be leading us to a two-tier system of wealth and poverty that is closer to traditional societies than to any dream of the future.

Recognizing the implications of technological change, we should be determining the amount and kind of labor we need and mobilizing capital to take advantage of the new opportunities. The swelling of the numbers of unneeded entry-level laborers, with the concomitant social and welfare costs, is probably an object to be avoided rather than pursued.

We have seen enough history to recognize that the "baby bust" children of the 1930s were able to find better jobs, with less dislocation, than their baby boom successors of the 1950s. Perhaps we should be studying how to save and invest enough to put the existing labor force to work rather than spending the money on raising more children to meet an imagined need some forty years away.

Our Crowded Future

The economist Kenneth Boulding coined a wonderful epigram: "Anyone who believes exponential growth can go on forever in a finite world is either a madman or an economist." How better could one dispose of all the verbiage that has been written on the topic of growth?

To propose more children or more immigration to maintain a high proportion of the working-age population to the old is—on a gigantic scale—akin to proposing a little drink to cure a hangover. We are presently working off the baby boom. There are various ways to accommodate the aging of that cohort without resorting to population inflation. Do we want to "solve" an anticipated problem that may not materialize when the baby boomers grow old, by generating more rapid population growth, and, eventually, more old people later on?

At some stage, we must ask how many of us we want. There is no mathematical formula for answering that question, but in retrospect 150 million does not look bad. That was the level in 1950, before the creation of most of the huge chemical dumps, before chlorofluorocarbons and acid rain, when carbon dioxide in the atmosphere was just beginning its rise to problem levels, nuclear energy was new enough to seem wholly benign, suburbs were within commuting distance of the cities, and the cities themselves seemed attractive places to live. The year 1950 was no idyll. We were already pursuing the habits that led to our environmental problems. But wouldn't it be attractive to face our present problems with that more manageable population? This sounds like nostalgia, but can anybody who was alive in the 1950s deny a certain regret at what has been lost?

Leading demographers a few years ago projected the population a century from now at about 255 to 259 million. It has already reached that vicinity (see Chapter 13). Fertility in the United States has recently risen to about "replacement level" (very roughly, the two-child family). Coupled with recent immigration trends, this could push the figure toward a half billion. Even without deliberately stimulating immigration or fertility, the prospect is for a more crowded rather than a less crowded society.

As Boulding reminds us, stabilize we must. The question is not whether, but when. Do we wait until our population density has reached that of India or Bangladesh? Opinions may differ about the population size that is desirable or practicable. We need to begin the debate and to translate the results into a population policy. It is remarkable that, on an issue so fundamental to our well-being, the nation has hardly begun the process.

Future Issues

When we have arrived at a consensus, there are real issues to be addressed. How do we shift from the support of children, which tends to be financed by parents, to the support of the old, which is usually a societal responsibility in this country, its cost painfully evident in every worker's Social Security deductions? Medical miracles are making it possible to keep more and more of the very old alive, but these miracles are very expensive. We have another debate ahead of us concerning our responsibilities to the old: how much life support is the nation morally obligated to provide to the very old?

More generally, how can creativity be maintained, with an older population? How do we maintain employment and economic activity without the stimulus of growth?

There is time for the debate. With the 1983 changes in the Social Security system, the Social Security Trust Fund is beginning to run a surplus that is expected to mount to almost unmanageable levels through the middle of the next century. As the third graph shows, the problem is not, as so many believe, that the Fund is in imminent danger of exhaustion. Rather, it is that the Fund is being used to help cope with

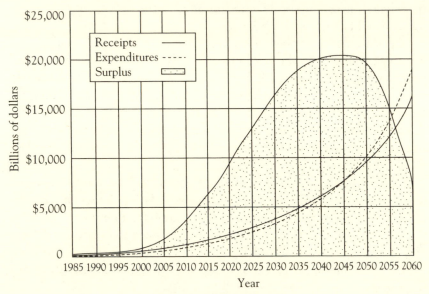

Social Security Trust Fund surpluses, 1985–2060.

the federal deficit rather than to make the productive investments that would support the aging when their numbers begin to mount steeply about a generation from now.

The Counsel of the "Prudent Man"

Those who argue for higher fertility or more immigration to support the aged are arguing for more population growth. It would take a very sharp drop in fertility indeed to justify their fears, and such a drop is not presently in sight. Let us not create future problems by embracing a single-track "solution" with such vast and unexamined ramifications.

HOW TO GET THERE FROM HERE

The Demographic Route to Optimal Population Size

LEON F. BOUVIER

The momentum of population growth is an awesome force, and it might take a century to turn it around even if the nation decided to do so.

It would be unfair to make the case for an optimum population and then to offer no thoughts on how the optimum could be achieved.

As a first step, Dr. Bouvier describes the impact of different fertility, mortality and immigration levels on future population size.

Our Love Affair with Growth

On the popular TV game show "Jeopardy" the college-level participants were asked which country would "surpass China in population within the next century." Two of the three contestants properly identified India. The third replied, "The United States." Such an answer from a Harvard student is surprising. But even more surprising was the comment of the host, Alex Trevek: "That is a noble thought, but unfortunately it is incorrect."

In January 1989 the U.S. Census Bureau published a new set of population projections.[1] Its middle scenario projected an eventual decline in population starting fifty years from now. The "neo doomsdayers," worried about population decline, jumped up in unison to sound the alarm. Journalist Ben Wattenberg, already on record as advocating more births to U.S. women, commented in *U.S. News and World Report:* "The surest way to break the downward momentum of the projections is through more immigration. And only more immigration can provide the stream of 'instant adults' to deal with the looming problems in a timely manner."[2] Economist Julian Simon, another supporter of higher fertility, has argued that immigration levels should be raised to perhaps two million annually.[3] The media generally viewed the prospect of declining population quite gloomily—never mind that the so-called middle range scenario of the Census Bureau was in fact a rather low projection, given current levels of fertility, mortality, and immigration.[4]

These two unrelated incidents point out the built-in bias for growth among many Americans. Texans proudly look forward to passing New York State in population, as Californians did in 1963. Chambers of commerce hail the latest population estimates showing their metropolitan area to have climbed two places. Suburbanites are gleeful when their city's population surpasses that of the older central city in their metropolitan area. We have forgotten E. P. Schumacher's words that "small is beautiful." Rather, we have been convinced, and were so particularly in the Reagan era, that "growth is good."

Such a turn of events is quite ironic. Twenty-five years ago most Americans who thought about population were concerned about explosive growth. The population of the United States was increasing at a rate we now associate with the third world, one that would have yielded over 400 million inhabitants by 2050. Many felt that the United States was growing too fast. Mortality was low and immigration moderate, but fertility was high. Consequently, the goal of zero population growth gained wide acceptance. In the intervening quarter of a century the perceptions of many Americans has turned about. From its baby boom peak of 3.7 in 1957, U.S. fertility fell below the level needed to replace the population and reached 1.8 in 1972. Baby boom had given way to baby bust. Even though the country has added 54 million people in the past two decades, a new and unfamiliar fear now troubles some Americans: population decline. Yet even the highly publicized "medium" projection of the Census Bureau shows a population of 292 million in 2080—some 40 million more than today's approximately 250 million.

Interestingly, those agonizing about population decline and advocating increased population growth seldom discuss the consequences of that growth. Alex Trevek is a thoughtful and intelligent individual. His comment on "Jeopardy" was made on the spur of the moment. No doubt, he would not advocate a U.S. population of over one billion people! Yet if our fertility reverted to that during the baby boom and if we did accept two million immigrants per year, the resulting growth rate would yield two billion Americans within the next century.

Even a more conservative set of assumptions yields a disturbing answer. If life expectancy increased slightly, if fertility rose to a mere 2.2 live births per woman, and if net immigration were constant at 800,000 annually (close to current levels), the U.S. population would surpass half a billion in just ninety years—and still be growing fairly rapidly!*

It may be difficult for Americans to accept the fact that not all growth is beneficial. The small world of certain growth-oriented economists is just that—a small world that fails to take into account the dangers to the environment and to the quality of life of all Americans that will result from continued population growth. So, like it or not, and while we may disagree on the eventual ideal number, sooner or later, population growth must come to an end. Those advocating continued rapid growth concede privately that, eventually, growth must cease, perhaps at some astronomical number. Those advocating negative growth must also favor eventual stationarity at some level smaller than the current population, of course—otherwise, the society will run out of people!

The Demographic Variables

This given agreement on the need for limits to growth begs a big question: "How do we get from here to there?" We get there by manipulating the three demographic variables that account for all the changes in population size: migration, mortality, and fertility.

*Since these projections were proposed, the fertility rate has already risen to over 2.0. The projections used in this chapter are based on the 1988 Census Bureau report.

Slight variations in any single demographic variable can have considerable impact on eventual population size. For example, according to the Census Bureau projections, if immigration is 800,000 per year rather than 500,000 (while holding fertility and mortality constant), there will be forty-one million more people by 2080. A gradual increase of seven years in life expectancy (holding immigration and fertility constant) means a difference of twenty million by 2080. The impact of fertility is particularly powerful. A gradual 20 percent increase in fertility from 1.8 to 2.2 live births (holding immigration and mortality constant) means 128 million more people by 2080!

Furthermore, in 2080, in all likelihood, the population would still be growing. Population momentum must thus be considered when looking at the three demographic variables. If an end to growth is desired, it cannot be achieved overnight. There is a built-in momentum for growth in any young population. A drop in the fertility rate does not necessarily mean that the number of births has fallen. The number of potential mothers is as important as the number of children each has. In the United States, for example, the number of births climbed from 3.1 million in 1978 to 3.8 million in 1987 although the fertility rate remained fairly constant at about 1.8 live births per woman. The reason is that in the 1980s there were proportionately many women in their childbearing years; the baby boom babies had become potential mothers. Interestingly, a momentum for population decline is also possible. If U.S. women were to average one child for the next generation, there would be very few women twenty-five to thirty years hence to have babies. If further population decline were not desirable at that time, these relatively few women would have to average at least three births for the population to stop falling.

Thus momentum is an important concept to consider when trying to determine how to get there from here.

Demographic Models

What do we mean by "there"? It can be both a number and a date. There is general consensus that population growth must end. Other writers in this volume believe that it should stop at a lower level than the present U.S. population. Demographers are supposed simply to give the facts, to describe the results of different sorts of demographic behavior. Demographers are people, too, and I confess to a certain sympathy with the view that eventual moderate population decline is desirable. However, my obligation is to demonstrate just how hard such a task will be and how long it will take. To be realistic, we limit our horizon to the next sixty to ninety years—to the years 2050 and 2080. What combinations of fertility, mortality, and migration behavior patterns will get us from here to there, whatever "there" is?

We begin by examining demographic mathematical models. These are not intended to serve as projections; rather, they illustrate what would occur under certain constant demographic conditions. Perhaps the best known of such models is the stable model developed by Dublin and Lotka early in this century.[5] Essentially, the model states that, in a closed population (that is, where there is no migration), a stable condition evolves if age-specific birth and death rates remain constant over a long period of time. A stable population exhibits a constant rate of growth and has constant birth and death rates. Note that a stable population can be growing, declining, or stationary. Herein lies the reason why demographers never use the word *stability* to mean "no growth." They reserve for that the term *stationarity*.

In 1982 the stable model theory was expanded to include migration, becoming the open stable model.[6] If age-specific birth and death rates are fixed, if fertility is below replacement, and if the yearly number and age and sex composition of immigrants are constant, then that population will evolve in the long run to a stationary state with a constant size. In other words, as long as fertility is below replacement and the level of immigration is constant, zero population growth will eventually occur.

Such models, while not appropriate for real-world projections, nevertheless point us in the right direction. This is particularly true for the United States which exhibits both below replacement fertility and net immigration. For example, if fertility were at 1.8 live births and if net immigration were limited to 400,000 annually, the eventual stationary population of the United States would be about 120 million. However, it would take two or three centuries to approach this goal, and we are more concerned with the twenty-first century. Using the demographic model as a guide, what demographic patterns are needed to attain our stated goal, whatever that may be?

The Projections

We first accept the fact that there is a momentum for growth in the current U.S. population. We then assume that life expectancy will increase in future years.

Admittedly, gains in life expectancy contribute to additional growth and more aging of the population and admittedly, life expectations could be depressed in the next ninety years by the environmental deterioration currently underway. Be that as it may, all of us, whether advocating massive increase or negative growth, favor extending the longevity of all Americans, and we should plan on it. The United States rates near the bottom of the list of all developed nations on such measures as life expectancy and infant mortality. The rate among certain U.S. minorities is particularly disturbing. One Census Bureau projection has life expectancy climbing gradually from seventy-five years today to eighty-eight years in 2080. This is a mere 1.5 years every decade, a reachable and

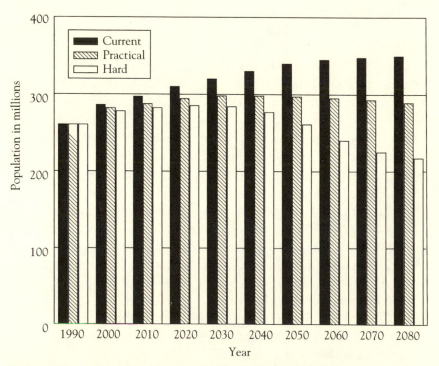

Alternative projection scenarios, U.S. population, 1990–2080.

desirable goal. In all further projections, such improvements in life expectancy are assumed. This leads to numbers slightly higher than those cited elsewhere in this book, since those projections use the Census Bureau's less optimistic median mortality projections. However, the nation hopes to reduce mortality and is spending heavily toward that objective. We should perhaps base our population projections on the assumption that we succeed.

A continuation of recent demographic trends (that is, fertility of 1.8 and net immigration of 800,000) would yield a population of 346 million by 2050 and 360 million by 2080, according to the Census Bureau projections. At that time the population would still be growing by about one million per year, as shown in the graph on alternative projection scenarios. Growth would eventually come to an end, as indicated by the demographic model, but only in the very distant future. This is an example of how to get from here to there following recent trends of demographic behavior. One hundred million more people in a mere sixty years is far too many for the nation to handle if its quality of life and its infrastructure are to remain at least at current levels, much less improve. It is not an optimal population.

THE "PRACTICAL" SCENARIO   I think that a maximum population of 300 million, with decline beginning well before 2080, is a practical and attainable goal. One of the Census Bureau's projections meets these requirements. Recall that life expectancy is assumed to increase to eighty-eight years by 2080. When that mortality is combined with fertility at about 1.8 and net migration of 300,000 per year, the population peaks at 300 million in 2040 and falls to 289 million by 2080. Beyond that year, the population declines slowly, reaching stationarity at about 120 million some three centuries later. But let us not concern ourselves with the twenty-second century any more than Americans of 1890 concerned themselves with our demographic problems!

THE 'HARD" SCENARIO   To those less patient with population growth, the numbers of the practical model may appear too high. Admittedly, adding fifty million Americans poses serious environmental problems.

Lowering fertility to 1.5 live births per woman, for example, is a possibility. Austria, Spain, and Italy exhibit rates below 1.5. Affluent Americans show similar fertility. It is the poor and the minorities who drive U.S. fertility up. Reductions in their fertility rates could result in an overall total fertility rate of 1.5 if government population policy encouraged such a change. With net migration reduced to 300,000, the nation's population would still grow to 278 million in 2020 before falling to 218 million in 2080 (see the graph). However, a majority of immigrants come from societies where fertility is high. With the resident U.S. birth rate below replacement, the proportion of the nation's population who are minorities will increase. We have projected elsewhere that by 2060 it is likely that no racial or ethnic group will constitute a majority of the U.S. population.[7] Thus, for overall fertility to fall to 1.5, some substantial reductions in the fertility of native-born Americans will have to occur to compensate for the growing proportion of minorities in the population.

Very few Americans advocate ending immigration entirely. Seeing ourselves as a "nation of immigrants," it is doubtful that we would accept such a policy. One alternative would be to take in only as many as leave the country in any given year. In other words, net migration of zero. The Census Bureau has prepared selected model projections of U.S. population assuming net migration of zero. With low fertility (total fertility rate [TFR] = 1.5) and life expectancy of 77.9 years, the population peaks at 255 million in 2010 and falls to 147 million by 2080. With moderate fertility (TFR = 1.8) and life expectancy of 81.2 years, the population peaks at 270 million in 2020 and falls to 220 million by 2080.

However, this would work only so long as there were a residue of emigrants from earlier in-movements. At most, one immigrant in three leaves the United States. (The number of native-born Americans who emigrate is negligible.) Eventually, the number admitted would be extremely small if based on the number leaving. This would in effect end immigration. For every 100,000 accepted, for example, only 30,000 may leave. Thus, it seems to me that zero net immigration is not a viable option. However, lower levels than 300,000 might be considered.

It remains for us to balance fertility and immigration. Fertility was remarkably stable for 16 years. It fell to 1.8 live births per woman in 1972 and remained at approximately that level through 1987. In 1988 the rate rose to 1.94, and in 1989 to about 2.0. Similar increases have been observed in Sweden and Germany. The fertility rate could rise in the future because of an increasing proportion of minorities in the population. Hispanics, in particular, have substantially higher fertility (about 3.0) than other groups. Gains in their share of the population could result in some increases in the nation's fertility.

Given these conditions, I feel it is unrealistic to project lower fertility in the United States for the immediate future. Americans could be encouraged to lower their fertility through more and better jobs for women, better and easier access to abortions, and wider availability of effective contraceptives. Much more could be done, through sex education, to lower the disturbingly high level of adolescent fertility. In a democratic society, specific fertility levels can never be enforced, nor should they be. However, a population policy encouraging lower fertility could prove effective.

Although compulsion cannot be used in the case of fertility rates, much can be done to determine the extent of immigration. Federal legislation limiting international movements, in one way or another, has been in effect in some form for over a century. Currently, about 650,000 legal immigrants enter the country annually. Additional hundreds of thousands enter illegally. We do not know the exact number, but conservative estimates put it at between 200,000 and 400,000. Nor do we know how many people leave the country in any given year. It could well be as high as 200,000. In balance, these figures suggest that annual net migration may be in the vicinity of 750,000 to 800,000. These numbers will undoubtedly grow in the 1990s as a result of 1990 legislation, which increases the level of legal immigration.

The Demographic Quandary

For those of us who would prefer that eventual zero growth be either at current population levels or lower, certain problems present themselves. First, while increases in life expectancy are favored by all, they contribute to additional numbers, as well as aging the society. Second, the built-in momentum for growth inherited from the baby boom means that some increases will occur. It would take drastic and unrealistic reductions in fertility to end growth immediately. Third, immigration could be ended, but most Americans, being either immigrants or descendants thereof, would undoubtedly disapprove of such governmental policies.

Together these problem areas limit the range of possibilities to a narrow band of fertility and immigration options. Recalling the open stable model, if fertility remains below replacement (below 2.1) and if some constant level of immigration is maintained, eventually a stationary population will emerge. However, the lower the fertility, the greater and more rapid the ethnic shift in the composition of the population. If the resident U.S. fertility remains below replacement, residents and their descendants will eventually be replaced by immigrants and their descendants.

That is the quandary facing Americans who desire an end to population growth in the near future. The other alternative is cultural amalgamation where widespread intermarriage occurs between groups. How long it will take before a "no majority" situation obtains depends on how low the fertility, how high the immigration, and the extent of intermarriage.

DEMOGRAPHIC BEHAVIOR RECONSIDERED   The population acts of millions of Americans and immigrants to this nation have given us today's United States population. By "population acts" we mean the fertility, mortality, and migration behavior of these millions of individuals. Today's and tomorrow's population acts will give us the population of 2000, 2050, and 2080—not only the numbers of people but their age and ethnic composition. Advocating a specific ideal size necessarily means also considering the age and ethnic composition of that ideal.

Equally important is the fact that, if the desire is to limit the size of the nation's population, the demographic dynamics assure us both increased age and heterogeneity. Aging and diversity are not problems to be avoided, however; they challenge society to better adapt to changing situations. It is up to us to adapt to demographic shifts as we enter the twenty-first century.

Conclusion

There is little agreement as to what "optimal population" means and what numbers best reflect the optimum. We must be realistic in our efforts to determine what population size is achievable, as opposed to optimal. Three, and only three, factors determine population size. One, mortality, is untouchable in that we all advocate increased longevity. A second, fertility, is in the hands of millions of U.S. population actors. While fertility declines should be encouraged, nothing can be done in a democratic society to enforce those suggestions. That leaves immigration as the most maneuverable variable. Yet even here, it is doubtful that Americans would allow an end to immigration. We must consider the age and diversity of the population almost as much as its size. Finally, we should not get carried away with long-term models and projections. The next fifty to ninety years are sufficiently long term—bearing in mind, of course, the potential for further exponential growth—to allow the development of specific demographic routes that will show us how to get there from here.

Ending population growth and beginning population decline will be rough, and it will be a slow process. If the problems described elsewhere in this volume are as real and as serious as their authors believe, I suggest that we begin to concentrate on the demographic dimension of the problem. From the evidence described in this chapter, it is clear that time is not on our side.

SUSTAINABLE IMMIGRATION
Learning To Say No
DAVID E. SIMCOX

In theory, at least, immigration should be the most easily managed of the three forces that determine population growth. Taking the necessary steps may not be all that easy, however.

1990 was a revealingly eventful year in the uncertain course of U.S. immigration policymaking, demonstrating in the extreme the varied political and emotional dynamics that have driven overall immigration to 900,000 yearly, with further growth likely.

• In February Gene McNary, Commissioner of the Immigration and Naturalization Service (INS) announced he was using his discreionary authority to grant the equivalent of limited permanent resident status to illegal aliens who are spouses of minor children of legalized aliens but themselves failed to qualify for the 1986 amnesty. By this particular stroke of pen, McNary added as many as 1.5 million people to the permanently resident population.

• Congressman Bruce Morrison, Chairman of the House of Representatives Immigration Subcommittee in February introduced his legal immigration reform bill that would boost the flow of newcomers in the 1990's to about 1.5 million a year—almost twice the current number. Morrison's bill also provided for the admission of some 250,000 temporary resident workers and their families, most of whom would ultimately become permanent residents.

• Early in 1990 INS and the State Department began admitting refugees from the Soviet Union and Southeast Asia who normally would not have qualified under the test of individual persecution provided in the 1980 Refugee Act. As Soviet emigration mounted because of eased rules, Congress grew concerned over the numbers denied refugee status under more stringent rules and legislated for them a blanket "presumption of eligibility." The nearly 20,000 who exceeded the authorized 125,000 refugee limits for the year would be admitted anyhow under the Attorney General's "parole" authority. U.S. agencies also began implementing a 1989 White House directive granting "enhanced consideration" to asylum seekers from China who claimed to be fleeing forced abortion or mandatory sterilization.

• In October 1990 Congress passed the first legal immigration reform act since 1965. The new law increases legal immigration by nearly 40 percent (to 700,000 a year) and authorized a new and ostensibly temporary category for the humanitarian admission of persons from countries troubled by generalized violence or environment disaster, with no requirement to prove individual hardship or risk. Congress directed that illegal aliens from El Salvador, as many as a quarter-million persons, be the first beneficiaries of the newly created "temporary protected status." The administration soon after added Liberia, Kuwait, and Lebanon to the lists of eligibles.

• As 1990 ended, arrests by INS for the year broke the one million mark, showing illegal immigration to be sharply rebounding after four years of decline. Factors in the resurgence of illegal entries were the continued explosion of the Caribbean Basin's working-age population and the reduced deterrent effect of employer sanctions caused by widespread falsification of ID documents.

* In 1990 the government further increased the intake of refugees for 1991 to 131,000, doubling annual admissions since 1986. As the year ended, major immigrant advocacies and foreign policy specialists were pressing for special legislation to resettle here some of the half-million Soviet citizens now expected to emigrate yearly in the 1990s.

Unlimited Immigration Demand

Driving the ad hoc concessions, the special exceptions and steady up-creep is a profound imbalance between the numbers abroad who want to live in the United States and the limits and conditions imposed on their coming by U.S. law. As world population has swelled by more than eighty million yearly, proliferating family migration chains have lengthened the waiting list for U.S. visas from 1.0 million in 1980 to 2.4 million in 1990.

Congress responds distractedly to these pressures, with special exceptions for relief measures to alleviate perceived refugee and asylee emergencies, putative labor shortages, or the clamor of powerful special ethnic interests. Cumulative concessions pushed total immigration to nearly 900,000 a year in 1990. But regularly missing from this ongoing legislative bazaar is concern for the long-range population effects of so many newcomers. The accompanying graph shows the population effects of different immigration levels.

Even allowing for emigration, immigration under current law and practice directly accounts for 32 percent of national population growth, and the proportion is rising. The 1990 Census is expected to show that the foreign-born population has grown from 4.7 percent in 1970 to 8.5 percent in 1990. Fears of labor shortages—although the U.S. 1990 unemployment rate of 5.8 percent was twice that of Japan—led Congress to approve expansions of immigration of both temporary and permanent workers in the 1990 legislation. Under that act, net annual legal and illegal immigration will climb to about 1.1 million by 1995, or more than 44 percent of population growth. Two to three million aliens amnestied under the 1986 law will convert to permanent status in the early 1990s, further swelling the permanent population as they bring their families to this country.

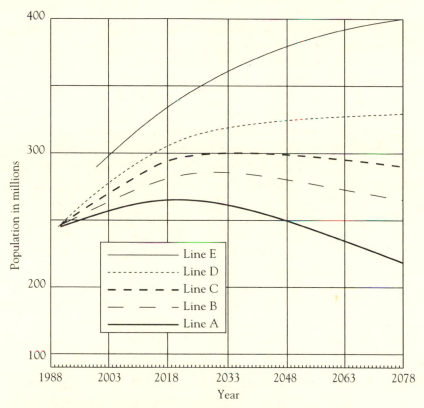

Immigration and projected U.S. population growth, 1988–2080. *Line A:* With immigration equal to emigration, the population of the United States would peak at 270 million in 2020 and would decline gradually to 220 million in 2080. *Line B:* With a net annual immigration of 300,000, the population would be 288 million in 2030 and 266 million in 2080. *Line C:* With a net annual immigration of 500,000, the population would peak at 302 million in 2040 and would decline slightly to 292 million by 2080. *Line D:* With a net annual immigration of 800,000, the population would pass 333 million in 2080 and would still be rising. This line represents a reasonable conservative estimate of today's net immigration levels. *Line E:* A net annual immigration of 1.5 million—which could result from current proposals—would lead to a population passing 403 million in 2080.

Sources: Lines A through D: Gregory Spencer, *Projections of the Population of the United States, by Age, Sex and Race: 1988 to 2080.* (U.S. Bureau of the Census, Series P-25, no. 1018, January 1989). Line E: Leon F. Bouvier and Cary B. Davis, *The Future Racial Composition of the United States* (Washington D.C.: Population Reference Bureau, August 1982). The assumptions in the two studies are comparable, though not identical. The latter study assumes a total fertility rate 0.092 lower than the Census study and life expectancies converging in 2080 at a figure 0.5 years lower. Both assume fertility below current levels substantially, and are therefore conservative.

Census data and immigration statistics understate the degree of population growth due to entries from abroad. The Census count disregards such categories as foreign students, long-staying temporary workers, and most illegal and commuter aliens—categories that add another million to the U.S. population on any given day. Furthermore, many of these immigrants have children, and their children have children, swelling the population base.

Census Bureau projections of future population growth use 800,000 as the "high" assumption of net yearly immigration.[1] In Chapter 13, Leon Bouvier notes that the high assumption is now more reasonable as a medium projection. Bouvier warns that if U.S. fertility rose only to the 2.2 replacement level, net immigration of 800,000 per year would push the U.S. population to 394 million in 2050 and 471 million by 2080.

Positing a low fertility of 1.8 and a "low" net annual immigration of 300,000, the Census projects that the U.S. population would peak in 2030 at 288 million and then gradually decline to 265 million in 2080.[2] Clearly, if the United States is to begin to reverse its population growth, net immigration of 300,000 or less is imperative. But as annual entries have crept up since the 1960s, we have come to see as the norm a net inflow of newcomers of at least twice that number.

The Psychic Function of Generous Immigration

Indeed, many Americans regard the accommodation of hundreds of thousands of immigrants and refugees as a peculiarly American mission in the world, one that is deeply intermingled with the nation's sense of self-worth and high moral values. For many others, immigration yields only positive benefits by reuniting families, bringing in needed labor or investors, or aiding our foreign policy. Underlying all these particular interests is the pervasive sense that our generous immigration policies are an ennobling American statement to the world. Thus basic immigration policy, as the Senate debates of immigration reform in the summer of 1989 demonstrated, is most often legislated on the basis of anecdotes, slogans, and impressions, vague notions about the nation's immigrant past, and a desire to use immigration law to affirm standards of charity and generosity. These sentiments becloud the national interest, edging out practical concerns for the nation's population future.

Commonly, long-term population concerns are dismissed with the argument that the ratio of immigrants to the general population is far lower now than in 1910. The implication is that as the U.S. population grows it should take in steadily more newcomers to maintain a historically ordained ratio. By that reasoning, the United States, to maintain the immigration–population ratio of 1910, should admit 3.5 million immigrants in 1990.

Immigration Austerity: Curbing Illegal Settlement

Given the diversity and intensity of the current demands on our national immigration system and the powerful sentiments involved, which of the many claimants would receive priority if the nation were to decide to reduce immigration to a more sustainable 300,000 or fewer per year? How could a democratic system fairly allocate the pain that would accompany a two-thirds reduction in immigration?

The first and most politically defensible step toward far lower immigration would be deep cuts in illegal immigration, now estimated by the INS to add some 200,000 a year to the settled population, though unofficial estimates go as high as 300,000. Firm commitment to enforcement of the immigration laws—so far never conscientiously attempted in the United States—could soon reduce this number by two-thirds. The task would demand a doubling of the money and manpower of the thirteen thousand-member, billion-dollar-a-year INS. But much of the added cost could be recovered by vigorous application of fines, service fees, and tax penalties on illegal aliens and their employers and sponsors in the United States.

But even an expanded INS could not successfully combat such a pervasive national problem unaided. The federal government must mobilize other agencies having regular contact with illegal immigrants and their employers, such as Internal Revenue, the Department of Labor, the Social Security Administration, the Department of Housing and Urban Development, and national law enforcement agencies. Federal funding and federal leadership would be essential to animate state and local labor, revenue, welfare, and police agencies to act against illegal alien employment and settlement.

Two new weapons against illegal immigration emerged in the 1980s. Penalties, or "sanctions," against employers of illegal aliens are intended to turn off the magnet of jobs. "Systematic alien entitlements verification," known by the acronym SAVE, uses computer matching and identity checks to deny welfare and public assistance to illegal aliens. Not surprisingly, both devices are under fierce attack from immigrant advocacy and civil rights groups. However, they need to be strengthened, with additional deterrents brought to bear. Among those worth considering are the following:

- Proof of legal status or citizenship as a condition for
    a. entering into real estate contracts, such as home purchases or leases,
    b. obtaining drivers' licenses, motor vehicles registration, or liability insurance,
    c. qualifying for professional and occupational licensing,
    d. enrolling in state or federally assisted colleges and universities, and
    e. securing business and alcoholic beverages licenses.

- IRS audits of employers found hiring illegal aliens and disqualification of wages paid to unauthorized aliens as deductible business expenses.

- Such internal controls to be matched by increased numbers of border patrol officers backed up by more expeditious procedures for deportation and summary exclusion of aliens entering illegally.

- Tightened strictures against illegal immigration, utilizing a tamper-proof system of identification and more rigorous controls over birth, death, and other vital statistics documents.[3]

Living with Lower Legal Immigration

While working to reduce illegal immigration to zero, federal policymakers would also need to reorder current priorities to reduce legal immigration and refugee flows from their present 600,000 to 700,000 a year to 300,000. As shown in the table on the allocation of immigration spaces, a sustainable annual immigration level of 300,000 could be organized around the three general streams that now dominate the current immigration system: refugees, family reunification, and independent immigrants. A reasonable and politically acceptable allocation among the three might be as follows:

1. Refugees and asylees, now entering at the rate of 130,000 yearly, could be reduced to 50,000 a year—the figure determined by Congress to be "normal flow" in the 1980 Refugee Act. The

privilege of refuge would be awarded by rigorous case-by-case examination of applicants of special concern to the United States and given only to those who demonstrate the clear probability of life-threatening harm. Unsuccessful applicants would have the option of competing as candidates for independent immigration.

2. Family reunification in 1988 brought in 220,000 quota-free immediate relatives of U.S. citizens and nearly 200,000 other immigrants claiming family relationships to citizens or legal resident aliens. Immigration austerity would require limits on the privilege of U.S. citizens to bring in immediate family members, reducing the inflow in this category (now 220,000 yearly and growing) to 100,000 a year. Preferential immigration of spouses and minor children would be limited to those whose marriages were contracted before the immigration of the petitioning U.S. citizen occurred. Parents of U.S. citizens, children over eighteen and married children of any age would no longer qualify for family reunification visas but could compete as independent immigrants. Neither native born nor foreign born U.S. citizens would be entitled to bring in newly acquired spouses for residence under this category, though they could seek independent immigrant visas for them.

3. A pool of 150,000 independent immigrants would serve the nation's most pressing needs for the importation of highly skilled workers and professionals, family members of U.S. citizens and residents not otherwise covered, and persons of special foreign policy interest. Visas would be awarded through a point system that would assign variable values for criteria such as skills, investment potential, adaptability, family connections, hardship, importance to foreign policy, and number of children (with smaller families receiving extra points).

Allocation of Immigration Spaces

Category	Current Law (1990)	Proposed Austerity Allocations
Family immigration	520,000	100,000
Refugees and asylees	140,000	50,000
Independent immigrants (Professionals and skilled workers, special immigrants)	170,000	150,000
Totals	830,000	300,000

Since refugee emergencies could not be ruled out, unforeseen urgent, presidentially certified refugee demands would be met by preempting numbers, first, in the independent category and then in the family category, until both were exhausted. For such emergencies, the President could also borrow up to two-thirds of the succeeding year's immigration numbers, but never for more than two consecutive years. (The outcry from those Americans with an interest in the regular flow of immigrants would probably ensure that no President would use this authority except in the most unusual circumstances.)

Heads of families authorized for independent immigration would receive a one-time allocation of the visas needed to bring their spouses and minor children with them, thus avoiding the need for subsequent special arrangements for family reunification.

Reduction of the supply of visas would have to be accompanied by measures to dampen demand. Applications of non refugee aliens should carry a sizable fee. Those successful in winning a visa should pay a front-end service charge of up to $5,000 per family unit. Employers sponsoring aliens for jobs should pay a surtax of 15 percent on the alien's earnings during their first five years here.

The Tough Scenario

If population pressures were determined to be unusually severe, could the United States manage even lower migration? Cutting inflow to 150,000 a year or lower, thus offsetting or falling below emigration, would significantly hasten population reduction if fertility stayed low. But it would leave national policymakers with excruciating choices. At such a low volume of immigration, three distinct categories would have little purpose. More appropriate would be a single comprehensive point system, with all types of applicants competing for a single pool of visas. Congress could periodically review and if necessary adjust the weightings given different migration criteria, such as persecution or political hardship, family connections, skills, or investment potential.

The nation's economic and cultural interaction with the world will continue to demand a sizable flow of foreign sojourners. The current immigration laws provide a range of specialized temporary, or "nonimmigrant," visa categories to meet this need (shown in the table on long-staying temporary workers), but these provisions are frequently abused to arrange de facto permanent residence for many who are ineligible or unwilling to compete for regular immigration slots.

A More Careful Count of Inflow

The Immigration Service logged 377 million entries into the United States in 1988, including returning U.S. citizens and repeat visits by aliens with border-crossing cards, aircraft crews, and the like. Sixty percent—225 million—were noncitizens. Of those persons, 14.6 million entered the United States with nonimmigrant visas. And of that number, the Immigration Service estimates that 255,000 stayed beyond the period allowed by the terms of their admission.

If population benefits are to be gained, overall cuts in legal and illegal immigration would have to be matched by more comprehensive methods of counting the total permanent alien population in the United States and keeping it within an overall ceiling. Policymakers must make less of the fictional legal distinctions between "permanent resident aliens" and nominally "temporary" longstayers, who can easily remain in the United States indefinitely. Notwithstanding the disparity of labels, the aggregate pressure of the foreign-source population on the environment,

Long-staying Temporary Workers (Not Counted as Immigrants)

Category and Visa Symbol	1984	1986	1988	Period of Admission
Treaty trader or investor (E-1, E-2)	22,419	30,424	31,920	Indefinite
Student (F-1, M-1)	136,129	137,573	159,406	4 years +
Temporary worker of distinguished merit and ability (H-1)	25,903	31,052	41,202	2–6 years
Other temporary workers (H-2)	5,828	8,725	6,656	Up to 1 year
Industrial trainee (H-3)	2,115	1,915	1,600	Up to 1 year
Exchange visitor (J-1, J-2)	97,652	129,563	157,994	2–4 years
Fiance or fiancee of U.S. citizen (K-1, K-2)	7,645	8,291	7,082	Permanent
Multinational company (L-1)	13,621	14,174	12,707	Indefinite
Total visas issued	311,312	361,717	418,587	

Source: Report of the Visa Office 1988, Washington, D.C.: Department of State, 1989.

demand for services, infrastructure, and consumption of resources is the same. Population planners should consider anyone who comes with the reasonable expectation of staying a year or more an addition to the population count, regardless of personal intentions or temporary category.

Worth exploring is the concept of "full-time equivalence" as a measure of the total foreign impact on population and resources. The full-time equivalence system would, for example, be a convenient way of measuring the presence of the transient and sojourner portions of the population in person-years. Two hundred thousand persons in the United States for six months yields 100,000 person-years. This type of measurement provides a far more revealing assessment of the effects of foreign-born persons on population and environment. The 1990 Census is expected to show twenty-one million of the nation's 255 million as foreign born. Under a full-time equivalence count, twenty-one million alien person-years would increase substantially with the addition of person-years for nearly one million foreign students, temporary workers and specialists, seasonal agricultural workers, and some two to three million long-staying tourists.

The Public and Immigration Levels: Wanting It Both Ways

Obviously, such a disciplined approach to the management of immigration will not come easily for a beleaguered Congress. National polls in the past two decades have consistently shown that a heavy majority of Americans support freezing immigration levels or rolling them back. A 1965 Gallup Poll, for example, at a time when legal immigration was less than 300,000, showed 72 percent favored allowing it to go no higher. Almost half of those favored reductions. In 1990, when legal immigration had surpassed 600,000, 77 percent of respondents to a Roper Poll felt it should go no higher.

Congress's mild response to what seems like clear public opinion on the issue suggests a greater public ambivalence. The electorate's strong but unfocused demand for lower immigration repeatedly yields to the highly focused demands of segments of the public for ad hoc responses to the short-term perceived needs for refugee admissions, farm workers, separated family members, and the like. Often wanting to respond compassionately to urgent needs, the general public—and its congressional representatives—take the view that "a few more can't hurt." Overlooked in the process are the higher future immigration demands that often result because of new precedents, additional family reunification chains, or the opening of new migration streams through "one-time" refugee relief measures.

The public needs to be made aware of the sizable long-range, cumulative population consequences of isolated short-term concessions. Only the discipline of a tight, all-inclusive immigration "budget" or ceiling can regularly force the trade-offs and tough choices that true immigration austerity will demand.

HOW TO INFLUENCE FERTILITY
The Experience So Far

JOHN R. WEEKS

The specter of coercion has made any discussion of conscious efforts to influence fertility politically untouchable, even though the nation inadvertently influences fertility through its decisions on a whole range of national policies. In fact, the experience of countries that have set out to influence fertility indicates that there are many non-coercive ways to do it.

We must bring the discussion into the open. The alternative is a willingness to resign ourselves to the blind operation of our procreative drives. In that event, as the editor of *Science* magazine editorialized, "ask not whether the bell tolls for the owl or the whale or the rhinocerous; it tolls for us."

The population of the United States is currently growing at a rate of 1 percent per year—well below the world average rate of 1.7 percent. The average number of children born per woman is, as is well known, right at 2.1— the level of replacement. Less well understood is the fact that the number of births each year in the United States is considerably higher than the number of deaths, owing to the demographic momentum built into the age structure. In 1990 U.S. women were giving birth to 3.8 million babies, while 2.1 million people of all ages were dying. Thus we are increasing by 1.7 million people each year just from natural increase. Net legal migration is estimated to be 600,000, and an additional 200,000 undocumented immigrants are also augmenting the total population.[1] The population of the United States thus continues to grow by 2.5 million people each year. In less than two years this country adds as many people as there are in Norway, and it would take only four years for the annual growth in the United States to equal the total population of Sweden. Some people react to such numbers with alarm because they think the rate of growth is too low. How can business expand when markets are not increasing at as rapid a pace as in the past? Others react to the numbers with a potentially xenophobic concern about the balance between natural increase and immigration: Shouldn't the birth rate be higher so that the rate of growth would be composed of a higher fraction of native-born babies and fewer imported workers? Still others react to the U.S. growth rate by noting that the average American consumes a vastly disproportionate share of the world's resources and so the impact of population growth in this country is far greater in the long run than is true of population growth in Asia, Africa, or Latin America.

This uncertainty about how to respond to our current demographic situation is both a cause and a consequence of the fact that the United States has never had a formal population policy, has never tried directly to influence the direction or size of the birth rate. On the other hand, we have sat back rather smugly with our relatively low levels of fertility and dispensed advice (often unsolicited) to other countries (mainly developing nations) about how *they* should proceed to lower their fertility. Could we lower ours? If it became clear that our national interest would be better served by a lower fertility rate, would we know how to go about designing a set of policies to influence fertility?

Developed nations have very little experience in directly influencing fertility levels to drop, but a great many things that governments have done in the West have serendipitously helped to generate lower fertility, and there may be much to be learned from these "accidental" or indirect policies. Most governmental efforts to influence fertility in developed societies have been attempts to *raise* levels that are perceived to be too low, and there is also something to be learned in the general failure of these policies to have much impact. However, most of the direct fertility policy lessons come to us from the developing world, and while the third world experience may not always be directly applicable to a country like the United States, some of the successes and failures may be guideposts to effective policy.

Direct and Indirect Policies Designed to Influence Fertility

Based on the detailed histories of fertility trends in Europe, Ansley Coale of the Office of Population Research at Princeton University has argued that there are three preconditions for a sustained decline in fertility: (1) the acceptance of calculated choice as a valid element in fertility, (2) the perception of advantages from reduced fertility, and (3) knowledge and mastery of effective techniques of control.[2] Each of these components has implications for population policy, as shown in the accompanying table. Some policy initiatives are aimed *directly* at influencing demographic behavior, while others are oriented toward trying to change social behavior, which will then *indirectly* have an impact on population processes.

RATIONAL CHOICE The first example of policy initiatives confronts the awareness of population issues at both the private and public levels. The principal barrier to recognition of personal freedom in determining reproductive goals is *tradition*, in particular the attitude that reproduction is in the hands of God or those of a woman's husband. It is a world view that does not admit to self-determination of family size. Rather, the view could be summed up by the phrase "children happen."

This is an attitude that is often associated in the western world with third world nations, especially Islamic nations,[3] but shades of it are evident in all human societies, because it is often associated with religious *fundamentalism*, regardless of the specific religious *preference*. In the United States, Christian fundamentalists (including both Catholics and Protestants) argue that certain aspects of reproduction (such as abortion or contraception for unmarried teenagers) should not be under the control of the woman herself.

Examples of Policies to Limit Fertility

Precondition for Which Intervention is Desired[a]	Examples of Policies	
	Direct	**Indirect**
Rational Choice	*Provide full legal rights to women *Increase legal age at marriage for women	*Promote secular education *Promote communication between spouses
Motivation for smaller families	**Incentives** *Payments for not having children *Priorities in jobs, housing, education for small families *Community improvements for achievement of low birth rate	**Incentives** *Economic development *Increased educational opportunities for women *Increased labor force opportunities for women *Peer-pressure campaigns *Lower infant and child mortality rates
	Disincentives *Higher taxes for each additional child *Higher maternity and educational costs for each additional child ("user fees")	**Disincentives** *Child labor laws *Compulsory education for children *Peer-pressure campaigns *Community birth quotas
Availability of means for limiting family size	*Legalize abortion *Legalize sterilization *Legalize all other forms of fertility control *Train family-planning program workers *Manufacture or buy contraceptive supplies *Distribute birth control methods at all health clinics *Make birth control methods available through local vendors *Establish systems of community-based distribution	*Public campaigns to promote knowledge and use of birth control *Politicians speaking out in favor of birth control

[a] See text for explanation of preconditions.

In order to change such behavior, policies can aim directly to grant women more freedom to act in their own interest (in combination with family interest, rather than solely on the basis of what others wish). This would include providing full legal rights to women, including the right to obtain birth control devices, an abortion, or a sterilization without having to obtain permission from the husband or some other family member. In Bangladesh, for example, a young women wishing to use contraception will typically have to do so through the cooperation of her mother-in-law, with whom she lives. This will almost certainly be called to the attention of her husband, and may well lead to considerable family strife. Thus, it is often easier for a woman to get pregnant than to risk the social ire of others by seeking contraception.[4]

Other legislation that might directly influence a woman's ability to think and act for herself would be the raising of the legal age at marriage, making it more difficult for a family to push daughters into an early marriage. These direct policy initiatives go hand-in-hand with indirect measures to raise the status of women and thereby increase the awareness that they, their husbands, and other family members have of the contributions that they can make to the family and to society, instead of simply being baby-machines. Articulating and attempting to alter the basic components of traditionalism (which is almost always pronatalist) would be one type of indirect population policy, albeit a vague and controversial one. Indeed, thus far, no one has explicitly promulgated such a policy, but mass secular education is the most successful antidote to the kind of traditional attitudes that prevent women (and couples) from exercising full control over their reproductive capacities. Associated with this is the need to promote communication between spouses on all matters, including reproduction. Without interpersonal communication, a spouse is more likely to assume that his or her partner holds the stereotypically traditional attitudes, and behavior will follow suit. Recent studies in rural Peru and in Burkina Faso have shown that, even in these geographically disparate societies, men appear to have more accurate knowledge about female reproduction than women and know nearly as much about contraception. However, cultural norms tend to maintain the traditional gender roles and limit the amount of such information that is passed between spouses.[5] Mass education helps to break down some of these walls by exposing both sexes to the same information in a context in which both men and women know that the other knows about reproduction and contraception and thus the subject is easier to broach and discuss.

The importance of education as a factor in reducing fertility cannot, in fact, be overstressed. Virtually every study ever done on the topic has revealed that higher education is associated with lower fertility, no matter what the cultural setting, geographic region, or religious preference of the respondents. In a recent review of four Latin American countries, for example, researchers concluded that improvements in female education alone could account for 40 to 67 percent of the fertility decline, other things being held constant.[6] Education works directly to lower a woman's fertility by delaying her exposure to intercourse and indirectly by showing her alternatives in life to early marriage and numerous children. More broadly and fundamentally, though, education changes the way all people think about their lives and the role that reproduction plays in life.

In a less-developed society, as in some areas in the United States, a sixteen-year-old female may appear in every way to be a *woman*. She has been raised with the expectation that she will be a wife and mother, and by age sixteen she is physically and socially ready to take on those roles that, when accepted, will hold her in virtual bondage for the rest of her life. Her family may be delighted at her marriage because, among other things, it relieves them of the worry that she will shame the family name by having an out-of-wedlock pregnancy.[7] By contrast, in a more developed nation, a sixteen-year-old female is still a *girl* with several years of schooling ahead of her and a job to start or career to establish before marriage and reproduction enter her social picture. Physically, of course, she is ready for parenthood and that is a dilemma that most developed countries except for the United States have dealt with by providing access to contraception (discussed below) for young people, who are literally bursting with hormones but are not yet ready to be shackled by premature parenthood. Parenthood at younger ages is only premature, however, because a more educated society redefines its terms and reorients its expectations.

MOTIVATION FOR SMALLER FAMILIES Self-determination of reproduction does not necessarily mean fertility limitation. Thus, the second precondition suggests policies oriented toward motivating a person or a couple to limit family size. If societal leaders are convinced that reducing fertility levels is an important way to reach desired social goals, then these policies are designed to reduce the gap between public needs (lower fertility) and private wishes (the maintenance of high fertility). Such policies include direct and indirect initiatives, within which we find both incentives and disincentives (rewards for small families, punishments for large families).

Direct incentives include payments to women or couples for not having a pregnancy during a specified interval (a practice on several tea estates in India),[8] or payments to individuals to undergo voluntary surgical contraception (VSC), as was instituted in the now famous vasectomy programs in India. Noncash incentives include priority for housing or for educational placement for first or second children but not for higher-order births. Broader still are incentives practiced in some rural areas of China, in which communities are rewarded with improved community infrastructure (a new school, paving of streets, and so forth) if they meet targeted birth rate levels. Of course, the farther away from the individual the reward for a small family, the more important the indirect policy of social pressure to encourage compliance with a low-fertility regimen.

In the developed nations the path to lower fertility has been alongside the road to economic development, and the classic statement of the demographic transition spotlights development as the major stimulus to fertility limitation. From that concept were born the maxims that "development is the best contraceptive" and "take care of the people and population will take care of itself."[9] The problem with development as a policy initiative is that it is a much slower process than imitation. But we do not need to imitate our past. We simply must extract the appropriate lessons. One of the crucial elements of industrialization was that it reversed the flow of income between children and parents: Children became economic liabilities rather than assets. Furthermore, it was built on the back of a better-educated labor force that increasingly moved toward maximizing human capital by bringing women into the paid labor force.

The lesson, then, is that economic development appears always to be associated with fertility declines because the process of development incorporates a complex set of direct and indirect incentives to limit family size along with direct and indirect disincentives to have large families. The task of the modern policy planner is to sort through those factors that may be implemented independently of the process of development and that, through diffusion rather than innovation, may lead to lower fertility. For example, the motivation to have a small family can be enhanced by indirect incentives such as greater opportunities for women to become educated and to enter the paid labor force. As I have argued elsewhere[10], economic independence is the key to raising the status of women, which, in turn, is a key element in the decline in fertility. Even direct public pressure may influence behavior by publicly changing norms in a manner not unlike the spread of fad and fashion in a society. Thus, governments that wish to lower fertility sometimes begin the process by "spreading the message" that small is beautiful when it comes to family size. There is evidence that fertility in Europe, for example, was subject to strong social influences independent of levels of socioeconomic development,[11] so the idea that family size preferences can be influenced at least to some extent by social pressure seems a reasonable one.

Since it is often argued that the development of high fertility norms in societies was a historically rational response to high death rates, it is reasonable to suggest that the lowering of infant and childhood mortality may help indirectly to lower fertility by reducing the pressure that couples feel to have several children so that a few will survive to adulthood. Of course, as I pointed out above, most societies are already devoting as many resources as they can to the lowering of mortality for purely humanitarian, if not social and economic, reasons, but the policy certainly can be explicitly incorporated into a population policy. Interestingly enough, there is some evidence emerging to suggest that lower levels of fertility themselves help to lower infant mortality (a reversal of the expected causal direction) by lengthening the interval between children and allowing a mother to concentrate her physical and social resources on her newborn child.

Disincentives may also be employed to limit fertility. Children may be taxed after the second one (in direct opposition to the pronatalist policy in the United States of permitting tax deductions for each child), and each successive child might result in higher "user fees" for maternity care, educational services, and other public resources. Indeed, subsequent children might result in a loss of specific benefits for a family, especially in a socialist state (such as China, where many resources are distributed through the government). Similarly, at the community level there could be punishments (such as less electricity or oil available or higher community tax rates) if a community did not meet a preestablished birth quota. As was true with incentives, these disincentives are most effectively implemented when combined with measures of indirect pressure on couples to use contraception or to abort a birth if it might cause the community to exceed its quota. This latter situation, which has the elements of coercive abortion, has apparently existed within some rural Chinese communities[12] and is the root of the Reagan and Bush administrations' unfortunate and misguided policy of withholding money from the United Nations Population Fund because the organization supports family planning programs in China. The United States is in the incongruous situation of withholding funds because those family planning efforts may include abortion, which is legal in the United States, as well as in China. Indeed, the abortion ratio in China (thirty-one abortions per one hundred pregnancies) is not significantly different from the level in the United States (thirty per one hundred).[13]

Draconian coercive measures may be implemented if quick results are required at the expense of individual freedom, but there is a variety of indirect disincentives that historically have had important long-term effects on the motivation for small families. Child labor laws, if rigorously enforced, help to lower (or at least delay) the economic benefit of children to their parents and thus may cause parents to think twice about the value of an additional child. Similarly, a societal mandate (again, when enforced) that children must attend school takes children out of the labor force, making them unable to contribute to their parents' income; moreover, schooling may cost money—for appropriate clothes, books and supplies, meals, and so on—either directly (cash spent on each child) or indirectly (through some system of taxation to pay for schooling).

AVAILABILITY OF MEANS FOR LIMITING FAMILY SIZE Even if a person is motivated to limit family size, implementing that desire is facilitated by the accessibility of effective means of fertility control. "Accessibility" includes knowledge of methods—what are available, where one gets them, and how one uses them. Thus, policies oriented to a direct implementation of this precondition for a fertility decline will be focused on legalizing all culturally acceptable methods of fertility control, including possibly, abortion, voluntary surgical sterilization, and other means of contraception. An ideal program of fertility control (and one that prevails in most Western nations) is to teach boys and girls about the reproductive processes of both sexes in what are often called fertility awareness classes and to have a wide range of highly effective chemical contraceptives (such as the pill and injectables) and barrier methods (such as the IUD, contraceptive sponges, and condom) available for those people who wish to delay pregnancy while still engaging in sexual intercourse. Postpartum breastfeeding accompanied by barrier methods of birth control enhance maternal and infant health by maximizing infant nutrition and spacing the next pregnancy. Voluntary surgical contraception for those who wish to avoid further pregnancies reduces the risk of unwanted children at older ages and permits societal resources for the more expensive chemical and barrier methods to be spent on the younger members of society.

The success of a fertility control policy aiming to make methods available to the citizenry depends upon the way in which such a policy is implemented. This is, of course, true for any policy, but the private nature of reproduction seems to highlight the importance of program effort in achieving success. For example, legalization of methods is but a first step. This must be followed by the training of people who can teach others to use a method, accompanied by the mechanism for manufacturing or buying a supply of the method, along with an organized distribution system. The various ways by which contraceptives (especially the more popular ones, such as the pill and condom) are distributed has been the subject of considerable evaluation over the past decade, and, while the results suggest that there are many different ways to successfully organize a program, female contraceptives have the highest continuation rate when a consistent supply is available through a discreet mechanism of personal transfer (such as a community worker making a personal delivery). Condoms are also most widely accepted when they are routinely available at stores and other outlets, such as street vendors. Vasectomy programs have proved successful even in strongly "macho" areas like Brazil if they are performed in high-quality, male-only clinics. Not surprisingly, vasectomy adopters are typically married men who are concerned about and have consulted with their wives on the adverse health consequences of an additional pregnancy. Thus we are reminded that these policies work best when we have gotten past the first two preconditions.

The idea that a motivation for a smaller family is perceived to drive the demand for effective contraception is a reasonable one, but it apparently does not exhaust the possibilities. There also appears to be a "supply side" factor in fertility limitation. That is to say, the availability of an effective program of contraception may, in fact, create its own demand. Discussing their experience with the large-scale Matlab demonstration project in Bangladesh, Phillips and his associates have pointed out that "an intensive service program can compensate for weak or ambivalent reproductive motives and create demand for services, leading to contraceptive adoption where it might otherwise not occur."[14]

For a program to have that kind of impact, however, it must have a broad base of support, which is typically generated or at least enhanced in two different ways: (1) by public campaigns that promote the knowledge and use of birth control and (2) by important politicians and other community leaders speaking out in favor of birth control. Political support is particularly important, often the leading edge in making resources available to mount and maintain a successful family planning program.

The preceding discussion sets out the range of possibilities for policies to limit fertility. Success will depend partly on the mix of strategies employed and partly on efforts to implement the policies. We now turn to an examination of some of these factors in the context of policies that have been put into place in various nations around the world.

Policies To Limit Fertility: The Evidence

Out of 170 countries surveyed by the United Nations in 1989, 68 (40 percent) perceived their rate of growth to be too high.[15] These countries included 64 percent of the population of the globe but did not include a single industrialized nation. In 1974, the year of the United Nations' first such survey, only 28 percent of countries (encompassing 59 percent of the total population) had perceived their growth to be too high. Most, although not all, of these countries had a government policy in 1989 designed to lower the fertility level. Thus, as of 1989, 64 countries, comprising 63 percent of the world's population, had some kind of policy designed to lower fertility.

In the abstract, of course, it is impossible to evaluate the efficacy of those policies, but we can note that between 1974 and 1989 the crude birth rate for the world declined from thirty-five births per one thousand population to twenty-eight per thousand,[16] a 20 percent difference. Objectively, then, the short-term past has not witnessed dramatic declines in fertility, but clearly the worldwide trend is in the direction of lower fertility. To assess these patterns, it is useful to examine the globe regionally and look at some representative instances of the implementation of policies designed to limit fertility.

EAST ASIA Eastern Asian nations have generally been the most successful in engineering short-term rapid declines in fertility. The decline in Japan, for example, seems to have been born of necessity. A population trying to rebuild a nation after war, but swamped with repatriated Japanese who had been living in occupied countries, needed demographic relief and found it in abortion. Between 1947 and 1957 the birth rate was cut in half in Japan, almost exclusively through the use of abortion, which had been legalized as part of the Eugenics Protection Act of 1948 in Japan (the act had been passed primarily to eliminate illegal abortions, which had been on the rise). Only since the 1960s have other forms of contraceptives (especially the condom and more recently the pill) increased in importance as a factor in keeping birth rates low. At present, fertility levels in Japan are below replacement level, and the government has no fertility control policy.

Singapore's fertility decline has somewhat different roots. Singapore is a city-state that used to be part of Malaysia, and more than three-fourths of its 2.5 million inhabitants are ethnic Chinese. Upon independence in 1965 there was governmental recognition that rapid population growth would deter the nation's ability to continue developing economically. The government first established a family planning program to make contraceptives available on the assumption that the demand for such services existed. The results were disappointing, however, and in 1969 the government adopted the slogan "Two Is Enough," while legalizing abortion and introducing direct disincentives for large families, including steeply rising maternity costs for each additional child, low school enrollment priorities for third- and higher-order children, withdrawal of paid two-month maternity leave for civil service and union women after the second child, low public housing priority for large families, and no income tax allowance for more than three children. The impact on fertility was dramatic, with the average number of children being born to women dropping from 4.5 in 1966 to 1.4 in 1988. So low did fertility drop that Singapore's Prime Minister began to worry that too many of the wealthier, better-educated women were cutting back on births, while too few of the poorer, less-educated women were doing so; as a result, in a plan that generated worldwide controversy, selective incentives were instituted to encourage "elite" women to increase their level of reproduction. Indeed, since 1986 the official government view has been that fertility is too low, and the policy is to try to raise it. Available evidence suggests that the birth rate is edging back up.

The People's Republic of China has instituted the most famous program of fertility control, although the one-child policy does not actually explain low fertility in that country. Fertility began to drop steeply in China as early as the mid-1960s, long before the one-child policy was established in 1979. Communism brought with it a significant restructuring of family and gender roles, particularly among younger people. Children became less of an economic asset, and women had increased access to education and to the labor force and were no longer so likely to be dominated by elders in the family. Thus, the motivation for fertility limitation had been growing, especially within the Han majority, for some time before the government moved in the direction of more coercive measures. The current policy is in essence designed to keep fertility low among those groups who already have low fertility and to extend the pattern of fertility limitation to rural areas and ethnic minority groups, where high fertility norms still persist. Thus, the one-child policy, with its mix of direct incentives for small families and direct disincentives for large families, enforced by the indirect mechanism of strong social pressure, has been viewed by the government as an interim measure to bring a halt to population growth, stabilizing the population size at a target of 1.2 billion, after which the controls can be eased just enough to maintain that numerical limit. Despite U.S. concern about abortion in China, the official statistics indicate that fertility is kept low by the use of the IUD until the family is completed, at which time voluntary surgical contraception is the norm. We should note in passing, that despite the one-child policy, China's fertility rate remains above the replacement level (at about 2.3 children per woman, virtually the same level as in 1980) because some groups, such as rural ethnic minorities, are exempted and some families do not comply.

Since one in five humans lives in China (although less than one in seven newborn babies is Chinese), world interest remains riveted on that part of the world. The government's policy continues to favor limitations on fertility, and the success of that policy will influence world growth rates for the foreseeable future. On the other hand, the Chinese have a disproportionately small impact on world resources because China is one of the poorest countries in the world, with a per person income that is less than 2 percent of the average income in the United States.

SOUTHERN ASIA   An additional one in five humans lives in the southern Asian subcontinent, which includes India, Pakistan, and Bangladesh. High fertility remains more firmly entrenched in this part of the world despite government policies designed to limit fertility. The average woman in India continues to bear four children, despite nearly forty years of official government effort to lower the birth rate and although per person income in India is virtually the same as in China. The major difference between the two countries is in the amount of effort and resources that the government has been able to mobilize to impact any of the three preconditions for a fertility decline. India's first family planning effort, in 1952, relied heavily on the rhythm method, whose high failure rate is well known.[17] Indeed, the old joke asks, "What do you call users of the rhythm method?" The answer is "parents." India's next major foray into family planning was with the vasectomy campaigns of the 1960s, but this program was hampered by the fact that many men who were sterilized had already fathered several children, and some had wives who were already past menopause. Furthermore, there were claims that men were being wrongly coerced into sterilizations by recruiters who (like the person undergoing the vasectomy) were rewarded with a transistor radio or similar premium. The IUD has been available in India since 1961, and abortion was legalized in 1971, but the pill is still not widely distributed. In various areas of India there have been experiments in paying women not to have babies by depositing money in a pension-type account for them for each month or year that they delay or avoid a pregnancy. Such schemes have been generally successful, but they have had neither the funding nor the local government backing necessary to make them widespread.

The contrast between China and India reveals that in poor populous countries beset by a variety of problems, including multiple ethnic groups and diverse linguistic and cultural practices, the birth rate can be dramatically lowered if the government insistently promotes a small-family norm, helps to generate a demand for fertility control by instituting social changes that undermine traditional pronatalist practices, makes it worth a young person's while to delay marriage and, within marriage, to limit the number of children, backing up these motivations with widespread availability of the means by which fertility can be limited. At the same time, as the case of China shows, a decline in fertility can be wrapped around a concomitant decline in mortality; China's leaders clearly understood that "barefoot doctors were the indispensable allies of intrauterine devices."[18] Indeed, in the mid-1950s China and India had virtually the same mortality and fertility levels. In 1990, China has mortality and fertility levels nearly comparable to those in Europe, while Indians continue to die at rates well above the world average. Yet during all of the this time, average income in the two countries has remained roughly the same.

Indonesia provides good evidence of the way that government support for subtle social change and effective delivery of family planning services can impact fertility. Indonesia is the fifth most populous nation in the world and the most populous Muslim nation. In a relatively short period of time women in Indonesia have brought their fertility down from 5.7 children per woman in 1960 to an average of 3.3 in 1990—higher than China, but clearly lower than anywhere on the Indian subcontinent. There is some evidence that oil-based development in Indonesia was beginning to build a latent demand for smaller families, but most analysts agree that the strong support of President Suharto and of Islamic religious leaders for the government's programs were crucial in its widespread adoption. A survey in 1971 suggested that only 3 percent of married couples of reproductive age were using contraception, whereas by 1987 the percentage had increased to 48 percent. Donald Warwick notes: "Of great importance in the country's achieving this shift was Suharto's support for the family planning program's budget even when, as in 1986, government revenues were falling."[19] The government accommodated Islamic religious beliefs by omitting abortion and sterilization from the family planning program; from the beginning, too, religious leaders were included in the policy-planning phases. They have thus been able to assist the program by assuring the community that family planning was in accordance with the Koran, by adding family planning messages into wedding ceremonies, and by actively telling individuals about the program. Educational levels are rising in Indonesia, and that has accompanied delayed marriage among women, along with a later start and earlier stop to childbearing. As is true throughout the world, this pattern of childbearing also helps to reduce infant mortality, which then circles back to reassure parents that they are safe in having a smaller family.

LATIN AMERICA Latin America (including the Caribbean) reveals considerable regional diversity in achieving low levels of fertility, ranging from a low of 1.7 lifetime births per woman in the tiny islands of Antigua and Barbuda to a high of 6.4 in Haiti, which shows that being an island is not necessarily a defense against high fertility. Several of the islands have been aided in achieving lower fertility by the outmigration of young people (especially males), many of whom head to the U.S. mainland to search for jobs. Cuba has not recently had the United States as a major migration outlet, but it did find some temporary relief in its military adventures in Angola and elsewhere, effectively removing young men from the island for substantial periods of time. In recent years this has facilitated a rise in the average age at marriage in Cuba, which, in combination with legalized abortion and access to free contraceptives, has pushed Cuban fertility below the replacement level.[20]

The government of Mexico has also become increasingly active in promoting small family norms and in providing family planning assistance through public and private outlets. For decades, if not centuries, women in Mexico had been bearing an average of seven to eight children; however, in the middle of the 1960s it appears, the birth rate began to drop, perhaps as economic development began tentatively to take root. In 1974 the government rather dramatically reversed its previously pronatalist position and the General Law of Population was rewritten to encourage "responsible parenthood" and to offer family planning services to Mexican couples. Less than fifteen years later, in 1987, a nationwide fertility survey indicated that fertility had dropped to a national average of 3.8 children per woman.

Conclusion: What Can The United States Learn?

Any policy oriented toward fertility limitation must keep in mind that population control is rarely an end in itself but rather an implementing strategy that helps in achieving other goals. Our eye is on the prize of a desired social order, and population policies must be kept in that perspective. Policies based on racism or elitism should be clearly unacceptable in U.S. society. Instead, policies need to focus on groups whose fertility is above average and ask (1) why these groups have higher fertility and (2) what policy lessons learned from elsewhere in the world can be applied to encourage lower levels of fertility within the context of a society in which the small-family norm is already well rooted.

In the United States, as in most areas of the world, fertility rates are highest among the least educated, the poor, and racial/ethnic minority groups. Using data from the U.S. Census Bureau's Current Population Survey in 1988 (the most recent data available as of this writing), we can see that, among women aged eighteen to twenty-nine (the years in which most childbearing takes place), women who had less than a high school education were almost twice as likely to have had a baby during the previous year as were college graduates. Women in families with income under $10,000 per year were nearly three times as likely to have had a baby in the previous year as those women in families with $50,000 or more income (see Chapter 1). Hispanic women were 25 percent more likely to have a child than were non-Hispanic women, and Black women were 40 percent more likely to have a child than were White women. These categories are not mutually exclusive, of course, since

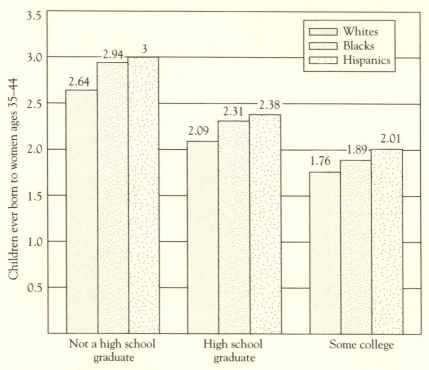

Fertility levels are highest among the least educated, regardless of race/ethnicity, United States, 1988. (Source: U.S. Bureau of the Census, *Current Population Reports.* Series P-20, no. 436, 1989).

racial/ethnic minority group members tend disproportionately to have lower levels of education and to have lower incomes. Indeed, these structural features explain much of the racial/ethnic differences in fertility in the United States. In the accompanying graph it can be seen that in the United States in 1988, the differences between racial/ethnic groups in fertility were much less than the differences in education.

Given the policy initiatives discussed, one could imagine a two-pronged approach to fertility limitation in the United States. Fertility could be brought down by increasing educational and income levels within society and by increasing the motivation of less-educated and less-well-off persons to have small families and increasing their access to effective means of fertility control. It must be recognized, though, that we are referring to a multicultural, multilingual group in U.S. society, and it is almost certain that no single approach will work best in all situations. In areas dominated by immigrant groups, some of the methods utilized in their own homelands may be effective when adapted to the U.S. environment. In inner-city areas, characterized by fractured families, high unemployment, and high crime, a system based on the Chinese "barefoot doctors" may be the model for the delivery of family planning, maternal, and infant health services. In Caroline County, Maryland, a page has been torn from the third world with an experimental program to pay high school girls not to get pregnant.[21]

However, before running off and designing a program only for the least-educated and poorest segments of the population, we should bear in mind that in the year prior to the 1988 survey referred to above, women with less than a high school education accounted for only 18 percent of all births in the United States, whereas those women who had graduated from high school but had not attended college accounted for 43 percent of all births. If we concentrated on the least-educated group and reduced their birth rate to the level of high school graduates, we would reduce the annual number of births by 3 percent. On the other hand, if we concentrated on lowering fertility of the high school graduates to the level of women who have attended college, we could reduce the annual number of births by 7 percent. Clearly the latter is the more effective strategy in terms of a quantitative impact on the birth rate. It is probably also more effective in terms of cost-efficiency because this is a group more likely to be amenable to policy pressure. Governmental policies that affect motivation for small families through taxation, the housing and consumer credit markets, and the availability of educational and labor force opportunities for women are more likely to find a response among the middle classes than among the group often labeled the underclass.

The experience of other nations suggests also that government policies influence family size decision making partly through their economic impact but partly through the social message they carry, too. Humans are inherently social creatures, not simply rational economic beings, and we are constantly looking about us for clues to social behavior. A consistent set of governmental initiatives aimed at lower fertility is almost certain to have the long-term effect of leading couples to think more consciously about their family size decisions. Such consciousness could be raised especially by the adoption of what has been called a demographic impact report (DIR). Analogous to the environmental impact reports (which initially contained the clear intention that demographic issues be addressed), the DIR would be required of all (or at least broad classes of) legislation to evaluate the proposed law's effect on either raising or lowering the fertility rate. The importance of the DIR lies in the fact that the demographic implications of most public policies are hidden to the untutored eye and only become apparent when it may be too late to overcome the consequences.[22] The DIR would have the effect both of actually promoting lower fertility (by rejecting legislative initiatives that would have the opposite effect) and of promoting low fertility *values* through the example set by legislative leadership.

Throughout the world the success of fertility limitation policies often depends upon the strength of leadership, and there is little reason to think that the United States would be an exception to this. The personal support of national leaders such as Suharto in Indonesia, Lee Kuan-yew in Singapore, and Bourguiba in Tunisia has seemed to have an unmistakable influence in the promotion of lower fertility in those countries. In this country, our complacency about low fertility has allowed national leaders to sidestep the population issue. Yet every addition to the population in a country like the United States yanks a vastly disproportionate hunk out of the world's storehouse of known resources. For this reason, policies that affect population growth in the United States have a major long-term effect on all aspects of the world's ecosystem.

We should assist globally in every way we can, and we should lead by example. We do that now *implicitly* by having low fertility, but it is not always clear to the world that we, as a nation, actually *prefer* the level of fertility we have. We exhibit considerable ambivalence about national fertility levels, and pronatalist voices are often louder than antinatalist voices. A mechanism like the DIR could be one part of a larger national policy condoning the concept of a small, healthy family that would generate a lower and more equitably distributed birth rate in the United States, while adding clout to our international assistance efforts by reducing the perception that those efforts are patronizing or even genocidal in their intent. In the words of the president of the Swiss National Bank, the United States would be offering "a frank and unashamed word in favor of family planning."[23]

ESCAPING THE OVERPOPULATION TRAP

ROBERT COSTANZA

For another way of looking at the problem of motivating people to want smaller families, let us pick up again the philosophical approach suggested in Chapter 4.

How do we communicate with the people who make the decisions—the potential parents—and escape the overpopulation trap? The elimination of social traps requires intervention, the modification of the reinforcement system. Indeed, it can be argued that the proper role of a democratic government is to eliminate social traps (no more and no less) while maintaining as much individual freedom as possible. Cross and Guyer list four broad methods by which traps can be avoided or escaped from: education (about the long-term, distributed impacts), insurance, superordinate authority (that is, legal systems, government, religion), and the conversion of the trap to a trade-off (that is, correcting the road signs).

Education can be used to warn people of long-term impacts that cannot be seen from the road. Examples are the warning labels now required on cigarette packages and the warnings of environmentalists about future hazardous waste problems. People can ignore warnings, however, particularly if the path seems otherwise enticing. For example, warning labels on cigarette packages have had little effect on the number of smokers.

The main problem with education as a general method of avoiding and escaping from traps is that it requires a significant time commitment on the part of individuals to learn the details of each situation. Our current society is so large and complex that we cannot expect even professionals, much less the general public, to know the details of all the extant traps. In addition, for education to be effective in avoiding traps involving many individuals, *all* the participants must be educated.

Governments can, of course, forbid or regulate certain actions that have been deemed socially inappropriate. The problem with this approach is that it must be rigidly monitored and enforced, and the strong short-term incentive remains for individuals to try to ignore or avoid the regulation. A police force and legal system are very expensive to maintain, and increasing their chances of catching violators increases their costs exponentially (both the costs of maintaining a larger, better-equipped force and the cost of the loss of individual privacy and freedom).

Religion and social customs can be seen as much less expensive ways to avoid certain social traps. If a moral code of action and belief in an ultimate payment for transgressions can be deeply instilled in a person, the probability of that person's falling into the "sins" (traps) covered by the code will be greatly reduced with very little enforcement cost. On the other hand, there are problems with religion and social customs as means of avoiding social traps: The moral code must be relatively static to allow beliefs learned early in life to remain in force later, and it requires a relatively homogeneous community of like-minded individuals. In modern, heterogeneous, rapidly changing societies, religion and social customs cannot handle all the newly-evolving situations; nor are they effective in regard to the conflicts between radically different cultures and belief systems.

Many trap theorists believe that the most effective method for avoiding and escaping from social traps is to turn the trap into a trade-off. This method does not run counter to our normal tendency to follow the road signs; it merely corrects the signs' inaccuracies by adding compensatory positive or negative reinforcements. A simple example illustrates how effective this method can be. Playing slot machines is a social trap because the long-term costs and benefits are inconsistent with the short-term costs and benefits. People play the machines because they expect a large short-term jackpot, while the machines are in fact programmed to pay off, say, 80 cents on the dollar in the long term. People may "win" hundreds of dollars playing the slots in the short run, but if they play long enough, they will certainly lose 20 cents for every dollar played. To change this trap to a trade-off, one could simply reprogram the machines so that every time a dollar was put in, 80 cents would come out. This way, the short-term reinforcements (80 cents on the dollar) are made consistent with the long-term reinforcements (80 cents on the dollar), and only the dedicated aficionados of spinning wheels with fruit painted on them would continue to play.

Balancing the Human Species in the Ecosystem

Balancing the human species in the ecosystem is therefore *in principle* a simple problem: Simply make the long-run, distributed, whole-system, *worst-case* costs and benefits of human population growth (and all other human activities) incumbent on all individuals in the short run and locally, at least provisionally until the worst-case impacts can be lowered. If your next child will be a net cost to the planet of *x*, you should be required to pay *x* , up front, for the right to have it, at least until it can be proved to have a lower impact. In a sense, this is an extension of the "polluter pays" principle to "polluter pays (at least provisionally) for uncertainty, too." If, and only if, this whole-system cost accounting (including uncertainty) is in place can we expect individual decisions about population growth to have any meaning for the planet as a whole.

Of course, *in principle* is very far from *in practice* in this particular case. The problems of devising cultural mechanisms to effectively communicate that cost to individual parents are daunting. But no one said it was going to be easy. The next stage of our cultural evolution must be the development of just this capacity to put back in the long-run constraints that the initial phase of cultural evolution appeared to release us from. We need to develop and use cultural "road maps" and "scouts" to counter our dependence on "road signs" in the tricky terrain in which we now find ourselves. I offer the following summary suggestions and challenge the anthropologists and sociologists to put their research to practical use in devising cultural mechanisms to implement them.

1. Establish a hierarchy of goals for national and global ecological economic planning and management. Sustainability should be the primary long-term goal, replacing the current GNP growth mania. Issues of justice, equity, and population are ultimately tied in with sustainability as preconditions. Only sustainable levels of human population are desirable. Economic growth in this hierarchy is a valid goal only when it is consistent with sustainability. The goals can be put into operation by having them accepted as part of the political debate and implemented in the decision-making structure of institutions that affect the global economy and ecology, such as the World Bank.

2. Develop better global ecological economic modeling capabilities to allow us to see the range of possible outcomes of our current activities, especially the interrelated impacts of population, per capita resource use, and wealth distribution.

3. Adjust current incentives to reflect long-run global costs, including uncertainty. To paraphrase a popular slogan, we should model globally, adjust local incentives accordingly. In addition to traditional education, regulation, and user fee approaches, a flexible assurance-bonding system has been proposed to deal specifically with uncertainty.[1] Curbing population growth requires that long-term worst-case ecological costs be made apparent to potential parents in a culturally acceptable way.

4. Tax natural capital consumption to halt the decline in the stock of natural capital. This policy will encourage the technological innovation that optimists are counting on, while conserving resources in case the optimists are wrong. Revenues can be used to mitigate problems (such as counteracting the economic forces for unwise population growth) and to ease up on income taxes, especially for the lower end of the income scale.

EUROPE IN THE ENERGY TRANSITION
The Case for a Smaller Population

When one has gotten used to something, the prospect of change can be unsettling. West Europe's population has probably been growing since the end of the Black Plague, and some writers are disturbed at the prospect that the trend may be reversing. Their concern may be misplaced. Let us look at the implications of that change for the well-being of Europe.

The Demographic Facts and Projections

Europe is crowded. The subregion of Western Europe (see the definitions in the Notes for this chapter) has a population of about 155 million—nearly two-thirds of that of the United States in an area about one-tenth as large. Despite the surge of third world populations, it is the most densely populated subregion of the world, except for Japan. In the Northern Europe subregion, the United Kingdom is even more densely populated. The population of the two subregions grew by almost one-quarter following World War II and has stabilized since 1980 at just under 240 million.

Perhaps the best indicator of coming demographic trends is the total fertility rate (TFR), a measure of how many children the average woman may be expected to bear. In modern societies, "replacement level TFR" is just above 2.0, that is two children per woman, with a small allowance for mortality and for the tendency to bear more boys than girls. At that level, a population will eventually stabilize; below it, the population will eventually decline, unless immigration makes up the difference.

In the so-called developed world, Poland, Romania, and the USSR are slightly above replacement level. All the non-Communist developed countries (except for Iceland and Ireland) are now below it. Japan has a TFR of 1.6; the United States is at 2.1; Canada at 1.7. (By contrast, the third world, excluding China, has a TFR of 4.6 and a current population doubling time of 29 years.) The lowest rates of all are in non-Communist Europe. Italy is at 1.3; Austria, Germany and Luxembourg at 1.4; the Netherlands and Spain at 1.5; and Belgium, Denmark, Portugal, and Switzerland at 1.6. These are the figures that lead to the concern about depopulation.

Why do I believe that the concern may be misplaced? First, there is the matter of perspective: These processes take a long time. For the next generation, European populations are on a plateau, not in rapid decline. The United Nations' projections illustrate this point and also remind us of the uncertainty of predicting TFRs. There are three projections. If fertility should stay roughly at its present levels, Western Europe's population in 2025 will have declined by only 1.8 percent. Even the low variant, with fertility well below current levels for most of the period, yields a projection of 92 percent of the present population, a little higher than the population in 1960, when West Europe was hardly underpopulated. The "high variant" assumes a return to 1960s fertility and yields a population *increase* of 4 percent. Europe has time to think about its demographic future.

Second, and more important; Europe may be wise to aim for lower population densities. Europe exported a sizable fraction of its population growth during its demographic transition and is probably better off for having done so. Now, rollback of population growth may be a benefit.

Someday the societies of Europe must decide how to bring fertility back to replacement levels if they are not to die out or be supplanted by immigrants—and European governments are not very receptive to immigration. In the meantime, however, they would do well to decide what population densities would serve their interests as they look into the next century.

Along with the rest of us, Europe faces an imminent energy transition away from petroleum-based economies. At the same time, it faces an environmental transition. Its own economic success has brought it face-to-face with resource and environment constraints that will limit its future options. These issues are interconnected, and it will take foresight to deal with both. My contention is that they can be better addressed with a smaller population.

The Energy Transition

World petroleum production will probably peak and begin to decline sometime in the next generation, the exact timing probably more dependent upon demand, prices, and technology than upon the discovery of new fields. For Europe, according to the International Energy Agency (IEA), the transition has already come.

In varying degrees since the start of the Industrial Revolution, west European countries have been paying for net imports of food, natural fibers, and energy through their possession of colonial empires, foreign investments, and technological superiority. Their overall energy dependence intensified, however, as petroleum supplanted coal. By 1973 non-Communist Europe was only 38 percent self-sufficient in primary energy.

Discovery of the North Sea fields gave Europe (and particularly the United Kingdom) a temporary boost, and non-Communist Europe reached 64 percent of self-sufficiency in 1985. That boost is winding down, however, and the IEA anticipates a 28 percent decline in European petroleum production during the 1990s. The United Kingdom expects to become a net importer again sometime in the mid-1990s. That may not be a happy time to be entering the market, since the monopoly position of the Persion Gulf as the residual supplier will become increasingly strong, particularly as U.S. imports continue to rise.

The Environmental Transition

Like the United States, but in a much tighter space, west Europe is struggling with urbanization and its consequences, with multiple by-products of industrialization such as toxic substances, and with the pollution generated by fossil fuels and nuclear energy.

The energy-related problems are perhaps the most pressing ones: world climate change and acid precipitation. World sea levels are rising, posing a particular threat to eastern England and the Low Countries. The effects of climate change upon European agriculture are still unpredictable. Acid precipitation, still little understood, is damaging the continent's forests and may affect its agriculture.

Europe must change its practices to preserve its environment if it is to maintain its livability. It starts these energy and environmental transitions with some penalties: The colonies are gone, and technology has fled to multi-national corporations seeking cheap labor. Europe has adjusted to these changes with considerable resiliency, but at the cost of an extremely intensive development of a small and crowded region.

In agriculture Europe has hedged its bets—at considerable economic cost—to avoid relying on imports. The deliberate pursuit of self-sufficiency has almost succeeded: The European Community (EC) has reached self-sufficiency in major foodstuffs. Non-Communist Europe as a whole runs a $20 billion annual deficit on its overall agricultural account, but this is a modest figure in $3 trillion economies, and the import gap has been declining.

Self-sufficiency has been achieved by subsidizing very high-yield, high-cost agriculture. In the EC direct subsidies constitute about 45 percent of the value of agricultural production. On top of that, consumers pay a premium of about 76 percent over world prices for agricultural products. Moreover, the system has a built-in conflict. In the EC, only Denmark, France, and the Netherlands are net agricultural exporters, and they are subsidized by Germany and the United Kingdom, the principal importers.

The high yields come at the cost of very high inputs. In most of west Europe, cereal yields exceed 5 tons per hectare (12 tons per acre) well above the U.S. level, but fertilizer inputs per hectare are more than double those in the United States. France alone uses almost as many tons of insecticides and fungicides as the United States, on one-tenth as much cropland. Italy uses even more. From the scattered data available (for example, on river-borne nitrates and phosphates) Europe's agricultural pollution problems are correspondingly serious.

Consider the intensity of energy use. West Germans use 15 percent as much energy as Americans, in less than 3 percent of the U.S. land area. They drive 13 percent as many vehicle miles in that same crowded area. (These are pre-unification data.) Individually, they do not use as much energy or drive as much, but the atmosphere has no way of knowing that. As a result of such disparities, the zone of extremely acid precipitation (below pH 4.7) covers substantially all of west Europe but less than one-fifth of the United States. No wonder the Germans find half their forests damaged.

One could go on with such examples. The United States lost about 18 percent of its wetlands between 1950 and 1980; West Germany and the Netherlands each lost more than 50 percent. The driving engine is the pressure to use the land.

The point is that the energy transition will be a much more complex process than simply finding substitutes for oil. The Europeans must find environmentally benign ways of running their energy economies. They must arrest the environmental attrition generated by industry and agriculture—at costs they can afford.

The Alternatives to Oil

West Europe faces a tougher transition than does the United States. Even if it can find ways to mitigate the environmental costs of using fossil fuels, its resources are very limited.

COAL Germany and the United Kingdom, the traditional coal suppliers, have remaining resources totaling perhaps 20 to 40 percent of U.S. resources, and those resources are substantially less accessible than ours. (Bear in mind, however, that fuel resource estimates are notoriously unreliable). The new Cool Water integrated coal gasification combined cycle (IGCC) technology or other new technologies may make it possible to exploit these reserves and still ameliorate acid precipitation, but they offer less comfort concerning carbon dioxide.

NATURAL GAS Most of the dwindling natural gas reserves are in Norway and the United Kingdom.

BIOMASS Biomass is the first natural alternative to fossil fuels. Before the advent of coal, biomass was already the principal non-animal energy source. Ideally, if it is harvested on a sustained yield basis, it can be neutral with respect to carbon dioxide, since it recycles the carbon dioxide between plants and the atmosphere rather than releasing it from fossil fuels. Unfortunately, here again, the Europeans are the victims of their own intense use of the environment. Where does one find the land to grow the biomass? Some 78 percent of Western Germany and 84 percent of France are already in cropland, pastureland, and forest. Every acre given to biomass production will involve tradeoffs with food or forestry production—and the forests are already in trouble. The European climate will not grow crops like sugar cane and corn which yield high tonnages of potential fuel. There is only limited opportunity here.

NUCLEAR ENERGY Nuclear energy once seemed the answer, but one need hardly belabor the concerns that it has generated. France, Germany, the United Kingdom, and Sweden are the only major west European countries to go heavily into nuclear power. In Sweden, even before Chernobyl, the electorate had voted to phase out of nuclear energy by 2010. The programs in Germany and the United Kingdom are in trouble. Only in France is there a major continuing commitment to the nuclear route; 80 percent of its electric power production is nuclear.

As a result, France, with one-quarter our population and only 6 percent of our land, already has over one-half as many cubic feet of spent fuel and radioactive wastes to be stored or reprocessed as does the United States. At any rate, nuclear energy is only a transitional fuel unless one goes to the breeder reactor, but that route is proving very expensive and poses dangers of operating safety and the diversion of plutonium to weapons. Nobody can yet say whether fusion-based energy is possible (it is not easy to harness a 90 million degree explosion) and we cannot yet assess the radioactivity problems or the environmental implications of using such a vast new source of energy.

HYDROPOWER Although Europe already uses 59 percent of the theoretical potential, more than any other continent, hydropower meets only 7 percent of non-Communist Europe's energy needs. The potential is marginal, and the social and economic cost of developing new sites is high.

SOLAR ENERGY Europe is the least favorably situated inhabited continent for direct solar energy. Almost all of Europe north of the Alps averages more than 50 percent cloud cover, and much of it is 70 percent cloudy or more. Moreover, due to its northerly location, Europe's days are very short when the energy is most needed.

WIND Think of windmills and one thinks of Holland. Wind power has potential: A NASA study once concluded that it is technically feasible to meet the United States' energy needs with wind power. However, since the potential energy varies with the cube of the wind speed, the cost rises exponentially when average wind speeds are low. Rising fuel costs justify the investment in wind power technologies, but west Europe, with its relatively placid climate, is not particularly well situated.

The Demographic Connection

Daunting as this brief survey is, Europeans are educated and resilient. They will experiment and come up with some currently unpredictable mix of sources, perhaps including exotics such as wave power and ocean thermal gradients. There will be an incentive to develop more efficient engines, such as the fuel cell, and to intensify energy conservation. (Back to bicycles?)

However, demography is fundamental to the size of the problem. At given levels of per capita consumption, technology, and conservation, the scale of the problem is proportional to the size of the population to be served. A reduction of, say, 20 percent in population would mitigate the pressure for high agricultural yields, in turn reducing the pollution problems, the high cost of food (with savings that could be invested in the energy transition), and the political tensions within the EC. Agriculture itself would require less energy, and land would be freed for possible biomass production for energy.

A population reduction would also generate comparable benefits from reduced requirements for new energy sources or from reduced costs in managing urban wastes and toxic substances. The benefits are not necessarily linear because the connections are complex. Europe might, for instance, choose to maintain food output to generate exports to pay for energy imports.

However, the direction in which population reduction would affect the management of the energy transition is unmistakable, and it is favorable.

The classical rebuttal is that labor creates wealth—the more people, the more wealth. But that is no longer the case. A mental model applicable to a less crowded world may not fit a crowded one. In the current technological revolution, a better model would be that capital, with a bit of intelligent direction, creates wealth. It is worth noting that the

Carter–Leontief UN world model tied production in the industrial societies to investment rather than to work force size. In the real world, Europe's problem has recently been unemployment, not labor shortages.

The Cannon Fodder Argument

The most popular argument for a larger population is that it is needed for military security. This "musket mentality" finds resonances in European countries that have been fighting one another and their neighbors for millennia.

The first response to that argument is that it ain't necessarily so. The argument is momentarily beguiling but unsupported by systematic historical research. A quick mental scan of the histories of Europe, the Americas, and Asia suggests that at least half of all wars have been won by the smaller adversary.

The second response is that wars have been getting prohibitively costly and destructive. A continuation of Europe's historical fratricidal behavior can only result in self-destruction. The EC is the testament to a driving desire to break the historical cycle, and it seems to be succeeding.

The USSR has more often been perceived as the threat necessitating military preparedness. In light of recent events, we are not hearing much currently from the proponents of this argument, but the present detente is not indestructible, so it would be wise to dispose of this argument, too. The deep national and ethnic tensions within the Soviet Union and between it and its erstwhile alliance have been dramatically displayed. It is time that we remember the mass defection of Ukrainians to the Germans in World War II. The Soviets would be embarking on dangerous seas indeed if they considered trying to escape their present difficulties by military adventure against the West. Even in that unlikely case, it is usually forgotten that even before East Germany switched sides, the total forces of NATO countries were 34 percent larger that those of the Warsaw Pact. For both sides, however, questions of cohesiveness and will are more important than crude numbers.

At the other extreme, any single European country is completely outnumbered by the USSR, and a population change of 20 or 30 percent either way would not substantially alter the equation.

If the apocalypse should come, the present assumption is that it would be a nuclear exchange and that troop strength would be of limited relevance. Even if the Soviets were willing to take that risk, the enticement depends upon the opportunities. A stable Europe adjusting successfully to the energy and environmental transitions is less likely to offer opportunities than a Europe riven by economic and resource problems—and I have already argued that a smaller population makes a successful transition more likely. Competitive fertility justified on military grounds may be self-defeating.

The "cannon fodder" argument rests in part upon the awareness that the population of the USSR is still growing. However, most of that growth is occurring among the Soviets' restive Asian minorities, whose loyalties would not be predictable in war. As the Soviets know, war regularly leads to results far different from the expectations of those who start it.

Finally, in an increasingly interdependent world, autarky becomes increasingly unattractive to both sides. The USSR is now a major importer of Western grains, paying for them in some part with energy exports, including natural gas to West Europe. The Soviets' relations with Europe are shaped by forces far different from the simplistic confrontation out of which NATO and the Warsaw Pact emerged, and strategic thinking must adjust to the change.

The Problems of Transition

There are problems of adjustment as population stabilizes, and they are more severe if there is a rollback, particularly if it happens quickly. How does one run a prosperous "steady-state economy" without the stimulus of population growth? How does one maintain innovation and creativity? How does one manage a changing age structure?

These issues have to be faced. Population growth cannot continue indefinitely in a finite world. You cannot avoid the energy transition or the environmental issues by ignoring them. The problems will eventually face all nations. West Europe (and Japan) have simply gotten there first.

Conclusion

If a sustainable society is judged by its success in living comfortably within its resources—in preserving the environmental and resource base that supports it—then Europe like the rest of the world has not yet achieved it. Fossil energy has made possible a period of very high productivity while its by-products have been sowing the seeds of destruction of the economies it has supported. The energy transition may be a blessing if it lessens that threat and forces us all toward sustainable energy policies.

It is ironic that when West Europe has just succeeded in

—stabilizing population growth,

—controlling a potentially dangerous dependency on imported food,

—adjusting to the transisiton from the colonial era, and

—positioning itself to deal with the energy transition,

there are those who are fearful of that very success.

There is no magic about "population stability," nor is it even attainable in the real world. When growth ends, there will be fluctuations, not a constant.

Europe, apparently, has entered that period, and the present demographic patterns help to meet the problems that they face. Bravo. We should be studying their experience and their solutions.

NEIGHBORS' PROBLEMS, OUR PROBLEMS

Population Growth in Central America

ROBERT W. FOX

By contrast with Europe, Central America is an example of the effects of uncontrolled population growth. It is hardly a unique example, but it is of particular interest because it is nearby and because the United States is and will be bearing some of the cost of a horrendous failure of foresight.

I was walking through the streets of Cartago, Costa Rica, some twenty years ago when the bells rang and the elementary schools let out. A thousand scrubbed and uniformed children flooded the streets. That Lilliputian world was a dramatic reminder that Costa Rica, like the rest of

Central America, is a nation of children. Nearly half the population is under fifteen.

Central America's population explosion was captured for me in that incident. Today, ever-larger numbers of children are pressing hard on small and shrinking economies. The eight million Central American children aged zero to fourteen in 1970 represented a large increase from four million in 1950. There are thirteen million now. If projections hold true, there will be nineteen million by 2025. As shown in the table on population estimates and projections, in one lifetime Central America's population is not just doubling or trebling, but rising by a factor of seven—if the ecology can support it. And growth will not stop in 2025. In the first half of the seventy-five year period from 1950 to 2025 a third of the expected increase occurred. The much larger share, nearly two-thirds, is projected between 1990 and 2025. Past 2025, the projections call for further increases of about one million annually. The amounts may seem modest compared to the population size and growth in the United States, but proportionately they are massive. With Central America's pace of growth, the United States' population would be one billion in 2025!

Population is yesterday's, today's, and tomorrow's issue in Central America. The population explosion that began in the 1950s and continues today is arguably Central America's most significant historical

Central America: Population Estimates and Projections
(in thousands)

	1950	1975	1990	2000	2025
Costa Rica	862	1,968	3,016	3,711	5,250
El Salvador	1,940	4,085	5,251	6,739	11,299
Guatemala	2,969	6,022	9,197	12,221	21,668
Honduras	1,401	3,081	5,138	6,846	11,510
Nicaragua	1,098	2,408	3,872	5,261	9,219
Panama	893	1,748	2,419	2,893	3,862
Central America	9,163	19,312	28,893	37,671	62,808

Source: United Nations, *World Population Prospects, 1988*, Population Studies no. 106, ST/ESA/ SER.A/106 (United Nations, New York, 1989). Belize, with 180,000 population, is not included in this study.

event, overriding in importance both the Spanish Conquest and the Independence Movement 270 years later. Not only is the *amount* of growth of serious concern but also the *speed* at which it is occurring. It is wreaking havoc on the region's cultures, economies, and social systems and on the natural resource base.

We would do well to turn from the issues that have heretofore demanded our attention—the failure of political systems, murderous civil wars, and economic depression and unemployment affecting as much as half the labor force. Our key debates should not be over exploitive landholding systems, where power is concentrated in the hands of a few export crop producers. Secondary, too, are the low levels of living and the miserable urban slums that appear to be clusters of smoking cardboard and tin boxes strung along the *arroyos*. We should not be distracted by the exodus of tens and hundreds of thousands headed north to cross the porous Mexican and U.S. borders in search of jobs. We should focus on the rise in population. Redoubling every twenty to twenty-five years, it has put an incredible burden on attempts to resolve old problems while creating new ones. In Central America today you must run faster just to stay in the same place.

How Did This Rise Occur, and Why Do We Not Read More About It?

Foreign writers on Central America seem genuinely unaware of the issue's strength and of the intertwining of demographic trends and political and economic issues. A glance through recently published books in English on the region turned up only a few references to the subject, and they simply recite the facts of population size. Why the inattention? There are at least two reasons. The writers have little exposure or training in the basic principles of demography and consider it a technical matter best left to the experts. Second, there has been a concerted effort to narrow down the topic and find it a niche; accordingly, population is invariably classified and bottled up in the health and family-planning arena.

Largely ignoring population as a theme, writers focus on the visible results of overcrowded societies—rapid urbanization and growing slum settlements, crowded labor markets and high unemployment, declining purchasing power, falling levels of living, and a rapidly deteriorating natural resource base. These major problems were exacerbated in Central America during the "lost decade" of the 1980s as the economies stagnated.

In the 1990s, the economies continue to lose ground, while population growth relentlessly moves ahead.

Why the Population Explosion?

Central America's recent demographic history is typical of most third world regions. Before the twentieth century, high fertility was coupled with high mortality; as a result, the gap between these levels was small, allowing very low growth—well under 1 percent annually. Population grew slowly during the sixteenth to nineteenth century colonial era, and in the first century of independence as well. By 1920 the number stood at five million; the pace quickened, and twenty years later the figure increased to seven million.

By the 1940s, major health improvements were underway as the age-old era of pestilence and plague faded and the modern one emerged. Field reports of the Pan American Health Organization now discussed the positive results of the installation of sewage and potable water systems, for example, rather than reports of plague or cholera outbreaks in port cities. Following World War II, massive resources were invested in the region to improve general health conditions, including medical treatment, food processing, sanitation, education, and efforts to control communicable and transmissible diseases. As a result, the death rate dropped sharply in a very brief period of time. The decline in deaths depended on imported technology such as medicines, pesticides and insecticides. The birth rate, meanwhile, which depended on slowly changing cultural norms, remained high. Compared to twenty-four births per thousand population annually in the United States in 1950, the rate was forty in Panama and in a higher range elsewhere, from forty-seven to fifty-four. By the mid-1970s, it dropped substantially in Costa Rica, but only modestly elsewhere. Today, the birth rate is still moderately high, ranging from two-thirds to three-quarters its 1950 level. Women in Central America in 1950 averaged six to seven children; the range today is from three to six. These differences narrow, however, in terms of *surviving* children when the sharp drop in child mortality is applied.

Population growth represents the excess of births over deaths (absent migration). There were on average 290,000 more births than deaths annually in Central America during 1950–55; the difference is now about 800,000, and by 2020–25 it is projected to increase to around one million annually. The further reason for the explosion is tied to the vast increase in the number of women of reproductive age, associated in turn with the region's very young age structure. In Central America in 1950 there were 2.1 million women of reproductive age. By 1990, they numbered 6.7 million; by 2000, 9.2 million are projected; and by 2025, 16.4 million. In essence, although individuals are having fewer children, the vastly greater *number* of women will produce many more children than before.

The population of Central America will continue to increase until these forces are played out and the number of births is equal to the number of deaths in any given interval. The youthful age structure, combined with its product, the rising numbers of females aged fifteen to forty-nine, as well as the fertility and mortality trends described, constitute the inertia that ensures this relationship will not be attained for decades in spite of a falling birth rate.

Out of this population well-spring flow enormous consequences for the deteriorating natural resource base (particularly the forests), for urbanization and labor force growth, and eventually for the pressures that lead to flight to the United States.

The Tropical Forests

The deforestation diagram shows the linkage between the destruction of Central America's tropical rainforest and population growth. To accommodate the region's growing numbers, the pressures on natural resources are severe. With few mineral or petroleum reserves and limited amounts of good agricultural land, mostly tied up in large estates, the region is heavily dependent on its few remaining resources, among which, the forests are prominent. The forest resource has been increasingly drawn on to generate income in the "productive" economic sectors by supplying raw materials for the manufacturing and processing industries. Precious woods are marketed abroad for making furniture, doors, beams, and carved figures. Local demand for less desirable wood is high. Sawmills provide timbers and finished lumber for house construction to shelter the burgeoning urban population. Charcoal sellers ply the streets of the cities. The forests are being harvested, but there is little new growth to ensure the resource's regeneration.

These forest incursions have led to a process of continuous deterioration. To bring out prized timbers such as mahogany, primitive logging roads are built. These become waterways fed by tropical downpours. The local population exacerbates the situation by harvesting the readily

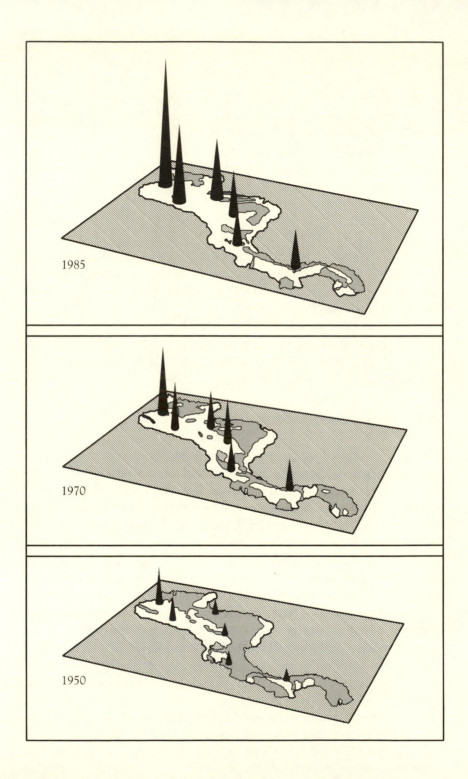

available wood on the slopes next to the road. Heavy erosion results, soils are lost in a widening radius, and gullies develop.

The roads also permit penetration into the jungle by "forest farmers" who apply slash-and-burn techniques to clear small plots. These techniques have been used for centuries. However, until recently there were far fewer people involved, and they farmed a plot for only a few years, moving on as erosion and mineral leaching depleted the land's fertility. Now, under conditions of rapid rural population growth, other farmers follow in their footsteps to try and coax one or two more crops out of the soil. Rather than allowing the land to rest for many years to rebuild its fertility, increased population pressure has led to further soil deterioration.

As patches of cleared jungle coalesce and the forest line retreats, it is valued only as pasture. From the early 1960s to 1987, the United Nations' Food and Agricultural Organization (FAO) reports, land in permanent pasture nearly doubled, increasing from 17 to 32 million acres, while land in forests and woodlands dropped from 67 to 42 million acres. The newly cleared land has supported a vastly expanded cattle industry. Much of the beef is exported: thus the "hamburger connection" is forged between tropical forest destruction and the economic demands of industrialized nations.

Deforestation in particular areas threatens to produce devastating results. Panama Canal operations depend on the water in Lake Gatun. Ships are raised from the Atlantic Ocean to the higher lake level through one set of locks; after crossing the isthmus they are lowered to the Pacific Ocean through other locks. Enormous amounts of lake water flush out to sea with these operations. Replenishing Lake Gatun's water supply is vital, and that depends on the heavy rainfalls that regularly sweep the area.

Canal authorities now worry about the amount of forest clearance taking place in the immediately surrounding watershed basin. With reduced tree cover, the hydrological cycle is disturbed. Evapotranspira-

The deforestation of Central America. The spikes represent each country's population. The dark land area is the tropical forest, and the light area deforested land. Less than 40 percent of the original forest remains, with two-thirds of the loss occurring since the 1950s. As much as 3 percent of the remainder continues to be taken down each year. Source: Robert W. Fox, Allen Carroll, and Melvin L. Prueitt, *Population Images*, 2nd ed. (United Nations Population Fund, New York, 1987).

tion is reduced, diminishing local water vapor recycling in the atmosphere. In the absence of tree cover, the increased reflectivity heats the atmosphere, counteracting cloud formation and rainfall. With the forest cover intact, the ground soaks up rainfall, releasing it slowly to the lake; without cover, however, water runoff increases, eroding the land and carrying soils that threaten to silt up the lake.

Central America faces a dilemma. The remaining forest must be preserved for its intrinsic value along with the vast genetic diversity it contains, undoubtedly a source of future medical and scientific discoveries. The tropics harbor many more times the number of species than exist in temperate climates. Tropical forests have taken millions of years to evolve into their extremely diversified biological states. Many species—plant, animal, and insect— survive symbiotically, that is, in mutual interdependence. The felling of one commercially desirable tree in the tropical rainforest may assure the destruction of an entire habitat and many of the distinct life forms it supports.

However, the region's explosive population growth exerts enormous pressures on this natural resource. The Central American nations are caught up in cycles that require income for new investments and old debt repayment. Earnings are needed to maintain current investments and to satisfy basic needs of very young populations. The difficulties of meeting daily national expenses are presently compounded by economic stagnation and economic instability. Short-term interests often prevail to the detriment of forest preservation.

Urbanization

The growth of Central America's major cities since 1950 was an early sign of the population explosion. Shunning near-feudal agricultural conditions, attracted by the city lights, and bused on good road systems in these relatively small countries, tens of thousands migrated to the cities. Voting with their feet, they continue today.

As the table on population of capital cities shows, Guatemala City, with around 340,000 inhabitants, was the "megalopolis" of Central America in 1950. Like the other capitals, including Tegucigalpa and Managua, it was compact and retained a distinct colonial-period feel. Quite suddenly, these cities, along with Panama City, San Salvador, and San Jose, faced growth onslaughts. Each increased three- to six-fold in population size between 1950 and 1980. What had been the entire city became the old, "colonial" part of town just a generation later.

Central America: Population of Capital Cities, Estimates and Projections (in thousands); see table on p. 212.

	1950	1980	2010	2025
San Jose, Costa Rica	146	508	1,150	1,525
San Salvador, El Salvador	213	858	2,050	3,200
Guatemala City, Guatemala	337	1,430	4,550	7,200
Tegucigalpa, Honduras	72	406	1,430	2,200
Managua, Nicaragua	109	662	2,550	3,750
Panama City, Panama	217	794	1,870	2,425

Source: Robert W. Fox and Jerrold W. Huguet, *Population and Urban Trends in Central America and Panama* (Inter-American Development Bank, Washington, D.C., 1977).

Burgeoning urban populations pressed for expanded services. Dusty streets, torn up for months and even years for the placing of water and sewer pipes, vied with overhead power-line installations for general disruptiveness. Moreover, in the 1960s expansive squatter settlements emerged on the cities' outskirts, particularly around the capitals of Guatemala, Nicaragua, and Honduras. Sharp conflicts with municipal authorities arose over two basic issues, ownership of the ground and legal recognition of the settlements, whose resolution was prerequisite to home improvements and the extension into the communities of water, sewage, and electrical lines. In San Salvador, makeshift dwellings built by squatters in the ravines radiated outward from the city core, threading their way through upper- and middle-class residential zones. Social class in San Salvador is literally tied to one's topographical position.

However, that massive urban growth was but a harbinger of the much greater increases to come. Practically all cities and towns have continued to grow rapidly, and there is no let-up in sight. In roughly half the seventy-five-year period (1950 to 1990), the urban population of Central America increased from 2.8 to 13.7 million; this net gain of eleven million, however, is just over a quarter of the expected total increase during 1950–2025. The much larger proportion, 73 percent, or some thirty million additional urban dwellers, lies immediately ahead.

The major cities often seem to have reached saturation and face significant constraints to further growth. Guatemala City is crowded onto a small plateau. San Jose's and San Salvador's further physical expansion threaten to take scarce and fertile adjacent lands out of agricultural production. Tegucigalpa is wedged into a small valley. Panama City is bordered on three sides by the Pacific Ocean, the canal, and the hills to the north. Managua, its vacant downtown area converted to cow pasture after the 1972 earthquake, reeling from the effects of a destroyed economy, must determine how to reconstruct a city around a hollow core, should confidence in the economy be regained and funds become available.

In addition, automobile and bus fumes, factory smoke, and nearby fires burning in the fields contribute to a steady decline in the quality of the urban environment. The once clear sky over Guatemala City, for example, is often gray with smog. Generally crowded conditions are apparent, affecting the public transportation system in particular as old and overloaded buses, belching black smoke, slowly thread their way through narrow city streets. Most shocking of all is the contrast between the clear upstream river and reservoir water before it passes through the cities and the black untreated sludge that pours into the stream beds at the other end and is used in the agricultural fields. Unfortunately, resources to remedy these and many other deteriorating urban conditions are nowhere in sight.

The urban share of the total population in all the countries was about one-third in 1950. (Honduras was less than 18 percent urban.) It has now risen to about one-half. By 2025 it is expected to range from two-thirds to three-fourths. It will continue to increase as rural areas approach saturation in the amount of population they will absorb and as the "redundant" rural numbers pour into the cities. In earlier times, rural saturation resulted from miserable rural socioeconomic conditions, including inequitable land ownership and tenure systems, rigid systems of social stratification and the absence of social mobility, a lack of rural schools and medical facilities, and the absence of rural credit and financing institutions. While these conditions have changed little, they have been compounded by rising rural population densities and a rapidly increasing labor force.

Growth of the Labor Force

A generation later, those children of Cartago, Costa Rica, are working or looking for work. Yet the region is in its second decade of a severe

Central America: The Economically Active Population (in thousands); see table on p. 212.

	1950	1975	1990	2000	2025
Costa Rica	295	637	1,050	1,338	2,016
El Salvador	685	1,349	1,743	2,295	4,277
Guatemala	966	1,767	2,630	3,666	8,234
Honduras	467	911	1,582	2,256	4,564
Nicaragua	367	722	1,204	1,776	3,674
Panama	315	588	873	1,111	1,597
Central America	3,125	5,974	9,082	12,442	24,362

Source: *Economically Active Population, 1950–2025,* vol. 3, *Latin America,* (International Labour Office [ILO], Geneva, 1986).

economic recession. Central American economies are in disarray as the value of the currencies and primary export commodities—coffee, bananas, timber, cattle, cotton and sugar—have fallen. Investors, jittery over unsettled political and economic conditions, have transferred capital to safer haven abroad. Disadvantaged by falling export commodity earnings, limited in natural resources, short on investment capital, and supported by outmoded technology, few of Central America's new labor force entrants are finding meaningful employment. And the number of entrants is indeed large as shown in the accompanying table.

Overall, labor force growth parallels the urbanization trend. About three-quarters of the 1950–2025 labor force increase will occur between 1990 and 2025. However, the relatively small agricultural labor force increase will throw the largest burden on the cities.

Should the poor economic growth climate persist, these massive urban labor force increases could result in unprecedented international labor force flows. This is already the case with El Salvador, where it is estimated that up to 15 to 20 percent of the total population has fled to the United States. Affecting this potential, however, are other key issues, including the as yet unmeasured capacity of the informal employment sector to absorb labor increases in the cities and the ability or the desire of the United States to absorb the flow.

Other Realities

For decades Central Americans have sought a proper place for the population issue in their social and economic institutions. This has been a tough, uphill battle, made more difficult by moral and ethical implications in predominantly Roman Catholic societies. It has been and continues to be a struggle.

Both as creed and operating mechanism, "economic development" has dominated Central America's view of its future since the 1960s. A fast pace of economic growth was expected to more than offset the demographic reality. It was to be fostered through export earnings, "soft" loans and grants from the multilateral banking community (World Bank and Inter-American Development Bank), by loans from Organization for Economic Cooperation and Development (OECD) nations, and by commercial bank funds. National policies focused on "development" in the context of an eventual fully integrated economic union, the Central American Common Market. This was to be supported by the Central American Bank for Economic Integration which was to attract the resources of the international lending community, then awash with petrodollars. Policies and programs were aimed at clearing the forests, colonizing and "developing" the land, and increasing export crops and livestock production levels. As the region's cities mushroomed in size, multiple urban industrialization options were advanced, some to deal with regional opportunities offered by the fledgling Central American Common Market, others to take advantage of the export market and the cheap and growing local labor force supply.

Such conscious policies for economic growth were not matched on the demographic front. Population growth was still considered a "given." The idea of slowing it down, of tampering with "natural" forces offended many and grated deeply on personal convictions. Besides, the notion of any "limitations" went completely against the grain of economic development and its corollary, "growth." Instead, commercial interests advanced the notion that growing markets would need more consumers. Rural interests stated that agricultural land remained to be developed. The military argued that more people were necessary to settle the fringes of national territory to prevent encroachments from the neighbors. Indigenous leaders railed at the thought that their groups would be targets of population "control" efforts.

Religious orders fought against the very notion of family planning and the provision of contraceptives. Many politicians behaved likewise in the male-dominated societies. Uncomfortable with the subject, they were often reluctant to discuss it. Outright hostility to family planning was not unknown.

It was always recognized that economic growth had to keep pace with population growth. If the economies faltered, the continuing population gains would slip right on by, producing lower and lower levels of living, and wiping out the forward momentum of the 1960s and 1970s. This is precisely what has happened. Living conditions in Central America have fallen back to 1960s levels.

The struggle to convey the demographic message in Central America in overwhelmingly "growth and development"–oriented societies has been difficult. The principal actors have very divergent views and interests in mind. Initially confined to the resolve of private organizations, the family planning base later broadened with its acceptance as a maternal and child health care issue in the ministries of public health. During the 1970s, several countries went so far as to create demographic evaluation units at the national planning level. Elevating the topic to that level was both an attempt to raise awareness and also to wrest control of it from economists, who more often than not considered population size and growth a given, an "externality" to their analyses.

Demographers have informed politicians that a very major problem is emerging for which there is no short-term solution. Further, it is guaranteed to continue to intensify for the next half-century and longer. Attempts to ameliorate it over the long term by implementing and supporting family planning programs will touch on and alter the deepest cultural sensitivities. All this, they argue, will contribute to unrest and eventually bring about profound changes in individual and family value systems.

Slowly but surely the old attitudes are changing. Recognizing the technical soundness of the population projections and making inescapable commonsense observations in the increasingly crowded streets, politicians increasingly realize that a serious and intractable problem has emerged. Their response has become, "I already know that there is a population problem. Don't bring me problems. Bring me solutions."

Conclusion

I have selected Central America as a typical case of the demographic forces at work in the third world. It has also been at the center of much foreign policy debate in the United States (including proposals recurrently made in Congress to enable various Central Americans, once here, to stay here) because the demographic future of Central America is linked with the United States' population future through immigration, and because the demographic trends in Central America imperil the prosperity and political stability of a region of considerable importance to the United States.

Much of what has been said about Central America could be said also of Mexico, which is three times as populous as all of Central America and shares a long border with the United States. High birth and rapidly falling death rates, a young age structure, and vast increases in the number of women of reproductive age are similar themes there.

The strongest distinction between Mexico and Central America is the Mexican government's deliberate decision in the 1970s to bring down its very high rate of population growth and to act quickly on this decision. Programs were drawn up and implemented and have since been reinforced by each successive national administration. The population target of 100 million by the year 2000 may be overshot by some six to ten million; nevertheless this number is more welcome than the earlier projection.

With shared features, Mexico has long realized that the demographic "passages" in store for Central America are also inevitable there. Appreciating that they have some control over the time required to work through these passages, Mexican authorities have made deliberate and concerted efforts to speed up the process. Accordingly, while the age structure has changed very little (the Mexican median age was slightly over eighteen years in both 1950 and today), the total fertility rate has dropped precipitously, from 6.7 children in 1950–70 to around 3.7 today. This represents enormous change in a very short period on the demographic scale of things. In Central America, only Costa Rica and Panama have had comparable fertility declines.

Nevertheless, with population momentum still driving their demography, neither Central America nor Mexico is likely to stabilize at a level and in time to take the pressures off its social, ecological and economic systems—or ours.

THE KINGDOM OF THE DEAF
It Can Happen Here

Let us look afresh at our huge nation, suspended between the runaway population growth of much of the third world and the matured demographics of Europe, and see what policy recommendations flow from the complex interweaving of viewpoints in this book.

To be more precise: It *is* happening here.

Even as this study was being written (1990), U.S. women's fertility moved back up from 1.8 to more than 2.0 children, making most of the population projections we have used look very conservative. Moreover, the proposed Immigration Act of 1990 will sharply increase legal immigration for the foreseeable future. Taken together, these rates would lead to a population in 2080 between 409 and 558 million.[1] The rates will change again, of course (and not necessarily downward), but the projection shows the direction in which we are presently heading.

There is a sardonic irony in current policies. The enthusiasm of the Reagan and Bush administrations for consumerism, taken together with their indifference or outright hostility to population limitation, is hastening the end of the era when their "Texas" view of consumption is supportable for any but a tiny fraction of the population. They are, in effect, encouraging the unrestrained growth of two of the three variables that determine the size of environmental and resource problems (population and per capita consumption), leaving technology as the only tool with which to address those problems.

In the process, the nation is limiting its options for the future and foreclosing the pursuit of what—if we stopped to think—would be the optimum.

To illustrate the point: Many of us favor policies that would discourage the use of private cars (by making their users pay their real social and environmental costs) and would promote the use of public transportation. This is not because we *like* to ride buses. Anybody who has waited in the snow for a homebound bus that never came or caught a winter cold from a fellow passenger sneezing in his or her face is not likely to idealize buses.

If we were to select the optimum transportation, in isolation from other considerations such as the environment or the energy transition, or the real world of snarling traffic jams, we would unhesitatingly choose an automobile. We advocate buses, however, because we recognize that we are past the population level that will tolerate our optimum mode.

Our country is being forced to make more and more of those less than optimum choices. We may not even recognize them as compromises. Necessity conditions us so deeply to think of the *possible* that we seldom distance ourselves sufficiently to ask "What is *desirable?*" If we will recognize that we can control population growth, we will find that we have more and better choices. Then perhaps we can begin to pursue the ideal, rather than choosing among unsatisfactory alternatives.

Most of our decisions have demographic consequences. The population change engendered by a decision on, say, immigration or welfare policy may imperil the pursuit of policies in some entirely different area, such as the integration of Blacks into mainstream U.S. society (Briggs), the protection of the environment (Ehrlichs), the preservation of the cities as good places to live (Speare and White), the productivity of the Chesapeake Bay (Tennenbaum and Costanza), or the preservation of the western high country from continued savaging (Brownridge).

How Many Americans?

The two most visible and perhaps the controlling restraints on population are energy and food. Environmental problems set a limit to the scale of economic activities, but it is not easy to say exactly where that line lies. Some very crowded places can prosper, particularly if they are surrounded by water or less developed countryside to absorb their effluents. Witness the success of South Korea, Taiwan, Hong Kong, Singapore, and Japan. These places all depend on a benign and open world economy to enable them to exchange their products for energy and food. In a sense, in a world trading system, they are the "world cities," trading with the "world countryside."

However, the assured availability of cheap energy is running out for all of us. In the present energy transition, because of the scale of its economy, the United States will be a major factor in deciding how abrupt and difficult the worldwide transition will be. Moreover, unlike those island economies, the United States does not have the luxury of simply assuming that food will always be there. We are the world's residual food supplier, and neither we nor the food importers have anywhere to turn if that source is imperiled.

ENERGY It is no wonder, then, that four of the authors in this study, quite independently, identify energy as a key factor in determining optimum U.S. population. They employ different reasoning but come to somewhat similar conclusions. The Pimentels come up with the range of from 40 to 100 million. Costanza reaches a "prudently pessimistic" estimate of about 85 million at current per capita consumption levels or twice that with a more energy-conserving "European" style of consumption. Similarly, the Ehrlichs propose a range of from 70 million, if we choose to remain profligate, to 135 million, if we do not. Werbos, in the most detailed energy analysis, offers a wider possible range, depending upon the progress of technology. He starts with a "pessimistic" figure of 60 million—which is the point at which direct solar energy would be needed for baseline electric power, driving the cost substantially upward—and puts the upper limit at 125 to 250 million, depending upon the performance of new technologies, with the cautionary note that environmental problems could be mounting at the upper end of that range.

Werbos also underlines the immense capital cost of adjusting in coming decades to the energy transition, beginning with oil. Because of that cost, he advocates population policies that would hold down the growth of demand, with national policies that would contribute to the rate of capital formation and enhance the productivity of labor. He believes that, as a nation, we are paying for the luxury of supporting the present pattern of differential fertility, in which the poorest and the least educated are the most fertile, and their children generate disproportionate social costs and transfer payments. He observes that wiser policies concerning immigration and fertility would lead toward something like the Bouvier "hard" scenario and an immediate slowing of population growth.

Notice that all four writers assume that *optimum* means renewables and conservation, with the end of the fossil fuel era and no prospect for nuclear power. The exclusion of fossil fuels is driven both by environmental constraints and by the fact that they are exhaustible and therefore transitional. If we face a mounting energy crisis, we also face an opportunity, since the ways we produce and use energy lie at the heart of many of our environmental problems.

Those who would interpose that nuclear power could fill the gap would be confusing the *possible* with the *desirable*. Given the dangers of nuclear energy that Werbos so eloquently states, would the world not be a better place without it, even if—because of a failure of population policy—we wind up without a better option?

Moreover, power from nuclear fission is also transitional because of the limits of uranium deposits, unless we go to the breeder reactor, which raises all the problems of safety and control in a much more concentrated form.

AGRICULTURE The Pimentels point to the agricultural limits on optimum population. We are mining our soils, drawing down the nation's groundwater supplies, and damaging the environment through concentrated use of fertilizers and pesticides. They recommend a 50 to 60 percent reduction of inputs in order to address those problems.

Farmland is limited. Some of it is too erosive for sustained cropping. Given the energy future already described, food production will compete with biomass for energy. Improved strains may possibly lead to yields comparable to the present, with less intensive inputs. Prudence would set this as an upper limit, however. The optimum population resulting from these calculations may be as low as half the present population.

HUMANS AND THE BIOSPHERE By definition, the nation is past the point of sustainability at the existing levels of population, per capita consumption, and the uses of technology—and is therefore over-populated. The proof lies in the documented deterioration of our environment—water, soils, air, wetlands. However, the authors in this volume do not present numerical calculations of optimum population on these grounds.

Proponents of conservation believe they have the cure. The problem with their "solution" lies in the trade-offs mentioned in the introductory chapter. Indeed, we could live an environmentally benign life with a lot more people if we cut consumption to Chinese levels (and, incidentally, managed our environment better than the Chinese are doing). The question is , of course, whether that is optimal. If it is not, where on the consumption scale is the optimum?

The technology buffs propose more technology, but, even when the investment costs are known, one needs to decide which technological solution would be best for each particular problem. The solution itself would also generate certain by-products that could contribute to other problems. If we reduce the demand side through population policy, we will be able to address multiple problems with one solution.

There are different combinations of population, consumption and technology that could, for instance, bring us back to desirable limits on ozone, acid precipitation sources, and greenhouse gases. Various scientific explorations underway, such as the NAPAP acid rain study,[2] will perhaps lead to a better understanding of the variables and may help a future effort to put a number on "optimum population," but such quantification is beyond the reach of this exploratory study.

We have put together some of the parts. Costanza demonstrates why the Chesapeake—and consequently the whole nation—would benefit from fewer people pressing on it. Brownridge makes a similar case concerning the high country of the West.

The Ehrlichs dramatize the United States' obligations to a shared planet. We are introducing a disproportionate share of the pollutants that threaten the Earth. For our own good and that of others, we are under particular pressure to reduce the perturbation that we generate.

LABOR FORCE AND POPULATION SIZE Briggs is concerned about the well-being and productivity of the labor force. He does not make an estimate of optimum population, and he expects to change his mind if the labor situation changes, but his recommendations on immigration and U.S. fertility would lead to something like Bouvier's "hard" scenario and an eventual turnaround in U.S. population growth.

Labor productivity is perhaps the most difficult area in which to attempt to calculate a theoretical optimum population, and Briggs is wise to avoid it. There are too many variables and value judgments. In principle, the optimum productivity (and, theoretically, earnings) might perhaps be seen in one of those famous Japanese factories, with robots and three or four supervisors, operating at night without even leaving the lights on. But what happens to the displaced workers? Who would buy the goods produced? And are maximum production and consumption optimal? We are in danger here of circling back to the fallacy of using GNP as a measure of well-being—the belief that bigger is necessarily better.

Those of us who try to define optimum population probably rely on some vague and intuitive feeling that optimal is the point at which workers earn a "decent" reward for their labor and at which there is little or no involuntary unemployment.

NATIONAL SECURITY Binkins does not try to derive an optimum figure from the security standpoint. He does, however, make the case that the Census Bureau's "lowest" projection (which leads to a U.S. population plateau for the next half century and therafter an accelerating decline) is compatible with U.S. security interests through 2040, which is as far ahead as he thinks one can look. He observes that military personnel requirements do not stand in the way if a population turnaround would enhance the national security broadly defined: a successful energy transition, a healthy agriculture, and a skilled and contented labor force.

Given the expense of modern arms, one wonders if the nation could afford to keep many more people under arms, as we did in World War II. A P-51 Mustang fighter cost less than $52,000 in 1944, complete. An F-15E costs about $24 million, without the weaponry. Even in the narrowest military sense, national security in the modern world may depend upon capital, technology, skilled labor, and energy resources more than on troop strength.

This brings us back to the question of energy, and it dramatizes the importance, in the real world, of an exercise like this one. If someone succeeds in the old dream of uniting the Arab world, we will soon need that leader's permission to embark on a military or peacekeeping mission, not just in the Persian Gulf, but anywhere, and even to ensure the flow of energy for our own economy. Our ships and airplanes and equipment operate on oil, which is increasingly becoming a monopoly of the Arab world. If you are interested in national security, managing the energy transition is a more important issue than troop numbers.

If we and the other industrial nations had had the foresight and the political nerve to begin to address the energy transition a decade or more ago, when it became apparent that oil was a dwindling natural resource, we would not be so vulnerable now to the ambitions of a Middle Eastern dictator. Moreover, by slowing down the rate at which remaining world petroleum resources are drawn down, we would have been in a better position to make a more orderly and less crisis-laden transition from reliance upon petroleum as an input for agriculture, transportation, power, and industry.

A population policy will not save us the pain of the energy transition. The oil is being depleted faster than demographics can keep up. It would, however, help.

ONE NATION, INDIVISIBLE U.S. public opinion seems to be, at a rather primitive stage. Although most of us feel that it is too crowded where we happen to be, we presume that people could, of course, go somewhere else. I hope that the chapters on the cities, the Chesapeake, and the high country demonstrate both that the big cities are indeed too big and that the extra people cannot be transported to the countryside or the "wide open West."

Population is not a local affair. It is a national issue, fed in large part by national policies and attitudes.

No author in this volume really comes to grips with the intangibles and the things that make up the "quality of life." Some of the them were touched in the first chapter, but an in-depth discussion of them is left perforce to a later study. Perhaps the best approach is to identify desirable circumstances and then, as Speare and White suggest, to consider what population densities would help achieve them.

We *have* identified some of the more tangible limits that define optimum population. At the very least, it becomes clear that a smaller population, and the lower levels of immigration and fertility required for its achievement, would benefit us in some of the critical areas of national policy.

I do not want to make impossible claims for population policy. The population of the United States in 1900 was just passing seventy-five million, less than one-third of the present population, yet we had already stripped most of the forest cover east of the Mississippi. We had inflicted damage on our settled farmlands from which they have yet to fully recover. Our urban population was tiny by today's measure, and yet cities suffered from poor water quality, waste disposal problems, and air pollution. And for all this damage, we were a poorer nation than we are today. So population policy is not the only issue. However, it may be the condition precedent to achieving the better world that most of us seek.

Having said all this, I will try my hand at a figure for optimum population: about half the present level, or 125 to 150 million, achieved over the next century.

This target lies within the population range of most of the estimates in this study. It is ambitious, but not impossible. By allowing a century, the target becomes achievable (if unlikely). As I will explain, a shorter time frame would generate severe transitional problems.

My target reflects optimism that we will learn to make better use of multiple energy technologies, including the wind, and that we will continue to find ways of diminishing energy inputs without serious deprivation. The timing is consistent with the transitional availability of coal, which will almost certainly be needed to accommodate the time lag involved in a shift to renewables. There are combustion techniques, such as coal gasification, that would substantially mitigate the environmental impacts of using the coal.

My target also reflects the hope that we can sequester more of the land from direct human exploitation, both for our own future good and for the preservation of a biosphere not totally dependent upon human goodwill and prudence.

I am quite prepared to raise my target if technology justifies more optimism, or to lower it if, as we learn more about the web of connections in which we live, it becomes clear that even fewer is better.

As a nation, we are not likely to reach my target—not, at the least, for a long, long time. (Barring a catastrophe, even Bouvier's "hard" scenario would leave us with 87 percent of the present population in 2080.) We may decide, along the way, that we do not want to achieve it, because we have learned to accommodate more people in a benign environment, because we decide that other goals, such as accommodating persecuted or hungry foreigners, are more important than optimizing well-being in the United States, because we are simply unwilling to pay the price in social engineering that might be necessary to achieve optimum population, or—most likely—because of inertia.

However, if for any of these reasons we do not try to head in the proposed direction, we have been warned.

Transitional Benefits

The reader may have noticed a curious harmony. Some writers in this series have addressed a future optimum population. Others have focused on current issues. In both approaches, however, the prescription is the same: sharply limited immigration aimed at acquiring skills in short supply and a leveling of fertility to bring the poor and less educated on a par with the better educated and more affluent.

Take, for instance, the example of labor. Briggs argues for these remedies as a way of stopping the pauperization of the poor and helping more Blacks enter the economic mainstream. I argue for them as a way of enabling society to concentrate on the better education and integration of smaller cohorts. Speare and White argue for them as a way of addressing the problems of the cities. Binkins says that the military needs skills, not raw labor, to operate modern weapons. Werbos argues the need for highly productive labor—with high savings and a reduction in the costs to society of an unemployed underclass—as a way of accumulating the capital needed to finance the forthcoming energy transition.

All of these are transitional arguments, but the effects would be to slow and eventually reverse population growth. Moreover, there is another reinforcement: Education and jobs for women rank at the top of Weeks's ways of achieving lower fertility. They also serve the immediate goal of improving the labor force.

I do not know whether this congruence between immediate and long-term goals is fortuitous. It may reflect a larger underlying unity that I do not understand. It does serve, however, to widen the support for a population turnaround. You do not need to select an optimum population to play this game. If you are concerned about any of the issues that have been raised in this study, you have reason to advocate the policies that point us in the direction of the optimum.

Excruciating Choices

The transitional and the long-term optimum might part company if a serious effort were launched to reach an optimum population much below 150 million in the next century. As I have noted, Bouvier's "hard" scenario would lead to a population still larger than 200 million in 2080. The Census Bureau's "low" projection uses the same fertility (1.5) and net immigration (300,000 per year). Although the Census Bureau projection is less optimistic about improvements in life expectancy, it results in nearly 200 million in 2080.

The only Census Bureau projection that would take population below 150 million in the next century is the low "zero immigration" scenario (series 28 in the 1988 study cited by Bouvier). With fertility at 1.5, it would lead to a population of 147 million in 2080, declining by about 1 percent a year. (The name is misleading, by the way. Because of emigration, there could still be immigration in these assumptions, but it would gradually decline as emigration declined.)

To translate these mathematics into policy terms, immigration would not contribute significantly to U.S. population growth if we limited gross annual immigration to 200,000 at first, gradually declining to about 100,000. These figures are generous by most world standards, but they are stringent indeed in terms of recent U.S. experience.

In Chapter 12 I rebut the argument that the United States needs more immigrants or higher fertility to take care of the old (themselves the legacy of the baby boom) a generation hence. Throughout this work we have reiterated the importance of persuading the poor and the less educated to bring their fertility down to the level that presently prevails among the educated and the middle class, about 1.5 children. Nevertheless, a fertility drop below 1.5, particularly if it were sudden, would skew the population structure toward old age so dramatically as to cause severe transitional problems. The "one child family" is indeed a desperate remedy.

This leaves the tightening of immigration, below Bouvier's "hard" scenario and the Census Bureau's "low" projection of 300,000, as a necessary element in moving the population much below 200 million in anything but a remote future. Simcox observes that this would leave national policy makers with some excruciating choices. Indeed it would, and as a nation we seem to have a hard time making tough choices. It is not simply that the cumulative voice of many interest groups tends to drive immigration up rather than down. We have a genuine moral dilemma: Rich in a world that is largely poor, can we justify restrictive immigration policies? I have resolved that dilemma to my own satisfaction.[3] In a world of nation-states, we have neither the authority nor the patent to save the rest of the world—though we should do more to help them address their own population problems. Our responsibility is to our own people, and to our descendants.

As we watch environmental and social problems unfold, and as the energy transition comes to the crunch, our society may come to realize that choices must be made. If so, this book may help us to understand the choices.

What Can Be Done?

We have seen that population momentum is a mighty force and that any change in direction will take most of a century to become apparent. We have also learned, however, that demographic change is not simply in the hands of fate or the Gods. Conscious social policy can affect it.

Weeks describes ways in which fertility can be influenced. Many of them center on raising the educational levels, the dignity and sense of self-respect, and job opportunities for women. If more direct motivation is needed, it can be provided through incentives and disincentives, such as priorities in jobs, educational opportunities and education for small families, taxation policies that discourage large families, and even direct payments for not having children. The means to limit child-bearing must be available, and women must know about them. Leadership is essential, and it must come from role models and those in authority.

These are some of the means, but they alone are not sufficient. We are unlikely, as a society, to devote such efforts to population limitation until we become aware of the ways that population growth will hinder the pursuit of other goals, and we need to become aware that we may be influencing fertility when we undertake policies that are superficially unrelated.

Enter **foresight** and the processes for handling complicated and interconnected issues.

The Uses of Foresight

How do we get a better fix on causes and connections in complex systems?

As a nation, we have come to resemble a pugnacious collection of single-interest groups. Our political discourse sounds like deaf men in a pit, shouting insults at each other. Perhaps, oddly enough, we have come to this point from an excess of self-righteousness. It is very easy and satisfying to promote a social objective into an absolute moral principle. Environmentalists oppose the development of power plants (particularly if they are nuclear). Few of them consider the connection between population and demand or the need for sufficient power to run the economy. Civil rights activists call others racist if they disagree with a particular formula to bring minorities into the mainstream. Right-to-lifers dismiss as "murderers" those who disagree with their proposals.

However, in human affairs few if any principles are absolute. Even the First Amendment has its limits. Good and reasonable objectives collide. When they do, "white hats" are pitted against each other, each absolutely certain of his or her total moral superiority.

I would like to persuade those antagonists to see the connections between their objectives and other social desiderata:

- To encourage environmentalists to recognize that their proposals may cause the poor to freeze until we can develop energy alternatives; to broaden their advocacy to include a population policy to address the fundamental source of demand.

- To persuade the civil rights activists that there are also other goals to protect. "Affirmative action" and "equal opportunity" for all (including the majority) are a see-saw balanced on a moral knife edge. There may be ways of achieving the first objective while limiting damage to the second. For example, if we could revamp the educational system and children's attitude toward it, we might help them become more competitive in the modern world. A new look at immigration might ease the competition for entry-level jobs, and the activitists might also take a new look at fertility among the poor, to give a smaller cohort a better chance.

- To bring the right-to-lifers into the population debate. Some or all of the arguments for a turnaround in U.S. population growth might strike them as reasonable. If they also understood that, historically, abortion has been—but is not necessarily—a principal method whereby population growth had been controlled, then perhaps they could be enlisted in the search for policies to influence fertility. Opposition to abortion implies either a commitment to other methods of birth control or an indifference to the well-being of the children who are born unwanted or in desperate circumstances. One can hardly take refuge in the advice to "just say no." It may be good advice, but it is folly to think that such advice will significantly affect the pregnancy rate of poor young girls, unless a lot of education and social training and other opportunities go with it.

The enemy is one-track thinking. The effort to address population change has been particularly vulnerable to it. Any proposals to intervene deliberately in human fertility have long been in conflict with the biblical injunction to "be fruitful and multiply," and now they have become ensnared in that most explosive of current U.S. moral and political issues: abortion. In this embittered environment, the process of "foresight" used in this study offers some hope of a return to moderation and good sense by requiring that issues be addressed in terms of their consequences rather than of preconceived moral absolutes.

If the debate were recast in these terms rather than in moral absolutes, perhaps the Bush administration would find heart to address the population issue.

The Environmental Protection Agency's Science Advisory Board has discovered that policies in one area generate consequences in other areas: "Changing Federal policies in sectors not traditionally linked with environmental protection could provide cost-effective environmental benefits that equal or exceed those that can be achieved through more traditional means. Environmental considerations should be an integral part of national policies that affect energy use, agriculture, taxation, transportation, housing, and foreign relations."[4] The same thing could be said about population considerations. I wish they had said it.

On occasion, the U.S. Government has tried to engage in that kind of thinking: the Rockefeller Commission report of 1972; the *Global 2000 Report to the President* of 1980. Neither had identifiable effects upon national policy, because their conclusions were not connected with other current policy issues.

There have been a few stalwart proponents of better ways of making the connections. In Congress, Senator Albert Gore, Jr., has been a tireless advocate. With various co-sponsors, he has introduced his Critical Trends Assessment Act into successive sessions. The most recent version was S1345, introduced in 1989. Like its predecessors, it died in committee.

If our governmental processes are ever to catch up with a fast-changing world, public advocacy groups and the citizenry would do well to learn about and advocate such reforms. Dull as these "process bills" may sound in competition with our daily TV fare, they are important.

There is one process already available, but it has never been used for the big decisions, and it has fallen into disuse even for the smaller ones. The Environmental Policy Act of 1969 specifically made the connections that we have been talking about in this study, and it required the preparation of environmental impact statements (EIS) to examine those connections before decisions were made. Although population was included in the Act, it was left out by the bureaucracy when the implementing regulations were prepared, so the population impacts of proposed actions have seldom been considered.[5]

We would have a process for bringing demography into our national thinking if:

—the Act were vigorously enforced,
—the regulations were amended to require that population be considered among the impacts, and
—the Act were extended to include Congress, as well as the Executive Branch.

The process of examination would force our society, case by case, to ask the question:"What is optimum population?" If the participants in this volume are right, examination would lead to a wide acceptance of the concept that population has gone too far already. I can hardly imagine, for instance, that in a debate over energy policy there would be much support for the idea that we need more people. If I am wrong, then it will come out in such debates.

The recent Kuwait crisis and the ongoing energy issue provide a dramatic example of why we need some way to put the issues together. In the midst of that crisis and with the budget impasse staring at them, Congress took time out in October 1990 to pass a bill raising immigration. Census projections suggested that, even without that law, the country's population would rise by about twenty-five million during this decade. The new law will add perhaps five to ten million more by increasing immigration quotas and promoting future chain immigration.[6] The bill also generates immediate new budgetary costs for federal and local governments. The question did not arise as to whether it is a good idea to bring in more oil consumers precisely when we are coming to recognize the fragility of the petroleum supply, nor did the connection between increased immigration and the effort to reduce government expenditures.

Another example, if one is needed, is the new "national transportation policy" of the Department of Transportation (DOT).[7] This "plan" was produced, after months of labor, in February 1990.

The DOT had an opportunity to address the large issues affecting transportation. There are environmental constraints on the ever-increasing use of fossil fuels. We must prepare for the transition away from petroleum, in any case. The Geological Survey warns that the country's remaining petroleum resources total just sixteen years' consumption at present consumption rates. Our dependence on the Persian Gulf is increasing very fast, with fundamental foreign policy and national security implications. DOT should have been asking how transportation policy relates to these issues. If transportation is the principal driving force in generating the energy demand that causes these problems, shouldn't we be seeking means to control that demand, and if population size is a major element in the total demand for transportation, doesn't DOT have an interest in policy proposals that affect the two demographic variables of immigration and fertility?

Did DOT address these questions? Hardly. The report touched on the environment only with a promise to minimize the destruction of wetlands. No other connection was addressed, and there was no indication that DOT had thought ever to be in touch with the Departments of State or Defense, the Geological Survey, or anybody else.

This is indeed the kingdom of the deaf.

Few people relate transportation to demography, but it can affect, not just where we live and work, but the level of fertility itself. The interdependence of issues requires a broader policy perspective, but the connections are not always so glaringly obvious. Take the rather mundane example of the Washington METRO. If the population impact had been addressed when the METRO subway was being planned, perhaps some population sociologist would have had the chance to point out (as Weeks does in this volume) that fertility declines when women have jobs and the dignity that goes with self-support. There is a circular connection between poverty and high fertility. Anybody interested in ameliorating the isolation and alienation of Blacks in the inner city should have had an interest in where the subway went.

What has happened? The METRO is nearly complete, but the last part of it—still with no completion date—is the "Green line" into Anacostia, the part of the city where it is most needed. Jobs have fled the inner city, and we need to help connect the inner city residents with jobs. Different priorities would have helped to address the social breakdown, the poverty, and teenage pregnancies and might have helped to stem the violence and drug traffic that bedevil the inner city. Because they have not yet learned to think across issues, the planners did not weigh these implications in their choice of construction priorities.

The process of foresight is not all-seeing. It cannot pretend to draw a map of the future. The object, rather, is to get away from the single-minded pursuit of sometimes conflicting goals. With greater foresight, we might see more of the connections, better weigh the effects of demography on the pursuit of other objectives and understand how other policies might influence demography.

Foresight can help us apply what vision we have to the issues before us.

Coda

The skeptic, comfortable in his or her affluence, seeks to put off remedial action with the argument that more study is needed. Humans seldom have the luxury, however, of knowing everything about a problem before they must do something about it. The nation is hardly likely to agree on a fixed number for optimum population if even a group of rather like-minded specialists have not done so, but I·think that we have made a pretty strong case that, whatever the number may be, it is smaller than the present population and much smaller than the population levels toward which we are presently heading. And the policies that would lead to an eventual turnaround in population growth are the same ones that would help us to address major social and economic issues now confronting us.

Change has accelerated, and vast forces are set in motion that cannot be easily directed. With population, it may take half a century or more to turn growth around. If there is good evidence that we are already too big, even immediate action may not be fast enough to achieve the optimum for generations to come, and delay compounds the problems and worsens the choices.

As the Pimentels show with respect to energy, human impacts on the environment have grown to the point where they may even exceed natural processes. This awesome power imposes corresponding responsibilities. As a tribe, the human race needs to learn an "unnatural" way of thinking. We are genetically conditioned to perceive and respond to sudden and fast-moving emergencies, such as a charging carnivore. We need to become sensitive to vaster but much slower changes, such as those in our environment. We need to establish baselines from which to measure change, and we need to condition our behavior to deal in a much longer time frame.

The professional optimists reassure us that the human mind can solve any problem. Costanza warns us, more prudently, that we had better use our minds to avoid problems before they become traps, and we are already at least part-way into the population trap.

The time is long past when, with Mr. Micawber and various economists, we could afford simply to hope that "something will turn up."

I wonder if anybody is listening, out there in the kingdom of the deaf.

THE AUTHORS

DR. MARTIN BINKIN is a senior fellow in the Foreign Policy Studies program at the Brookings Institution. His chapter was written while he was on sabbatical, serving as the Secretary of the Navy Fellow in the Economics Department, U.S. Naval Academy. He has written extensively on defense manpower issues.

DR. LEON F. BOUVIER is currently a Visiting Professor of Sociology at Old Dominion University and Adjunct Professor of Demography at Tulane University School of Public Health. He is a former Vice President of the Population Reference Bureau, and he served as demographic consultant to the U.S. House of Representatives Select Committee on Population and the Select Commission on Immigration and Refugee Policy.

DR. VERNON M. BRIGGS, JR., Professor of Human Resource Economics at the New York State School of Labor and Industrial Relations of Cornell University, has written extensively on the subject of immigration policy and the U.S. labor force. He is a former Chairman of the National Council on Employment Policy.

DR. DENNIS BROWNRIDGE teaches at The Orme School in Arizona and writes on western resource and environmental issues. He formerly taught geography at the University of California at Santa Barbara.

DR. ROBERT COSTANZA is an Associate Professor at the University of Maryland's Chesapeake Biological Laboratory. He is chief editor of the journal *Ecological Economics*. He is also president and cofounder (with Herman Daly) of the International Society for Ecological Economics. He edited *Ecological Economics. The Science and Management of Sustainability* (Columbia University Press, New York, 1991).

DR. ANNE HOWLAND EHRLICH is a senior research associate in biology and associate director of the Center for Conservation Biology at Stanford. She has written or coauthored many technical and popular articles and books on issues such as population control, environmental protection, and the environmental consequences of nuclear war. She is the recipient of many honors, including selection for the United Nations' Global 500 Roll of Honour for Environmental Achievement.

DR. PAUL R. EHRLICH is Bing Professor of Population Studies, Stanford University, and author or coauthor of many articles and books, including (with Anne Ehrlich) *The Population Explosion*. Among his many awards are the 1990 Crafoord Prize in Population Biology and the Conservation of Biological Diversity and a MacArthur Prize Fellowship, 1990–95.

ROBERT W. FOX has been on the staff of the Organization of American States and the Inter-American Development Bank. He is presently coauthoring a series of reports that capture world population growth issues in three-dimensional computer graphics and text.

LINDSEY GRANT is a retired Foreign Service Officer and former China specialist. During his government career, he was an NSC staffer, member of the Department of State's Planning and Coordination Staff, Deputy Assistant

Secretary of State for Environment and Population Affairs, and Department of State coordinator for the *Global 2000 Report to the President*. He is the author of *Foresight and National Decisions: The Horseman and the Bureaucrat* (Lanham, Md.: University Press of America, 1988) and of various other publications on governmental decision making and on population, resource, and environment issues.

DR. DAVID PIMENTEL is a Professor in the College of Agriculture and Life Sciences at Cornell University. He has published extensively and has chaired panels dealing with food, energy, population and natural resources, for the National Academy of Science, the American Association for the Advancement of Science, and the U.S. Department of Energy.

DR. MARCIA PIMENTEL is Senior Lecturer (retired), Division of Nutritional Sciences in the College of Human Ecology at Cornell. She has authored a book and several papers dealing with nutrition and human populations.

DAVID E. SIMCOX is currently Director of the Center for Immigration Studies, a Washington, D.C., think tank that examines the effects of immigration on the broad social, economic, demographic and environmental interests of U.S. society. During a twenty-nine-year career in the Department of State, he specialized in labor and migration issues in Latin America.

DR. ALDEN SPEARE, JR., is Professor of Sociology at Brown University. His research interests are in the areas of international migration and population aging. He has coauthored (with William Frey) a 1980 census monograph, *Regional and Metropolitan Decline in the United States*.

STEPHEN E. TENNENBAUM has a master's degree in environmental engineering from the University of Florida and is presently engaged in doctoral study at the Department of Ecology and Systematics at Cornell University.

DR. JOHN R. WEEKS is Professor of Sociology and Director of the International Population Center at San Diego State University. He is author of *Population: An Introduction to Concepts and Issues* (Belmont Calif., Wadsworth), now in its fourth edition. Currently, he is completing a federally funded research project on infant health outcomes among low-income immigrants in California.

DR. PAUL J. WERBOS is a program director at the National Science Foundation. He was with the Energy Information Administration of the U.S. Department of Energy for a decade. He served on the interagency Task Force on Models and Data convened to respond to the problems identified in the *Global 2000 Report to the President*.

DR. MICHAEL J. WHITE is Associate Professor of Sociology at Brown University. His current research is in the areas of internal migration and U.S. immigration. He is author of the 1980 census monograph *American Neighborhoods and Residential Differentiation*.

Notes

CHAPTER 1

1. Peter M. Vitousek et al., "Human Appropriation of the Products of Photosynthesis," *BioScience*, June 1986, pp. 368–373.

2. UN World Commission on Environment and Development, *Our Common Future* (Oxford University Press, 1987).

3. See, for instance, World Resources Institute, *World Resources 1988–1989* (Basic Books, New York, 1988), and individual reports by the World Resources Institute, 1735 New York Avenue, Washington D.C. 20006. Also see Lester R. Brown et al., *State of the World 1989* (Norton, New York, 1989), and other Worldwatch papers (Worldwatch Institute, 1776 Massachusetts Avenue NW, Washington D.C. 20036).

4. The Commission on Population Growth and the American Future, *Population and the American Future* (GPO, Washington, D.C., 1972).

5. Julian Huxley, cited in Donald Mann, *A National Policy to Reduce U.S. Population* (Negative Population Growth, Inc., New York, 1980).

6. See Chapter 17.

7. See Noel Hinrichs, ed., *Population, Environment and People*, and S. Fred Singer, ed., *Is There an Optimum Level of Population?* (both from McGraw-Hill, New York, 1971).

8. To their credit, several economists have experimented with changes in the national accounts calculations to bring resource depletion or expansion into the accounts. See, for instance, Robert Repetto et al., *Wasting Assets: Natural Resources in the National Income Accounts* (World Resources Institute, Washington, D.C., June 1989).

9. See Chapter 12.

10. For a survey of the cross-sectoral processes of foresight, alternative futures studies and systems analysis, see Lindsey Grant et al., *Foresight and National Decisions: The Horseman and the Bureaucrat* (University Press of America, Lanham, Md., 1988).

11. R. Boyer and D. Savageau, *Places Rated Almanac, 1985* (Rand, McNally, Chicago, 1985).

12. *Urban Stress Test* (1988). Zero Population Growth, 1400 16th Street NW, Suite 320, Washington D.C. 20036.

13. *Science*, May 5, 1989, p. 5517.

14. *New York Times*, July 16, 1989, p. A1

15. Gregory Spencer, *Projections of the Population of the United States, by Age, Sex and Race: 1988 to 2080*, U.S. Bureau of the Census, Current Population Reports, Series P-25, no. 1018 (January 1989).

16. Study cited in Robert Repetto, "Population, Resources, Environment: An Uncertain Future," *Population Bulletin*, 42, no. 2 (July 1987), p. 19.

17. Brown et al., *State of the World*, p. 15.

CHAPTER 2

1. R. P. Ehrlich and J. P. Holdren, "The Impact of Populaton Growth," *Science*, vol. 171 (1971): pp. 1212–17; D. H. Meadows, D. L. Meadows, J.

Randers, and W. W. Behrens III, *The Limits to Growth* (Universe Books, Washington, D.C., 1972); Council on Environmental Quality, *The Global 2000 Report to the President, Technical Report, vol. 2* (GPO, Washington, D.C., 1980) [hereafter CEQ, *Global 2000 Report*]; N. Keyftiz, "Impact of Trends in Resources, Environment and Development on Demographic Prospects," in *Population, Resources, Environment and Development* (United Nations, New York, 1984), pp. 97–124; P.G. Demeny *Population and the Invisible Hand*, Working Paper no. 123 (Center for Policy Studies, Population Council, New York, 1986); G. Hardin, 1986. "Cultural Carrying Capacity: A Biological Approach to Human Problems, *BioScience*, vol. 36 (1986), pp. 599–606.

2. Population Reference Bureau, *World Population Data Sheet* (PRB, Washington, D.C., 1986) [hereafter PRB, *Population Data Sheet* 1988].

3. Population Reference Bureau, *World Population Data Sheet* (PRB, Washington, D.C., 1986) [hereafter PRB, *Population Data Sheet* 1986].

4. D. Wen and D. Pimentel, "Energy Flow Through an Organic Agroecosystem in China," *Agriculture Ecosystem Environment*, vol. 11 (1984), pp. 145–160. Wen and Pimentel use hectares rather than acres in their computation. An acre is approximately 0.4 hectares.

5. D. Pimentel and C. W. Hall, eds., *Food and Energy Resources* (Academic Press, New York, 1984); D. Pimentel and C. W. Hall eds., *Food and Natural Resources* (Academic Press, San Diego, 1989).

6. W. K. Kinzelbah, "China: Energy and Environment, *Environ. Management*, vol. 7 (1983), pp. 303–310; V. Smil, *The Bad Earth, Environmental Degradation in China* (M. E. Sharpe, Armonk, N.Y.: 1984).

7. Pimentel and Hall, *Food and Natural Resources*.

8. L. K. Lee, "Land Use and Soil Loss: A 1982 Update," *Journal of Soil and Water Conservation*, vol. 39 (1984), pp. 226–28.

9. D. Pimentel, J. Allen, A. Beers et al., "World Agriculture and Soil Erosion," *BioScience*, vol. 37 (1987), pp. 277-283.

10. R. F. Follett and B. A. Stewart. *Soil Erosion and Crop Productivity* (American Society of Agronomists, Crop Science of America, and Soil Science Society of America, Madison, Wis., 1985).

11. Ibid.; Office of Technology Assessment, *Impacts of Technology on Productivity of the Croplands and Rangelands of the United States.* (OTA, Washington, D.C., 1982) [hereafter OTA, *Impacts*].

12. OTA, *Impacts*.

13. Pimentel et al., "World Agriculture and Soil Erosion."

14. Pimentel and Hall, *Food and Energy Resources*; Pimentel and Hall, *Food and Natural Resources*.

15. H. F. Mataré, *Energy: Facts and Future*. (CRC Press, Boca Raton, Fla., 1989).

16. Mataré, *Energy: Facts and Future*.

17. H. D. Schilling and D. Weigand, "Coal Resources," in *Resources and World Development*, D. J. McLaren and B. J. Skinner, eds. (Wiley, New York, 1987), pp. 129–56; U.S. Bureau of the Census, *Statistical Abstract of the United States: 1987*, 108th ed. (USBC, Washington, D.C., 1988) [hereafter USBC, *Statistical Abstract*].

18. L. Leyton, "Crop Water Use: Principles and Some Considerations for Agroforesty," in *Plant Research and Agroforestry*, P. A. Huxley, ed. (International Council for Research in Agroforestry, Nairobi, Kenya, 1983) pp. 379–400.

19. National Academy of Sciences, *Alternative Agriculture* (NAS, Washington, D.C., 1989).

20. Ibid.; Council on Environmental Quality, *Environmental Quality 1983*, 14th Annual Report. (GPO, Washington, D.C., 1983) [hereafter CEQ, *Environmental Quality 1983*].

21. United States Water Resources Council, *The Nation's Water Resources 1975–2000*, Summary and vol. 1 (GPO, Washington, D.C., 1979).

22. CEQ, *Global 2000 Report*.

23. D. Pimentel, S. Fast, W. L. Chao et al., "Water Resources in Food and Energy Production," *BioScience*, vol. 32 (1982), pp. 861–67.

24. Environmental Protection Agency, *National Air Pollutant Emission Estimates, 1940–1984*, EPA—450/4-85-015 (Office of Air Quality Planning Standards, EPA, Research Triangle Park, N.C., 1986) [hereafter EPA, *National Air Pollution Emission Estimates*].

25. D. Pimentel and L. Levitan, "Pesticides: Amounts Applied and Amounts Reaching Pests," *BioScience*, vol. 36 (1986), pp. 86–91; D. Pimentel, L. McLaughlin, A. Zepp, et al., "Environmental and Economic Impacts of Reducing U.S. Agricultural Pesticide Use," *Handbook of Pest Management in Agriculture*, 2d ed. (CRC Press, Boca Raton, Fla., 1991), pp. 679–718.

26. D. Pimentel, E. Garnick, A. Berkowitz et al., "Environmental Quality and Natural Biota," *BioScience* vol. 30 (1980), pp. 750–55.

27. Biomass Panel, Energy Research Advisory Board, *Report on Biomass Energy* (ERAB, Washington, D.C. 1981) [hereafter ERAB, *Report on Biomass Energy*]; Energy Research Advisory Board, Department of Energy, *Solar Energy*

Research and Development: Federal and Private Sector Roles (ERAB, Washington, D.C., 1982) [hereafter ERAB, *Solar Energy Research and Development*].

28. D. Pimentel and M. Pimentel, *Food, Energy and Society* (Edward Arnold, London, 1979).

29. D. Pimentel, L. Levitan, J. Heinze, et al., "Solar Energy, Land and Biota," *Sun World*, vol. 8 (1984) pp. 70–73, 93–95.

30. Ibid.

31. D. Pimentel, D. Nafus, W. Vergara et al., "Biological Solar Energy Conversion and U.S. Energy Policy," *BioScience*, vol. 28 (1978), pp. 376-82.

32. ERAB, *Report on Biomass Energy*.

33. Ibid.

34. Pimentel et al., "Solar Energy, Land and Biota."

35. ERAB, *Report on Biomass Energy*.

36. Ibid.

37. U.S. Department of Agriculture, *Agricultural Statistics 1987* (GPO, Washington, D.C., 1987).

38. Pimentel et al., "Solar Energy, Land, and Biota."

39. ERAB, *Report on Biomass Energy*; D. Pimentel, A. F. Warneke, W.S. Teel, et al., "Food Versus Biomass fuel: Socioeconomic and Environmental Impacts in the United States, Brazil, India, and Kenya," *Advances in Food Research*, vol. 32 (1988), pp.185–238.

40. Pimentel et al., "Food Versus Biomass Fuel."

41. Ibid.

42. Pimentel et al., "Solar Energy, Land and Biota"; J. M. Ogden and R. H. Williams, *Solar Hydrogen: Moving Beyond Fossil Fuels* (World Resources Institute, Washington, D.C., 1989).

43. USBC, *Statistical Abstract*.

44. Mataré, *Energy: Facts and Future*.

45. Pimentel, D. Environmental and Social Implications of Waste in U.S. Agriculture and Food Sectors." *Journal of Agricultural Ethics*, 3: 5-20, 1989.

46. Pimentel et al., "Environmental and Economic Impacts of Reducing U.S. Agricultural Pesticide Use."

47. Pimentel et al., "Food Versus Biomas Fuel."

48. D. Pimentel, L. M. Frederickson, D. B. Johnson, J. H. McShane, and H.-W. Yuan, "Environment and Population: Crises and Policies," In *Food and Natural Resources*, D. Pimentel and C. W. Hall, eds. (Academic Press, San Diego, 1989), pp. 363-89.

CHAPTER 3

1. The views expressed in this essay are personal judgments, and do not in any way reflect the official views of my employers, past or present.

2. Energy Information Agency, *Monthly Energy Review* (National Energy Information Center, Washington, D.C., February 1990), pp. 7, 13, 91 [hereafter EIA, *Monthly Energy Review: February 1990.]*

3. Ibid.

4. N. Glickman, *Econometric Analysis of Regional Systems* (Academic Press, New York, 1977).

5. EIA, *Monthly Energy Review: February 1990.*

6. Ibid.

7. Energy Information Agency, *Annual Energy Outlook 1990,* (National Energy Information Center, Washington, D.C., 1990), p. 41, 46. [hereafter EIA, *Annual Energy Outlook 1990].*

8. Energy Information Agency, *Annual Energy Review 1989,* (National Energy Information Center, Washington, D.C., 1989), [hereafter EIA; *Annual Energy Review 1989].*

9. Energy Information Agency, *State Energy Data Report*, national aggregation of public-use computer tape.

10. Paul J. Werbos, *Documentation of the Transportation Energy Demand (TED) Model,* DOE/EIA-MO13 (National Energy Information Center, Washington D.C., 1987). Almost exactly the same equations were used in the subsequent "spreadsheet" model of transportation demand.

11. EIA, *Annual Energy Review 1989.*

12. Werbos, *Documentation of the TED Model.*

13. Charles Gary and Jeffrey Alson, *Moving America to Methanol* (University of Michigan Press, Ann Arbor, 1985).

14. Jack Faucett Associates, *Methanol Prices During Transition,* JACK FAU-86-322-8/11 (Jack Faucett Associates, Bethesda, MD., April 1987).

15. Ross Lemons, "Fuel Cells for Transportation, *Journal of Power Sources*, vol. 29 (January 1990), pp. 251-264.

16. EIA, *Annual Energy Outlook 1990*.

17. Office of Technology Assessment, *Energy for Biological Processes*, OTA-E-124 and -128 and vol. 3 (OTA, Washington, D.C., 1980) [hereafter OTA, *Energy for Biological Processes*].

18. Solar Energy Research Institute, *Fuel from Farms*, SERI/SP-451-519 (National Technical Information Service, Washington D.C., 1980), p. D-6.

19. OTA, *Energy for Biological Processes*.

20. EIA, *Annual Energy Review 1989*.

21. J. Weyant and P. Werbos, "An Overview of EMF8 on Industrial Energy Demand, Conservation and Interfuel Substitution," in *Proceedings and Papers of the Eighth North American Conference of the International Association of Energy Economists*, David Wood (MIT) ed., 1987; P. Werbos, "Econometric Techniques: Theory Versus Practice," *Energy: The International Journal* (March/April 1990); P. Werbos, "Industrial Structural Shift: Causes and Consequences for Electricity Demand," *The Changing Structure of American Industry and Energy Use Patterns*, Faruqui and Broehl, eds. (Battelle Press, Columbia, Ohio, 1987).

22. M. Mesarovic and E. Pestel, *Mankind at the Turning Point: The Second Report to the Club of Rome* (E. P. Dutton, New York, 1974).

23. B. Prinz et al., *Forest Damage in the Federal Republic of Germany*, LIS Report no. 28. (Landesanstalt für Immissionsschutz de Landes Nordrhein-westfalen, Essen; 1982); R.F. Huettl, "Research Methods and Preliminary Results in the Black Forest of Germany," in *Proceedings of Mid-South Symposium on Acid Deposition*, available from Prof. Blackmon or Beasley (eds.), Forest Resources Department, University of Arkansas, Monticello, Ark. (April 1986).

24. "Quickening the Pace in Clean Coal Technology," *EPRI Journal* (January/February 1989).

25. D. L. Meadows et al., *Dynamics of Growth in a Finite World*. (Wright-Allen Press, Cambridge, Mass., 1974); Office of Technology Assessment, *Global Models, World Futures and Public Policy: A Critique* (April 1982), Appendix C.

26. EIA *Annual Energy Review 1989*.

27. Mesarovic and Pestel, *Mankind at the Turning Point*.

28. National Academy of Sciences, *Issues in Electric Energy Systems* (National Academy Press, Washington, D.C., 1986).

29. P. Glaser, "A Solar Power Satellite Built of Aluminum Materials," *Space Power*, vol. 6, no. 1 (1986).

CHAPTER 4

1. P. Vitousek, P.R. Ehrlich, A. H. Ehrlich, and P. A. Matson, "Human Appropriation of the Products of Photosynthesis," *BioScience* vol. 36 (1986), pp. 368-73. They estimate that humans now directly control from 25 to 40 percent of the total primary production of the planet's biosphere. Human activity is also beginning to have an effect on global climate and the planet's protective ozone shield.

2. Including, but not limited to, the "tragedy of the commons" (cf. G. Hardin, "The Tragedy of the Commons," *Science*, vol. 162 (1968), pp. 1243-48), and the "prisoner's dilemma" (cf. R. Axelrod, *The Evolution of Cooperation* (Basic Books, New York, 1984).

3. J. Platt, "Social Traps," *American Psychologist* vol. 28 (1973), pp. 642-51; J.G. Cross and M.J. Guyer, *Social Traps* (University of Michigan Press, Ann Arbor 1980); A.I. Teger, *Too Much Invested to Quit* (Pergamon, New York 1980.) J. Brockner and J.Z. Rubin, *Entrapment in Escalating Conflicts: A Social Psychological Analysis* (Springer-Verlag, New York, 1985; R. Costanza, "Social Traps and Environmental Policy," *BioScience*, vol. 37(1987), pp. 407-412.

4. This particular positive reinforcement has in the past few years begun to turn into a negative one. As smoking becomes less socially acceptable, we should expect the number of new smokers to fall and many old smokers to escape the trap. But the process of escape is much more difficult than the process of avoidance.

5. G. Hardin, "Cultural Carrying Capacity: A Biological Approach," *BioScience*, vol. 36 (1986), pp. 559-606. P.R. Ehrlich and J.P. Holdren, "The Impact of Population Growth," *Science*, vol. 171 (1971), pp. 1212-17; P.R. Ehrlich and A.H. Ehrlich, *The Population Explosion* (Simon and Schuster, New York, 1991.)

6. H.E. Daly, *Steady State Economics* (W.H. Freeman, San Francisco, 1977).

7. Notable examples are Paul Ehrlich and Garrett Hardin. Herman Daly is a rare economist who shares this view.

8. H.J. Barnett and C. Morse, *Scarcity and Growth: The Economics of Natural Resource Availability*, (Johns Hopkins University Press, Baltimore, 1963); D.H. Meadow, D.L. Meadows, J. Randers, and W.W. Behrens, *The Limits to Growth* (Universe, New York, 1972).

9. See Chapter 2.

10. J.L. Simon and H. Kahn (eds.), *The Resourceful Earth: A Response to Global 2000* (Basic Blackwell, New York, 1984).

11. This is still an underestimate, because we are currently using at least

5 percent of renewable fuels in the form of wood and hydropower and because solar energy runs the ecosystems that provide life-support functions.

12.   R. Costanza, "Embodied Energy and Economic Valuation," *Science.* vol. 210 (1980), pp. 1219-24.

13.   All British thermal units are equal in their ability to raise the temperature of water. A Btu is defined as the amount of heat energy required to raise 1 pound of water 1 degree Farenheit. A Btu is equal to 0.252 kilocalories, 1,054 joules or 0.0002929 kilowatt-hours. But in terms of ability to do useful work, the concentration or quality of of the energy is important. Because sunlight is very dispersed relative to fossil fuel, it takes about 2,000 Btu of sunlight to grow enough trees to produce as much electricity as 1 Btu of oil. H.T. Odum, and E. C. Odum, *Energy Basis for Man and Nature* (McGraw Hill, New York, 1976).

CHAPTER 5

1.   The calculation here is confined to male youths since, under present policies, they will continue to constitute about 90 percent of all military personnel. Obviously, if the armed forces expanded the role of women beyond the current goals, a smaller proportion of the male population would have to be attracted.

2.   For a description of this methodology, see Martin Binkin and John D. Johnston, *All-Volunteer Armed Forces: Progress, Problems, and Prospects*, prepared for the Senate Committee on Armed Services, 93 Cong., 1 sess. (GPO, Washington, D.C., 1973), pp. 40-42, 59-60.

3.   For a further discussion of these factors, see Martin Binkin, *America's Volunteer Military: Progress and Prospects* (The Brookings Institution, Washington, D.C., 1984), pp.13-14.

4.   The annual number of births began to rise in 1975, not because of increases in fertility rates but rather because of the delayed "echo effect": More baby-boom women reached their childbearing years. Once this generation passes beyond childbearing, starting in the 1990s, annual births will decline again, barring larger-than-expected increases in fertility rates.

5.   See, for example, William W. Kaufmann, *Glasnost, Perestroika, and U.S. Defense Spending.* (The Brookings Institution, Washington, D.C., 1990).

6.   According to the conventional wisdom, the supply of women who are interested in military service is too small to support anything more than a modest expansion. Recent research indicates, however, that higher recruiting goals for women could probably be met if the same enlistment incentives, recruiting techniques, and advertising strategies that have been used for attracting male

volunteers were applied to females. See James R. Hosek and Christine Peterson, *Serving Her Country: An Analysis of Women's Enlistment* (RAND Corporation, Santa Monica, CA., January 1990).

7. For a discussion of this issue, see Martin Binkin, *Military Technology and Defense Manpower* (The Brookings Institution, Washington, D.C., 1986).

CHAPTER 6

1. Oxford Analytica, *America in Perspective* (Houghton Mifflin, Boston 1986), p. 20.

2. Vernon M. Briggs, Jr., *Immigration Policy and the American Labor Force* (The Johns Hopkins University Press, Baltimore, 1984).

3. Gregory Spencer, *Projections of the Population of the U.S., by Age, Sex, and Race: 1988 to 2080*, U.S. Bureau of the Census, Current Population Reports, Series 25, no. 1018 (GPO, Washington, D.C., 1989), projections 14 and 29. This calculation assumes annual net immigration of 800,000, a conservative estimate of the current level.

4. Elizabeth Bogen, *Immigration in New York* (Praeger, New York, 1987), p. 60.

5. Select Commission on Immigration and Refugee Policy, *U.S. Immigration Policy and the National Interest* (GPO, Washington, D.C., 1981), pp. 2, 5.

6. Richard M. Cyert and David C. Mowery, eds., *Technology and Employment* (National Academy Press, Washington, D.C., 1987), ch. 4.

7. John M. Culbertson, *The Trade Threat and U.S. Trade Policy* (21st Century Press, Madison, Wis., 1989).

8. William E. Brock, "Address to the National Press Club," Washington, D.C. (March 5, 1987), p. 8.

9. Cyert and Mowery, *Technology and Employment*, ch. 5.

10. George T. Silverstri and John M. Lukasiewicz, "A Look at Occupational Employment Trends to the Year 2000," *Monthly Labor Review* (September 1987), pp. 46-63.

11. Cyert and Mowery, *Technology and Employment*, ch. 5.

12. Jonathan Kozol, *Illiterate America*. (Anchor Press, Garden City, N.Y., 1985), pp. 4, 115.

13. Neal C. Peirce, "Unique Opportunities for the Nation's Blacks," *Ithaca Journal* (April 19, 1989), p. 8.

CHAPTER 7

1. U.S. Bureau of the Census, "Population Estimates for Metropolitan Areas, 1988," *Current Population Reports*, P-26 (GPO, Washington, D.C.).

2. The Gallup Organization, *The Gallup Opinion Index*, October 1989.

3. William Frey and Alden Speare, Jr., *Regional and Metropolitan Growth and Decline in the United States* (Russell Sage Foundation, New York, 1988).

4. John Long, *Population Deconcentration in the United States* (U.S. Bureau of the Census, Washington, D.C., 1981).

5. William Frey and Alden Speare, *Regional and Metropolitan Growth and Decline in the United States*, (Russell Sage Foundation, New York, 1988), pp. 40, 69.

6. Alden Speare, Jr., "The Role of Immigration in U.S. Population Redistribution," paper presented at the annual meeting of the Population Association of America, Chicago, 1987.

7. U.S. Immigration and Naturalization Service, *1987 Statistical Yearbook*, (GPO, Washington, D.C., 1988); U.S. Bureau of the Census, *Statistical Abstract of the United States* (GPO, Washington, D.C., 1986).

8. Ronald L. Moomaw, "Firm Location and City Size: Reduced Productivity Advantages as a Factor in the Decline of Manufacturing in Urban Areas," *Journal of Urban Economics*, vol. 17 (1985), pp. 73–89.

9. J. Vernon Henderson, "Efficiency of Resource Usage and City Size," *Journal of Urban Economics*, vol. 19 (1986), pp. 47–70.

10. Mark R. Montgomery, "The Effects of Urban Population Growth on Urban Service Delivery," paper presented to the meetings of the American Academy for the Advancement of Science, February, 1990.

11. D. Kotchman, T. McMullen, and V. Hasselblad, "Adequacy of a Single Monitoring Site for Defining Mean Outdoor Concentrations of Fine Particles in Demarcated Residential Communities," *International Journal of Air Pollution Control and Waste Management*, vol. 37 (April 1987), pp. 377–81.

12. Zero Population Growth, "Urban Stress Test," 1988. Air Quality was measured by the number of EPA long-term and twenty-four hour standards violations for seven possible pollutants; water was assessed for both abundance and lack of pollutants; sewage was judged by the extent of wastewater treatment and hazardous waste in EPA-reported hazardous waste sites within city limits.

13. We were provided these data on metropolitan area income inequality by Hilary Silver, Department of Sociology, Brown University.

14. Frank Levy, *Dollars and Dreams* (Russell Sage Foundation, New York, 1986).

15. U.S. Bureau of the Census, *Census of Population and Housing 1980, Detailed Characteristics* (GPO, Washington, D.C., 1984).

16. Claude Fischer, *The Urban Experience* (Harcourt Brace Jovanovich, New York, 1980), p.104.

17. Current Population Reports, *Fertility of American Women, 1988,* Table 2.

18. U.S. Bureau of the Census, *Current Population Reports,* P-20, no. 429, School Enrollment.

19. U.S. Office of Vital Statistics, *Vital Statistics 1987: Mortality* Table 2-10. (Washington, D.C., National Center for Health Statistics).

20. Michael J. White, *American Neighborhoods and Residential Differentiation* (Russell Sage Foundation, New York, 1987).

21. G. V. Fuguitt and J. J. Zuiches, "Residential Preferences and Population Distribution," *Demography,* vol. 12 (1975), pp. 491–504.

22. Katherine L. Bradbury, Anthony Downs, and Kenneth A. Small, *Urban Decline and the Future of American Cities* (The Brookings Institution, Washington, D.C., 1982).

23. Frey and Speare, *Regional Metropolitan Growth and Decline,* pp. 108–144.

24. Richard Boyer and David Savageau, *Places Rated Almanac,* (Prentice-Hall, New York, 1985 and 1989).

25. Joe R. Feagin, *Free Enterprise City: Houston in Political-Economic Perspective,* (New Brunswick, Rutgers University Press, 1988).

26. Frey and Speare, *Regional Metropolitan Growth and Decline,* p. 51.

CHAPTER 8

1. V. K. Tippie, "An Environmental Characterization of Chesapeake Bay and a Framework for Action" in *The Estuary as a Filter,* V. S. Kennedy, ed. (Academic Press, Orlando, Fla., 1984), pp. 467–88.

2. Chesapeake Bay Program, *Chesapeake Bay Program: Findings and Recommendations* (Environmental Protection Agency, Washington, D.C., 1983). Chesapeake Bay Program, *The State of the Chesapeake Bay: Third Biennial Monitoring Report—1989.* (Environmental Protection Agency, Washington, D.C., 1989).

3. U.S. Department of Commerce, *U.S. Statistical Abstract 1977* and *1986*. (GPO, Washington, D.C.).

4. W. Boynton, J. Garber, and M. Kemp, "Patterns of Nitrogen and Phosphorus Input, Storage, Recycling, and Fate in the Chesapeake Bay and Selected Tributary Rivers." In preparation 1990.

References

Bureau of the Census. *County and City Data Book 1952, 1972 and 1988.* GPO, Washington, D.C.

U.S. Department of Agriculture. *1954 Census of Agriculture.* GPO, Washington, D.C., 1954.

1974 Census of Agriculture. GPO, Washington, D.C., 1974.

1987 Census of Agriculture. GPO, Washington, D.C., 1987.

U.S. Department of Commerce, *U.S. Statistical Abstract* [various years]. GPO, Washington, D.C.

VanDyne D., and C. Gilbertson. *Estimating U.S. Livestock and Poultry Manure and Nutrient Production*, USDA, Washington, D.C., 1978.

CHAPTER 9

1. Unless otherwise noted, figures in this essay are from the following sources: *Statistical Abstract of the United States, 1989* (U.S. Bureau of the Census, Washington, D.C.); *Historical Statistics of the United States, Colonial Times to 1970* (U.S. Bureau of the Census, Washington, D.C.); *Goode's World Atlas* (Rand McNally, Chicago, 1990).

2. *High Country News* (Paonia, Colo.), February 12, 1990, p.1.

3. Commercial forest is defined as capable of growing at least 1.4 m^3/ha (20 cubic feet per acre) per year of commercially useful species.

4. Old-growth forest is defined, in part, as containing at least twenty 200-year-old trees per hectare (8 per acre). See Rowe Findley, "Will We Save Our Own?" *National Geographic*, vol. 178 (September 1990), pp. 106–36.

5. U.S. Environmental Protection Agency, *The Solid Waste Dilemma: An Agenda for Action*, Draft Report (September 1988).

6. *Arizona Republic* (Phoenix, Ariz.), October 14, 1990, p.1.

7. *High Country News* (Paonia, Colo.), March 12, 1990, pp. 6–8.

8. National Wildlife Federation, *Our Ailing Public Lands: Condition Report 1989.* (NWF, Washington, D.C., 1989).

9. Wilderness Society, *1989 National Wilderness Preservation System* (map) (Washington, D.C.). De facto wilderness is defined as roadless areas of 20 km² (about 6,000 acres) or larger.

CHAPTER 10

Documentation for many of the statements found in this article can be found in P. R. Ehrlich and A. H. Ehrlich, *The Population Explosion*, (Simon and Schuster, New York, 1990), and *Healing the Earth* (Addison-Wesley, New York, 1991). We thank Gretchen C. Daily for helpful comments on the manuscript.

1. Technically the economic system would not have worked quite that way since demand varied, but the point is valid nonetheless.

2. John P. Holdren, "Energy in Transition," *Scientific American* (September 1990), pp. 157–63.

3. Most likely it produces a net decrement, since the high total fertility rates of the immigrants tend to fade in a generation or so but presumably would have remained higher in the country of origin.

4. See P. R. Ehrlich, D. L. Bilderback, and A. H. Ehrlich, *The Golden Door*, (Ballantine Books, New York, 1979).

CHAPTER 11

1. See *The Cornucopian Fallacies* (The Environmental Fund, Washington, D.C., 1982). Excerpts printed by permission of Population Environment Balance, Inc., 1325 G Street NW, Washington D.C. 20009, successor to The Environmental Fund.

2. *Science*, 208, (June 27, 1980), pp. 1431–37.

3. Julian Simon, *The Economics of Population Growth* (Princeton University Press, Princeton, 1977).

4. Herman Kahn, William Brown, and Leon Martel, *The Next 200 Years* (William Morrow, New York, 1976). See especially Figure 5 on p. 56 and the accompanying text.

5. Gerald O. Barney, *The Global 2000 Report to the President: Entering the Twenty First Century* (GPO, Washington, D.C., 1980). Three-volume report prepared by the Council on Environmental Quality and the Department of State, with the cooperation of other U.S. government agencies. The data in the report are dated. See Note 2 of Chapter 1 for more current data. The interactive analysis, developed through cooperation among specialists in different fields, has not subsequently been matched in the United States.

6. Ibid., vol. 12, p. 64.

7. Kahn et al., *The Next 200 Years*, pp. 75–176.

8. Julian Simon, *The Ultimate Resource* (Princeton University Press, Princeton, 1981), p. 49.

9. U.S. Geological Survey, *Estimates of Undiscovered Conventional Oil and Gas Resources in the United States—A Part of the Nation's Energy Endowment* (GPO, Washington, D.C., 1989). This study was based on current prices and recovery efficiency, but the analysis (see p. 22 of the report) did not suggest dramatic differences between "recoverable" and "economically recoverable" quantities. The study was reviewed by a panel of oil experts including representatives from the industry.

10. Julian Simon, "Energy Supply Scaremongers," *Washington Times*, February 5, 1991, p. G4.

11. See Barney, *The Global 2000 Report*, vol. 2, Chap. 13.

12. Albert A. Bartlett, "Forgotten Fundamentals of the Energy Crisis," *American Journal of Physics*, 46 (September 1978).

13. See, for example, Kahn et al., *The Next 200 Years*, p. 93, or Simon, *The Ultimate Resource*, pp. 32–33.

14. Simon, *The Ultimate Resource*, p. 47.

CHAPTER 12

Data for this paper were taken primarily from the *Statistical Abstract of the United States, 1987 and 1989*, the World Bank, "World Population Projections 1985"; and the United Nations, *World Population Prospects: Estimates and Projections as Assessed in 1984* (UN Department of International Economic and Social Affairs, New York, 1986). A concise summary of projections of the U.S. population is contained in Leon Bouvier, "Will There Be Enough Americans?", Backgrounder no. 1 (Center for Immigration Studies, Washington, D.C., July 1987). The estimate of the cost of raising children is from Thomas Espenshade, *Investing in Children* (Urban Institute Press, Washington, D.C., 1984). The population pyramid is derived from 1980 Census and Bureau of Labor Statistics data. The graph of the Social Security Trust Fund is from *Population Today* (March 1985).

CHAPTER 13

1. Gregory Spencer, *Projections of the Population of the United States, by Age, Sex and Race: 1988 to 2080*, U.S. Bureau of Census, Current Population Reports, Series P25, no. 1018 (GPO, Washington, D.C., 1989).

2. B. J. Wattenberg, "The Case for More Immigrants," *U.S. News and World Report*, February 13, 1989, p. 29.

3. J. Simon, "Getting the Immigrants We Need," *Washington Post*, August 3, 1988, p. 4.

4. L. F. Bouvier, "The Census Bureau's 1989 Projections of Future U.S. Population: Which Scenario Is Reasonable?" (Backgrounder, Center for Immigration Studies, Washington, D.C., 1989).

5. L. I. Dublin and A. J. Lotka, "On the True Rate of Natural Increase," *Journal of the American Statistical Association*, vol. 20, no. 105 (1925), pp. 305-39.

6. T. J. Espenshade, L. F. Bouvier, and W. B. Arthur, "Immigration and the Stable Population Model," *Demography*, vol. 19 (1982), pp. 125-33.

7. L. F. Bouvier, *Peaceful Invasions: Immigration and Changing America* (University Press of America, Lanham, Md., 1991).

CHAPTER 14

1. Gregory Spencer, *Projections of the Population of the United States, by Age, Sex and Race: 1988 to 2080*, U.S. Bureau of Census, Current Population Reports, Series P25, no. 1018 (GPO, Washington, D.C., 1989).

2. Ibid.

3. David Simcox, *Secure Identification: A National Need—a Must for Immigration Control*, (Center for Immigration Studies, Washington, D.C., 1989).

CHAPTER 15

1. U.S. Bureau of the Census, "Estimates of the Population of the United States to March 1, 1990," *Current Population Reports*, Series P-25, no. 1056 (1990); "Population Profile of the United States, 1989," *Current Population Reports*, Special Studies, Series P-23, no. 159 (1989).

2. Ansley Coale, "The Demographic Transition," *Proceedings of the International Population Conference, Liege*, vol. 1, pp. 53-72.

3. I have discussed elsewhere the fact that the prevalence of these attitudes in Islamic nations appears to be more a matter of social structure than of religion per se. See John R. Weeks, "The Demography of Islamic Nations," *Population Bulletin*, vol. 43, no. 4 (1988).

4. James Phillips, Ruth Simmons, Michael Koenig, and J. Chakraboty, "Determinants of Reproductive Change in a Traditional Society: Evidence from Matlab, Bangladesh," *Studies in Family Planning*, vol. 19, no. 6 (1988), pp. 313-34.

5. Gisele Maynard-Tucker, "Knowledge of Reproductive Physiology and Modern Contraceptives in Rural Peru," *Studies in Family Planning*, vol. 20, no. 4 (1989), pp. 215–24; Therese McGinn, Azara Bamba, and Moise Balma, "Male Knowledge, Use and Attitudes Regarding Family Planning in Burkina Faso," *International Family Planning Perspectives*, vol. 15, no. 3 (1989), pp. 84–87.

6. Mary Booth Weinberger, Cynthia Lloyd, and Ann Klimas Blanc, "Women's Education and Fertility: A Decade of Change in Four Latin American Countries," *International Family Planning Perspectives*, vol. 15, no. 1 (1989), pp.4–14.

7. Saad Gadalla, *Is There Hope? Fertility and Family Planning in a Rural Community in Egypt* (Carolina Population Center, Chapel Hill, N.C., 1978).

8. J. Satia and R. Maru, "Incentives and disincentives in the Indian Family Welfare Program," *Studies in Family Planning*, vol. 17, no. 3 (1986), pp. 136–45.

9. Quoted in Michael Teitelbaum, "Relevance of the Demographic Transition for Developing Countries," *Science*, vol. 188 (1975), pp. 420–25.

10. John R. Weeks, *Population: An Introduction to Concepts and Issues*, 4th ed. (Wadsworth, Belmont Calif., 1989).

11. See, for example, Ronald Lesthaeghe, "On the Social Control of Human Reproduction," *Population and Development Review*, vol. 6, no. 4 (1980), pp. 549–80.

12. John Aird, *Slaughter of the Innocents* (American Enterprise Institute for Public Policy Research, Washington, D.C., 1990).

13. Stanley Henshaw, "Induced Abortion: A World Review, 1990," *Family Planning Perspectives*, vol. 22, no. 2 (1990), pp. 76-89.

14. Phillips, et al., "Determinants of Reproductive Change in a Traditional Society," p. 323.

15. United Nations, *Trends in Population Policy*, Population Studies, no. 114 (United Nations, New York, 1989).

16. Data for 1974 are from the "World Population Estimates" prepared by the Environmental Fund; those for 1989 are from the Population Reference Bureau's "World Population Data Sheets."

17. The rhythm method must be distinguished from more modern methods of periodic abstinence, such as the sympto-thermal method, which have failure rates that are similar to the condom.

18. United Nations, *World Population at the Turn of the Century*, Population Studies, no. 111 (United Nations, New York, 1989), p. 122.

19. Donald Warwick, "The Indonesian Family Planning Program: Government Influence and Client Choice," *Population and Development Review*, vol. 12, no. 3 (1986), p.455.

20. See, for example, Paula Hollerbach, Sergio Diaz-Briquets, and Kenneth Hill, "Fertility Determinants in Cuba," *International Family Planning Perspectives*, vol. 10, no. 1 (1984), pp, 12–20.

21. "Pregnancy Propositions—Dollars for Those Who Don't," *New York Times*, May 29, 1990, p. 1.

22. This is example of "foresight" in public policy making, and I am indebted to Lindsey Grant for suggesting this line of thought.

23. Quoted in *Popline*, vol. 6, no. 4 (1984), p. 1.

CHAPTER 16

1. R. Constanza and C. H. Perrings, "A Flexible Assurance Bonding System for Improved Environmental Management," *Ecological Economics*, vol. 2 (1990), pp. 57–76.

CHAPTER 17

I follow the UN usage: Western Europe includes Austria, Belgium, France, Germany, Luxembourg, the Netherlands, and Switzerland. Northern Europe consists of Denmark, Finland, Iceland, Ireland, Norway, Sweden, and the United Kingdom. For convenience, I describe these two subregions as "West Europe." Some of the generalizations are made for all of non-Communist Europe, since OECD and some other sources present their data on that basis.

The data for this article were taken from the *UN Statistical Yearbook 1986*; *World Population Prospects: 1988* (UN Deptartment of International Economic and Social Affairs, New York, 1990); *1990 World Population Data Sheet* (Population Reference Bureau, Washington, D.C.); UN Food and Agriculture Organization, *1985 Production and Trade Yearbooks*, *1984 Fertilizer Yearbook*, and *1951 FAO Yearbook: Production*; *1989 Statistical Abstract of the U.S.*; *Energy Policies and Programmes of IEA Countries* (OECD, Paris, 1987); *OECD Environmental Data Compendium 1987*; *Coal Information 1987* (OECD, Paris, 1987); Luther J. Carter, *Nuclear Imperatives and Public Trust* (Resources for the Future, Washington, D.C., 1987); International Institute for Environment and Development and World Resources Institute, *World Resources 1987* (Basic Books, New York, 1987); *The Global 2000 Report to the President*, vol. 2; WAES, *Energy: Global Prospects 1985–2000* (McGraw-Hill, New York, 1977); Paul R. Ehrlich et al., *Ecoscience* (W.H. Freeman, San Francisco, 1977); New York Times, September 27, 1987, p.E3, J. Goldemberg et al., *Energy for a Sustainable World* (World Resources Institute, Washington, D.C., 1987).

CHAPTER 19

1. Leon F. Bouvier, *The Impact of Immigration on U.S Population Size* (Population Reference Bureau, Washington, D.C., 1981). The two figures are based upon annual net immigration of one and two million, respectively.

2. National Acid Precipitation Assessment Program (NAPAP), 722 Jackson Place NW, Washington, D.C. 20503.

3. See my concluding chapter, "How Many Americans?" in David E. Simcox ed., *U.S. Immigration in the 1980s: Reappraisal and Reform* (Westview Press, Boulder, Colo., 1988).

4. Environment Protection Agency Science Advisory Board, "Reducing Risk: Setting Priorities and Strategies for Environmental Protection," recommendation 8 (EPA, Washington, D.C., September 1990), p.23.

5. For a detailed discussion of the methods and history of foresight, see Lindsey Grant, *Foresight and National Decisions: the Horseman and the Bureaucrat* (University Press of America, Lanham, Md., 1988).

6. See Center for Immigration Studies, "Updated Estimates of Immigration Under Current Legislative Options, 1991–1995" (1424 16th Street NW, Suite 603, Washington, D.C. 20036, March 1990), for projections of the five-year impacts of different legislative proposals then before Congress.

7. *Moving America: New Directions, New Opportunities: A Statement of National Transportation Policy Strategies for Action* (U.S. Department of Transportation, Washington, D.C., February 1990).

INDEX

DATE DUE